WORKING ACROSS DIFFERENCE

WORKING ACROSS DIFFERENCE

SOCIAL WORK, SOCIAL POLICY AND SOCIAL JUSTICE

DONNA BAINES, BINDI BENNETT,

SUSAN GOODWIN &

MARGOT RAWSTHORNE

© Donna Baines, Bindi Bennett, Susan Goodwin, Margot Rawsthorne and The Authors, under exclusive licence to Springer Nature Limited 2019

All rights reserved. No reproduction, copy or transmission of this publication may be made without written permission.

No portion of this publication may be reproduced, copied or transmitted save with written permission or in accordance with the provisions of the Copyright, Designs and Patents Act 1988, or under the terms of any licence permitting limited copying issued by the Copyright Licensing Agency, Saffron House, 6–10 Kirby Street, London EC1N 8TS.

Any person who does any unauthorized act in relation to this publication may be liable to criminal prosecution and civil claims for damages.

The authors have asserted their rights to be identified as the authors of this work in accordance with the Copyright, Designs and Patents Act 1988.

First published 2019 by
RED GLOBE PRESS

Red Globe Press in the UK is an imprint of Springer Nature Limited, registered in England, company number 785998, of 4 Crinan Street, London N1 9XW.

Red Globe Press® is a registered trademark in the United States, the United Kingdom, Europe and other countries.

ISBN 978–1–352–00640–7 paperback

This book is printed on paper suitable for recycling and made from fully managed and sustained forest sources. Logging, pulping and manufacturing processes are expected to conform to the environmental regulations of the country of origin.

A catalogue record for this book is available from the British Library.

A catalog record for this book is available from the Library of Congress.

Contents

List of Figures and Tables	xi
List of Contributors	xii
Acknowledgements	xix

1 Introduction   1
Margot Rawsthorne

References   9

PART 1   ABORIGINAL PERSPECTIVES   11

2 Invisible from the Start: Australian Aboriginal People's Experiences of Difference and Aboriginal Community-Controlled Organisations   13
Sigrid Herring and Jo Spangaro

Further readings	23
References	23

3 Transforming Classrooms: Developing Culturally Safe Learning Environments   26
Mareese Terare

Introduction	26
Background	27
Aboriginal historical experiences with the colonial education system and resultant current outcomes	30
Political human rights: Epistemologies, ontologies and axiologies	31
Adult learning theories	32
Cultural safety	34
Reflections	36
Conclusion	37
Further readings	37
References	37

4 Ownership and Protection of Aboriginal Knowledge: Academic Response and Responsibility   39
Bindi Bennett

The analogy	39
The 'collaborative' omelette	41

When does the use of Aboriginal knowledge in academia become
    cultural appropriation? ... 42
What is intellectual property? ... 43
What is Indigenous knowledge? ... 44
So what? ... 46
Case studies ... 47
Reflective questions ... 48
Further readings ... 48
References ... 49

PART 2   CRITICAL PERSPECTIVES ON CULTURAL DIFFERENCE   53

5 Islamophobia and Social Work Collusion   55
Lobna Yassine and Linda Briskman

Introduction ... 55
Islamophobia in Australia ... 56
Locating ourselves ... 56
What is Islamophobia? ... 58
The politics of Countering Violent Extremism (CVE)
    policies and programs ... 59
Problematising Countering Violent Extremism (CVE)
    policies and programs ... 60
Control through 'community' and 'Australian-ness' ... 60
Fixing dangerous minds ... 62
The Countering Violent Extremism (CVE) industry ... 63
Colour-blind policies and the State as 'neutral' ... 64
A critical social work perspective ... 65
Conclusion ... 67
Further readings ... 68
References ... 68

6 Pushing Back Against Stereotypes: Muslim Immigrant Women's Experiences of Domestic Violence   71
Nafiseh Ghafournia

Introduction ... 71
Domestic violence among immigrant and refugee women ... 72
Theoretical framework ... 73
Method ... 74
Findings ... 74
Discussion ... 80
Implications for social work practice and policy ... 81
Conclusion ... 82
Further readings ... 82
References ... 83

7	**Working with Cultural Differences: Teaching First-Year Undergraduate Students to Unpack Unjust Power** *Jioji Ravulo*	85
	Introduction	85
	Theory and approaches	86
	Deconstructionism and différance	86
	Power/discourse/marginalisation	87
	Epistemologies of ignorance	89
	Social justice education	90
	Transformational learning	91
	Case study: Working with cultural differences	92
	History and context of the Working with Cultural Differences (WWCD) unit	92
	Teaching content (lecture and tutes)	94
	Embrace differences (social media inclusion and Facebook page)	97
	Areas of development and possible future direction	97
	Conclusion	98
	Further readings	98
	References	98

PART 3   CRITICAL PERSPECTIVES ON GENDER DIFFERENCE   101

8	**Allyship and Social Justice: Men as Allies in Challenging Men's Violence and Discrimination Against Women** *Alankaar Sharma*	103
	Allyship and social justice	104
	Men as allies	105
	Relationship with feminism and feminist women	107
	Relationship with self	110
	Guilt	110
	Positivity towards self	112
	Relationship with other (profeminist) men	113
	Politicising MVDAW and resisting depoliticisation	114
	Conclusion	115
	Further readings	116
	References	116
9	**Women and Older Age: Exploring the Intersections of Privilege and Oppression Across Lifetimes** *Tina Kostecki and Selma Macfarlane*	120
	Introduction	120
	Theoretical orientations for intersectional research	121
	Problematising women's later life experiences	122
	An intersectional approach to research on women and ageing	125

Challenges in intersectional research practice	128
Conclusion	132
Further readings	133
References	133

10 Uncovering Games of Truth: A Collaborative Exploration of the Ways Transgender and Non-Binary Young People Access Health Care and Support 137
Rebecca Howe, Amy Harper and Sekneh Hammoud-Beckett

Our collaborative process	139
What sort of 'games' are we talking about?	139
Being trans is a medical condition	142
Listening for truths and openness	146
Conclusion	148
Further readings	150
Acknowledgements	150
References	150

PART 4   CRITICAL PERSPECTIVES ON NORMALITY AND DIFFERENCE   153

11 Accepting My Illness? Problematising the Claims of Mental Health Anti-Stigma Efforts 155
Emma Tseris

Introduction	155
Examining key messages	157
Mental illness as a common experience	159
Mental illness can affect anyone	159
Mental illness does not define you	159
The general public needs educating	160
Effective help is available	161
Recovery is possible	161
Talking about one's own experience of mental illness is empowering	162
Reflexivity and lived experience	163
Order and legitimacy	164
Rigidity and meaning-making	166
Conclusion	166
Further readings	167
References	168

12 Supported Employment and Social Inclusion: An Analysis from the Perspective of People with Intellectual Disabilities 170
Barbara Soares e Madureira

Introduction	170
Work	171
Disability as difference	171

Supported employment	172
Social inclusion	173
Method	174
The experience of work	175
Relationships	175
Personal and social changes as a result of employment	177
Training and further opportunities for employment	177
Community participation	177
Discussion and conclusion	179
Further readings	181
References	181

PART 5   POLICY WORK ACROSS DIFFERENCE — 183

13 Feminist Gains Lost: Public Policy and the 'Genericising' of Women Survivors of Domestic Violence — 185
Susan Heward-Belle

Introduction	185
Domestic violence, homelessness and housing	187
Feminist activism and the women's refuge movement	187
The policy context	188
The Going Home, Staying Home (GHSH) 'reform'	190
The study	191
Overview of the reform experience	192
Gains lost for domestic violence service provision	193
Gains lost for children and young people	194
Gains lost for domestic violence recovery and survival	195
Gains lost for Aboriginal and Torres Strait Islander and migrant women	196
Gains lost for the domestic violence workforce: Specialist knowledge and skills	197
Gains lost for workers	198
Gains lost for the feminist movement	198
Conclusion	199
Further readings	200
Acknowledgements	200
References	200

14 Who Can Argue with Blue Sky? The Questionable Alliance between Difference and the Market in Disability Policy — 203
Amanda Howard

Choice and control, reasonable and necessary	205
Human rights and the market	207
Operationalising tensions	209
Rise of the National Disability Insurance Agency (NDIA): the state and the market	209

The very managed market in implementation	210
Where to go from here?	215
Further readings	216
References	216

15 Collisions Between the State and the Evil Spirit: Home Care in Indigenous Communities — 218
Frank T.Y. Wang and Sheng-Pei Tsai

Background	219
Literature review	219
Research design	221
The Tao people and their Anito belief	221
Findings	223
Discussion and conclusion	227
Further readings	229
References	230

PART 6   RESISTANCES AND REFLECTIONS — 231

16 Concepts, Theories and the Politics of Difference: A Discussion of Select Terms — 233
Susan Goodwin

Binaries/binarism/binary thinking	235
Decolonisation/decolonising theory	236
Difference/the politics of difference	236
Diversity	237
Other/Othering	238
Postcolonialism	239
Poststructuralism	240
Privilege/white privilege	241
Settler colonialism	242
Conclusion	243
References	243

17 Afterword: Resistance, White Fragility and Late Neoliberalism — 247
Donna Baines and Fran Waugh

Introduction	247
Code of Ethics and the neoliberal context of practice	249
Vignettes from practice	252
Conclusion	258
Further readings	258
References	258

Index — 261

LIST OF FIGURES AND TABLES

Figures

9.1	Intersectionality wheel	128
9.2	Second intersectionality wheel	130
15.1	Temporary house for a Tao elderly person	223

Tables

7.1	WWCD Learning outcomes	93
7.2	WWCD Weekly topics	94
7.3	Three domains of learning via Reflect/Review/Refocus	96

LIST OF CONTRIBUTORS

Donna Baines, University of Sydney
Donna Baines is a cisgender, white female. Her family originally immigrated to Canada from many parts of Europe, in some cases fleeing arrest for union organising and, in others, fleeing poverty and religious persecution. Donna has joined many social justice movements and activities in her life. She moved with her family to Australia to be part of a social justice school of social work. Her work draws on anti-oppressive, feminist, anti-racist, intersectionalist and Marxist approaches. Donna is Chair and Professor of Social Work and Policy Studies at the University of Sydney.

Bindi Bennett, University of the Sunshine Coast
Bindi Bennett is a Gamilaraay woman who is a social work lecturer at the University of the Sunshine Coast. Her interests include equine therapy, trauma, Aboriginal social work, Aboriginal identity and well-being, as well as increasing cultural responsiveness in social work education. She has small aims of decolonising the world and emancipating Aboriginal peoples. Bindi is also a mother, a partner, a friend and a horse lover.

Linda Briskman, Western Sydney University
As the Margaret Whitlam Chair of Social Work at Western Sydney University, Linda Briskman works to uphold the reform traditions of the Whitlams. She conducts research, publishes and advocates in three areas critical to human rights – Indigenous rights, asylum seeker rights and challenging Islamophobia. She works from the premise that social work needs to engage with politics to be effective in contributing to social justice and social change.

Nafiseh Ghafournia, University of Sydney
Nafiseh Ghafournia is a Muslim immigrant woman. Her minority and religious status places her at a similar level with the research participants. During the data collection process, most of the women expressed the comfort they felt sharing their experience with her because of her familiarity with Islamic values and culture. Nafiseh recently completed her PhD at the University of Sydney.

Susan Goodwin, University of Sydney
Susan Goodwin is a white Australian woman who came to Sydney to work in feminist services and feminist policy machinery. She is passionate about the power of ideas and ways of thinking, and regards her research, teaching and community engagement as political practice. She works with communities in Australia and countries in the region to participate in shaping the knowledge, policies and practices that impact on their lives through community-led and action research. Her work is informed by poststructural and feminist theory.

Sekneh Hammoud-Beckett, Therapist and Activist
Sekneh Hammoud-Beckett is an Australian woman of Lebanese Muslim ancestry who holds a position of curiosity in her work as a therapist and activist, which she uses to explore and honour people's creative acts of resistance. Sekneh's community work spans more than 20 years. She teaches both nationally and internationally at reputable universities and has received international recognition for her 'inviting people in' concept. Sekneh is passionate about the therapeutic work in which she engages with young people of diverse cultures, religions, genders and sexualities. She considers the therapeutic process a privilege, and is committed to researching the potential of young people and their families when navigating the grips of a problem. Sekneh believes her 'work is love made visible'.

Amy Harper, Youth Counsellor
Amy Harper is a white Australian queer person living and working in Sydney. Amy is a LGBTQIA+ youth counsellor, which has had a large focus on navigating services for trans and non-binary young people. Prior to this, Amy worked for many years in adult recovery-oriented mental health services. Amy's approach is largely conversational and collaborative – honouring the person's experience, perspective and strengths. Amy believes in a holistic, compassionate and non-pathological practice that is informed by social justice principles. She is very interested in topics around community connection, identity and healing.

Sigrid Herring, Community Worker
Sigrid Herring is a Gomeroi woman from northwest New South Wales with Welsh and Scottish heritage, the third generation of her family born off Country, her childhood was spent in Ngarigo and Ngunawal Countries and since then on Darug Country. Sigrid has worked in family and community development in community-based settings for more than 20 years and in educating workers to support families and communities

for 15 years. She works for the reinstatement of Aboriginal men and women's agency and recognition as world leaders in parenting, child development and protection and as cultural designers of happy, healthy, sustainable lives for families and their environments.

Susan Heward-Belle, University of Sydney
Sue's family originally immigrated to Canada from the Ukraine and Scotland. Sue grew up in northern Canada, living mainly in Edmonton and Yellowknife. She immigrated to Australia in the 1990s where she has worked as a social worker and educator in the area of child welfare and domestic violence. Sue completed her PhD and joined the University of Sydney in 2014. Her research, teaching and advocacy are underpinned by principles of social justice, human rights and gender equity, and aim to develop socially just institutional responses that honour the inherent dignity and resistance of people who have experienced violence.

Amanda Howard, University of Sydney
Some of Amanda Howard's family came to Australia in 1800 as convicts; some others came later selling soap. They worked as itinerant labourers, members of Parliament, doers of washing and ironing, parents, cooks, soldiers, brumby riders, taxi drivers and secretaries. They came from oppression and poverty but were also oppressors as part of colonisation. This has shaped Amanda's passion for understanding complex contradictions in communities. Amanda now lives near a big old hospital from which people are moving into the community after a lifetime institutional care. She wonders what does the National Disability Insurance Scheme (NDIS) really mean for this group of community members? Amanda works at the University of Sydney in Social Work.

Rebecca Howe, University of Sydney
Rebecca Howe is a white settler-Australian, queer, cisgendered person who experiences a chronic illness. Rebecca has 15 years' experience in the youth homelessness sector, nine of which as a facilitator of social support programs for young people who identify within and beyond the LGBTQIA+ acronym. Her work has enabled the development of a theoretically grounded, constantly evolving practice that incorporates fierce youth advocacy with a critical queer intersectional lens. Working alongside young people has had such a transformational impact on her life it defies explanation; it has also meant she has never had to stop swearing when she gets passionate about something. Rebecca is working on her PhD at the University of Sydney.

Tina Kostecki, Victoria University
Tina Kostecki is a cisgender woman of Polish descent, and this cultural heritage has formed a strong part of her identity. Tina's parents came to Australia following World War II as 'displaced persons' (as they were then known). Their experiences of war taught her about the nature of systemic violence and its impact through generations. Tina chose social work as a way to engage with issues of social justice and worked for many years in women's services (family violence and sexual assault).

Selma Macfarlane, Deakin University (Emeritus)
Selma Macfarlane is of Norwegian-American descent and grew up in a working-class family in a small town in northern California, immigrating to Australia as a young woman shortly after the dismissal of Prime Minister Gough Whitlam. She saw what she believed to be social democracy in action, and since then has watched its demise. Selma obtained her social work degree and PhD as a single parent of three; and, after some work in community mental health, came to academia by an unexpected act of serendipitous kindness. Over the years she has learned more about the intersections of privilege and oppression that shape lives and societies and has tried to write and teach about these things. She is grateful to all those who work to make social justice a reality.

Barbara Soares E Madureira, University of Sydney
Barbara is a social worker from Brazil, where she studied and practised Radical Social Work. She came to Australia in 2007 and works with people with intellectual disabilities as a social worker, advocate and direct support worker. Barbara believes in social change and social justice.

Jioji Ravulo, Western Sydney University
Jioji Ravulo's father is iTaukei – an Indigenous Fijian from the village of Nayavuira, located in the province of Nakorotubu, in the region of Ra on the main Island of Viti Levu, Fiji. His mother is Anglo-Australian, who was born and raised in Sydney, Australia. Similar to his mother, Jioji was brought up in and among Western systems, but always knew his difference as a person of colour through the way he was treated beyond the comfort of his loving family environment. It is through this dual lens that he has become more and more aware of the tensions between the two; the need to compete in an individualistic society while upholding collectivist views and indigenous yearnings. Within this context, Jioji's involvement in social work continues to evolve, desiring to help marginalised individuals, families and communities navigate their own voice and space across society.

Margot Rawsthorne, University of Sydney

Margot Rawsthorne's family trace their time on Australia to the 1820s when Thomas arrived as a convict. He was among the first white people to cross the Blue Mountains and since the late 1800s the family has lived on Wirajuri land in Central Western New South Wales. Margot now lives and works on Gadigal land and pays her respect to Elders past, present and emerging. Her work focuses on how people working collectively can bring about change. Her teaching explores listening and learning; participation and action; and disrupting power and privilege. Margot's research also explores the lived experience of inequality, shaped by location, gender, sexuality and class.

Alankaar Sharma, University of Sydney

Alankaar Sharma writes from the position of a brown, cisgender, migrant man who was born and educated in India, and has lived, studied, and worked in many different parts of the world, including the USA and Australia. His interest in social justice, anti-oppressive and feminist approaches to social work is influenced by his personal experiences of transgressing and challenging heteropatriarchal gender norms and his family's history of forced displacement. He is a lecturer in social work, and his academic interests lie at various points of intersection between genders (particularly, men and masculinities), sexualities, childhood and violence.

Jo Spangaro, University of New South Wales

Jo Spangaro comes from Italian and British parents who were part of waves of migration to Australia in the 1920s and 1950s. Her social work practice has focused on gender-based violence where she has worked with both those who have experienced and those who have perpetrated violence, as well as in education and policy roles. Her feminist and trauma-informed outlook is informed by a commitment to bringing the experiences of Aboriginal and Torres Strait Islander people into view. Jo is a Senior Lecturer in the social work programme at the University of New South Wales, Sydney Australia.

Mareese Terare, University of Sydney

Mareese Terare is Bundjalung and Geonpul woman from Tweed Heads, Fingal – northern New South Wales and North Stradbroke Island – southeast Queensland. Mareese has more than 20 years' experience in the teaching and development of the curriculum in community education, registered training organisations and higher education sectors. She is passionate about ongoing process of decolonisation within social work education and research processes, and is committed to developing social work practices based on deeper understanding of Aboriginal world views, cultural humility and reflexivity.

Sheng-Pei Tsai
Influenced by her childhood experience living in the countryside with her grandparents, Sheng-Pei Tsai is interested in care and social welfare for the elderly, and the long-term care policy in Taiwan, especially for Aboriginal people in rural and remote areas. As most community care work is determined by higher-status actors, she stands and writes from the perspective of care recipients and caregivers, who are mostly women. She now works as a home care worker, trying to observe and interpret how the front line interacts with policy and bureaucratic management; meanwhile, she works to develop strategies to mend the gap between policy and reality.

Emma Tseris, University of Sydney
Emma Tseris is passionate about exploring critical perspectives on madness and distress (usually called 'mental health'), particularly in relation to women and young people – whose viewpoints are often dismissed or reinterpreted within psychiatric services through the lenses of patriarchy, classism and white privilege. As she writes from a positioning of being both white and unmarked by psychiatric diagnosis, she aims to imbue her research with processes of collaborative meaning-making, reflexivity and multiplicity.

Frank Wang, National Chen Chi University, Taiwan
Frank Wang's family immigrated to Taiwan from China in 1949 with the Nationalist government. As a sibling to a sister with spinal injury, Frank shifted his career from engineering to social work in his twenties, with the belief that social work is committed to social justice. He is passionate about the critical analysis of social work practices for Indigenous peoples. His work draws on feminist, anti-oppressive and Foucauldian poststructuralist approaches. Frank is a Professor at the Graduate Institute of Social Work at National Chengchi University in Taiwan.

Fran Waugh, University of Sydney
Fran Waugh's family originally immigrated to Australia from the Republic of Ireland and Great Britain (1850s onwards) in search of a better future. For more than 20 years Fran practised as a nurse and then a social worker, working with marginalised groups prior to joining the Social Work program at the University of Sydney in 2000. Her work, underpinned by critically reflective practice, draws on a range of theories and approaches

to understand and make sense of the inequities and injustices facing individuals, groups and communities. Fran is a Professor in Social Work.

Lobna Yassine, University of Sydney
Lobna Yassine is a Muslim Australian with Lebanese heritage. Her parents originally immigrated from Lebanon in the late 1970s due to war and in pursuit of a better life for themselves and for their children. Lobna is in the final stages of her PhD in Social Work at the University of Sydney. Her thesis is concerned with juvenile penality and the role of risk assessments, drawing on concepts of governmentality to analyse the shaping of subjectivities. Lobna is currently undertaking a Teaching Fellowship at the University of Sydney, in the School of Education and Social Work.

ACKNOWLEDGEMENTS

We acknowledge the original social justice fighters, the Aboriginal First Nation Sovereign peoples of Australia, and worldwide, and further, we thank the Ancestors and Elders who have gone before us. The editors also gratefully acknowledge the contributions of the authors and their goodwill in meeting deadlines. On behalf of the authors and ourselves, we would also like to thank the community members and research participants who contributed their experience and insights to our research. Funding for the conference where we first presented these chapters is gratefully acknowledged from the Sydney Social Sciences and Humanities Advanced Research Centre (SSSHARC), University of Sydney. Many thanks also to Gabriella Skoff who added her formatting and manuscript clean-up skills to the final draft. We would also like to thank our Red Globe Press editor, Peter Hooper, and the Red Globe Press team. Finally, we would like to thank our families for putting up with us and sharing our commitment to social justice and equity.

1
Introduction

Margot Rawsthorne

> *As editors we wish to start this book with an acknowledgement of the ongoing history of dispossession and deliberate attacks on the cultures and spirituality of Australia's First Peoples. This history gives us great pain and enormous regret at the devaluing of knowledge acquired by the First Peoples during 70,000 years of continuous life on this land. The inability of non-Indigenous Australians to learn from First Peoples is to our collective detriment, whether through inclusive social norms or communal forms of child-rearing, the demise of soil, or threats of extinction of unique fauna.*

Social work practice is implicated not only in the discounting of Aboriginal knowledge and an unwillingness to learn from it but also in the destructive intervention in the lives of generations of Indigenous Australians (Bennett, 2015; Briskman, 2016). Working across difference with Australia's First Peoples requires urgent attention. Accordingly, the book includes several chapters written by or with Indigenous Australians. These chapters are not presented as 'the' Aboriginal perspective but offer insight into the experience of multiple 'differences' in settings as diverse as academia, health, community and violence against women services. For non-Indigenous (white) readers these chapters provide an opportunity to listen and learn from Indigenous Australians, from a position of cultural humility.

This book arose from our shared struggles in practice, theory, research and teaching to 'work across difference'. The term 'differences' denotes a set of highly politicised, socially constructed, social relations that reinforce inequity, dominance and oppression. Difference benefits racially stratified, patriarchal capitalism but are simultaneously a site of struggle, something to work with and across, something that we inhabit and may inadvertently reproduce through daily practice and something that can be challenged and dealt with more equitably with a goal of social justice and fairness.

Writing from her social positioning within the intersections of race, gender, class and homophobia, the late Audre Lorde (2012) argued that

> Certainly there are very real differences between us of race, age, and sex. But it is not those differences between us that are separating us. It is rather our refusal to recognize those differences, and to examine the distortions which result from our misnaming them and their effects upon human behaviour and expectation. (p. 17)

Social work and policy studies in Australia are increasingly called on to work across differences in ways that promote social justice and challenge growing inequity. However, as Lorde (Lorde and Rich, 1981) noted, we have no patterns for relating across human differences as equals and, as she argues further, 'Institutionalized rejection of difference is an absolute necessity in a profit economy which needs outsiders as surplus people' (Lorde, 2012, p.115).

This quote highlights the way in which larger social systems benefit from both the denial of difference and our lack of strategies for identifying and working across real and imagined differences. These 'differences' justify inequity, harm and divide us and thrive off the existence of disposable people and regions of the world that can be exploited, destroyed and left to decline (Giroux, 2015). Lorde argues further that

> it is not the differences that separate us, it is our denial of their existence and our inability to critically examine and challenge their impact on social and individual actions and ideas. Too often, we pour the energy needed for recognizing and exploring difference into pretending those differences are insurmountable barriers, or that they do not exist at all. This results in a voluntary isolation, or false and treacherous connections. (Lorde, 2012, p.115; reprint from a 1977 speech delivered to the Modern Language Association)

This book is aimed at ending isolations of all kinds and building interconnections that recognise and celebrate differences, redistribute resources and ensure voice and representation in the building of equity-directed social justice practices and policies.

In this collection, the term differences is also used in Lorde's (2012) sense that much of the work of changing social relations lies with those who are more powerfully positioned within intersecting oppressions:

> Black and Third World people are expected to educate white people as to our humanity. Women are expected to educate men. Lesbians and gay men are expected to educate the heterosexual world. The oppressors maintain their position and evade their responsibility for their own actions. There is a

constant drain of energy which might be better used in redefining ourselves and devising realistic scenarios for altering the present and constructing the future. (p. 92)

Unearned privilege underlies these dynamics. This privilege is not distributed equally but accumulates along axes of power such as maleness, whiteness, gender, immigrant status, able-bodiedness and so forth (Mehrotra, 2010). These socially constructed relations form intersecting nodes of power and privilege that operate without the conscious instigation of those accorded this power in our society. For example, light-skinned immigrants do not wake up in the morning and decide to make use of white-skin privilege; it is part of everyday interactions without the need for conscious activation. Part of working across difference includes recognising and 'un-doing' this invisible but omnipresent privilege (Kennedy-Kish et al., 2017; Pease, 2010).

The contributors to this book highlight the need for intersectionality in our analysis, as critical race theorists have identified, as a tool for resistance (Carbado et al., 2013; Crenshaw, 1989). Intersectionality recognises that oppressions never operate singly; rather they overlap, reinforce, undermine and contest in complex and ever-changing webs (Mehrotra, 2010). Dismantling the many, intersecting threads of these webs requires a crisp, critical analysis and openness to new ways of challenging inequity and building social justice.

This collection does not provide a prescription for working across difference; instead it problematises intersecting differences and privileges in numerous contexts, and offers insights into more equitable ways of undertaking social work and making social policy. Working across difference is more than simply having promotional material in other languages, scattering around a few rainbow flags or employing the occasional non-white person. The task of 'working across difference' requires profound, ongoing, consistent efforts to make any meaningful progress towards our shared commitment to social change and equity. Oppression and privilege are deeply embedded through the hegemony of binary genders, settler colonialism, racism, ageism and ableism (Allan et al., 2009; Kennedy-Kish et al., 2017).

Despite social work's genuine concern with the experience of those subjected to oppression and 'othered', it remains too often uncritical of its own privilege and power, and its participation, often unintended, in sustaining oppressive relations (Bennett, 2015; Briskman, 2016). In this book we take a critical stance to the social work profession's current and historical 'social justice project'. We question the extent to which the actions of social workers and social policy makers have challenged structural oppressions. We ask, what would decolonised practice look like? How do we respond to mental distress without resorting to power/privilege/violence? In what ways do our practices disable? How do we disrupt the 'marking' of some identities as less than? This critical questioning of our role as social workers, policy makers and community activists needs to inform our ongoing 'social justice project', which may provide a pathway for rethinking social work beyond merely 'doing good'.

In rethinking social work beyond unintentionally doing harm while intending to be 'doing good' we are also reclaiming the centrality of the profession's ethical pursuit of human rights and social justice (IASSW, 2004). The danger of human rights and social justice becoming optional in social work practice (Ife, 2012) is even greater in the current context of austerity and late neoliberalism (Baines, 2017; Mullaly, 2010). Neoliberalism is understood in this collection as simultaneously a project, an ideology and a process (Dean, 2010; Harvey, 2007). The ideology of neoliberalism has introduced 'a new model of citizenship in which societal rights and responsibilities transform social problems into the failures of the individuals rather than that of society' (Birch and Mykhnenko, 2009, p. 7).

Taking this further, Roy (2014) argues that neoliberalism reconceptualises poverty as an 'identity problem', negating the systemic causes of inequality: 'Poverty ... is often framed as an identity problem, as though the poor have not been created by injustice but are a lost tribe who just happen to exist' (p. 37). Neoliberal ideology is so pervasive that it becomes almost impossible to challenge (as it is presented as the only option), saturating mass cultural and political realms, and creating new social norms and monoculture (Gray and Webb, 2013; Harvey, 2007). Under neoliberalism, power relations are reconfigured such that individuals internalise the state's 'marketisation' objectives through self-regulation and self-governance (Foucault, 1984). As such power is decentred, as opposed to being exclusively and overtly hierarchical and authoritarian, as it has become embedded in the beliefs, fears, desires and aspirations of the population (Brown, 2006). This has made neoliberalism almost invisible and the assimilation of social workers into the neoliberal political project less contested than it should be (Gray and Web, 2013; Mullaly, 2010).

Social service organisations and practitioners have been deeply challenged by the doctrine of small government, marketisation, individual responsibilisation, growing inequality and attacks on collective responses and resistance (Fawcett et al., 2010). Social work responses to neoliberal discourses' marking of certain groups as 'different' (read inadequate and unworthy) are often constrained by bureaucratic standardised practices which purport to be neutral (Allan et al., 2009; Gray and Web, 2013; Kennedy-Kish et al., 2017). These standardised practices often target those who social workers seek to work alongside in our social justice work, through imposing income support sanctions, rationing access to support, and/or criminalising and removing children. It is sobering to consider that more Indigenous children are currently in state 'care' than during the period known as the 'Stolen Generation' (Long and Sephton, 2011). In their putative neutrality these practices depoliticise social work practice, remaking it as a technical profession rather than a social justice-engaged vocation (Baines, 2017; Mullaly, 2010).

Through this book and in collaboration with our contributors we sought to explore how social work may repeat, reject, resist or rupture exclusionary practices based on difference. In doing so we deliberately privilege the perspectives of those positioned as 'different', through race, ethnicity, sexuality, gender and ability. In privileging these perspectives we are not suggesting that 'difference' is only a concern of those in dominant cultural positions. Our goal is to open up dialogue and debate concerning notions of difference with a view to the co-creation of new forms of social work practices. We acknowledge the risk of totalising the identities of 'others' through this and have tried to highlight the intersection of multiple (and at times contradictory) positionalities among ourselves and the people we work alongside (Mehrotra, 2010). Through adopting an intersectional stance we aim to resist collapsing difference under universal categories (Tong, 1989) and acknowledge as Lorde does that 'her shackles may look very different to my own' (Lorde, 2012, p. 124). This signals a rejection of the neoliberal discourse of a benign, uncontested 'diversity' which serves to obscure the very real, day-to-day structural inequality and oppression experienced by non-white, distressed, older, disabled and other marginalised people. Though we draw on concepts and strategies from the postmodern and poststructural critique, we consciously seek to avoid the paralysing effect of postmodern perspectives that do not provide the basis for collective political actions (Ramazanoglu and Holland, 2002). Our contributors seek to avoid identity politics that fail to acknowledge the material subjugation of those 'othered' (Zuffery, 2015) or the benefits that accrue to privileged groups through this. Rupturing exclusionary practices requires more than linguistic shifts or clever deconstructing. It requires structural as well as cultural and political solutions, including a concrete, material redistribution of resources, practices, policies, representation and access to affirming identities and cultural practices (Kennedy-Kish et al., 2017).

Though each situation and context requires its own unique strategies rather than a standardised response, the following points are helpful in thinking about and working across difference:

1. Recognising that multiple, intersecting differences exist in every interaction and context (Mehrotra, 2010).
2. Developing a critical lens for analysing these differences and understanding why they exist in any given context, who they benefit/harm and how to use this analysis to build consensus for action.

3. Working as an ally with those socially positioned as less powerful and less privileged (Bishop, 2012; Mullaly, 2010). Building conscious ties of support.

4. Accepting the leadership of oppressed groups and providing active, not passive, support for their social justice initiatives and critiques of power and privilege.

5. Using one's privileged position and the power that is socially accorded to this positioning in alliance with oppressed groups (Baines, 2017).

Working across differences, using these five points, can be accomplished through: direct practice with groups, individuals, families and communities; social policy; community and social policy projects; social activism; critical pedagogy; and theory.

We hope this book will be of interest and use to students, practitioners, policy makers and educators. It is likely that readers will focus on specific chapters reflecting their own priorities. To more fully comprehend the goal of this book, however, we would encourage readers to explore a range of chapters. In this way it will be clearer how 'difference' is structured, highlighting the commonalities in the struggles of young people of diverse sexualities, Aboriginal academics or Muslim women, for example. Each contributor has been asked to problematise normative and instrumental approaches which reproduce top-down toolbox approaches to working across difference. In doing so the contributors have drawn heterogeneously on anti-oppressive theories, including Indigenous knowledges, queer theory, intersectional feminism, critical mental health and critical race theory. Of course, one chapter can only be a taster – for those wishing to explore further issues raised by the contributors a list of resources is included.

For educators, we suggest chapters are paired, with student learning supported by guiding questions. Again we would encourage the pairing of diverse chapters in order to enable more sophisticated critical engagement. Guiding questions (for students but also others) might include:

➢ How are oppression and/or privileges structured and/or experienced by various groups of people?

➢ How is difference marked by neoliberal discourses or practices?

➢ How can the insights of each chapter be used to challenge inequity in social work practice and policy?

The book is divided into six parts. Reflecting our commitment to foregrounding the experience of difference and engaging with Indigenous knowledges, Part I focuses on Aboriginal Perspectives. It comprises three chapters incorporating the knowledge of practitioners, educators and academics. Sigrid Herring and Jo Spangaro (Chapter 2) bring into focus the experiences of Aboriginal community-controlled health organisations. The chapter highlights the contradictory experience (which appears common) of those both marked as requiring intensive state scrutiny and simultaneously unworthy of acknowledgement. Mareese Terare (Chapter 3) inspires educators to embrace difference within learning environments as a resource for transformational learning. The chapter argues that developing cultural safety is not merely about creating space for marginal voices but also about creating space for those with privilege. In this way these learning and teaching moments can reject, resist or rupture exclusionary practices based on difference. The final chapter in Part I by Bindi Bennett (Chapter 4) explores the tensions and risks of 'incorporating' Indigenous knowledges into white academia. The chapter challenges us to consider how non-Indigenous practice, sometimes unintentionally (sometimes not), leads to cultural appropriation. All three chapters in Part I engage with the impact of white privilege on Aboriginal Australians, highlighting the constant vigilance required not to replicate oppression and providing strategies for 'doing better'.

Part II explores the experiences of those marked as 'culturally different', through language, cultural practices and religion. Two of the three chapters in this section foreground the assumed difference of non-Christian Australians. Lobna Yassine (Chapter 5) and Nafiseh Ghafournia (Chapter 6) write from the position of Muslim women at a time of cultural hostility, challenging social workers to critically reflect and engage with the political task of confronting racist stereotyping. The chapter by Yassine and co-author Linda Briskman (Chapter 5) documents the collusion of leading social work organisations with efforts to vilify and marginalise Muslim people and suggests that we all have a role to play in resisting oppression in its professional and personal manifestations. Jioji Ravulo (Chapter 7) provides inspiration to educators seeking to engage with this political task in the classroom and through their teaching.

Part III shifts our focus to gender as a site of political struggle and contest. Alankaar Sharma (Chapter 8) questions the co-option of feminist positioning by men in challenges to men's violence and discrimination against women. He advocates for a position of allyship whereby men hold themselves and each other accountable for gendered violence. Tina Kostecki and Selma Macfarlane (Chapter 9) provide a tool for practitioners and researchers alike in uncovering older women's life stories. Readers are invited to experiment with the 'Intersectionality Tool' in their practice to avoid creating a static, monochrome picture. Rebecca Howe, Amy Harper and Sekneh Hammoud-Beckett (Chapter 10) draw on Foucault's notion of 'Games of Truth' in a powerful collaboration with transgender and non-binary young people. The chapter demands we interrogate our role in creating 'truth' for 'others'.

Part IV asks us to consider how the concept of 'normality' shapes the experiences of those outside that 'norm'. Emma Tseris (Chapter 11) adopts a critical stance in exploring social work practice with those people marked by psychiatry as 'mentally ill'. She confronts social work's co-option by psychiatric discourses that can lead to socially unjust practice. Barbara Soares e Madureira (Chapter 12) examines the social inclusion potential of supported employment for people with intellectual disabilities, highlighting first-person lived experiences.

In Part V our contributors turn their attention to policy responses to 'difference' across a wide terrain. Susan Heward-Belle (Chapter 13) questions policy assumptions that all homelessness is the same. Her research with refuge workers reveals that the specific experiences of women survivors of domestic violence cannot and should not be 'generalised' as simply homelessness. Amanda Howard (Chapter 14) takes a critical stance on the marrying of market forces and human rights within the National Disability Support Scheme (NDIS). She highlights how this marrying has rendered silent significant concerns about neoliberal marketisation. The lived experience of policy is Frank Wang and Sheng-Pei Tsai's focus in the final chapter (Chapter 15) of Part V. Highlighting Indigenous aged care practices in Taiwan, they reveal the possibility of conflict between the 'social justice' policy and self-determination.

In the final part of the book, Part VI, we provide some reflections and explore resistances. Susan Goodwin analyses select poststructural and postcolonial terms in Chapter 16. Though not all authors in the book used poststructural theory, the concepts she highlights are very useful in the analysis of socially constructed difference. The chapter can be used as a glossary or as a thought piece to spark further critical engagement with some of the concepts and ideas used in the book. Donna Baines and Fran Waugh provide an Afterword in Chapter 17, in which they confront the very real risk of ultra-right challenges to our social justice project and the pervasiveness of white fragility in the face of resistance and challenge from those marginalised within existing systems. Drawing on two extended vignettes the chapter seeks to undercover resistances in everyday social work practice. It asks, what tools can social workers use in the context of late neoliberalism to find spaces for critical reflection and generate alternative, social justice-engaged, diversity-embracing practices and policies? The Afterword concludes that resistance is still possible and avidly pursued by many in the social justice social work endeavour.

References

Allan, J., Briskman, L. and Pease, B. (2009). *Critical Social Work: Theories and Practices for a Socially Just World.* Melbourne: Allen & Unwin.

Baines, D. (Ed.) (2017). *Doing Anti-Oppressive Practice: Social Justice Social Work,* 3rd Edition. Halifax, NS: Fernwood.

Bennett, B. (2015). Stop deploying your white privilege on me! Aboriginal and Torres Strait Islander engagement with the Australian Association of Social Workers. *Australian Social Work,* 68(1), 19–31.

Birch, K. and Mykhnenko, V. (2009). Varieties of neoliberalism? Restructuring in large industrially dependent regions across western and eastern Europe. *Journal of Economic Geography,* 9(3), 355–380.

Bishop, A. (2002). *Becoming an Ally: Breaking the Cycle of Oppression in People.* London: Zed Books.

Briskman, L. (2016). Decolonizing Social Work in Australia: Prospect or Illusion. In J. Coatles, M. Grey and M. Yellowbird (Eds.), *Indigenous Social Work around the World* (pp. 111–122). London: Routledge.

Brown, W. (2006). American nightmare: Neoliberalism, neoconservatism, and de-democratization. *Political Theory,* 34(6), 690–714.

Carbado, D.W., Crenshaw, K.W., Mays, V.M. and Tomlinson, B. (2013). Intersectionality: Mapping the movements of a theory. *Du Bois Review: Social Science Research on Race,* 10(2), 303–312.

Crenshaw, K. (1989). Demarginalizing the intersection of race and sex: A black feminist critique of antidiscrimination doctrine, feminist theory and antiracist politics. *University of Chicago Legal Forum,* 1(8), 139–167.

Dean, M. (2010). *Governmentality: Power and Rule in Modern Society,* 2nd edition. London: Sage.

Fawcett, B., Goodwin, S., Meagher, G. and Phillips, R. (2010). *Social Policy for Social Change.* Melbourne: Palgrave.

Foucault, M. (1984). *The Foucault Reader.* New York: Pantheon Books.

Giroux, H.A. (2015). *Against the Terror of Neoliberalism: Politics beyond the Age of Greed.* London: Routledge.

Gray, M. and Web, S. (2013). *The New Politics of Social Work.* London: Palgrave.

Harvey, D. (2007). *A Brief History of Neoliberalism.* Oxford: Oxford University Press.

Ife, J. (2012). *Human Rights and Social Work: Towards Rights-Based Practice.* Cambridge: Cambridge University Press.

IASSW (International Association of Schools of Social Work) (2004). *Ethics in Social Work, Statement of Principles.* https://www.iassw-aiets.org/wp-content/uploads/2015/10/Ethics-in-Social-Work-Statement-IFSW-IASSW-2004.pdf.

Kennedy-Kish, B., Sinclair, R., Carniol, B. and Baines, D. (2017). *Case Critical: Social Services and Social Justice in Canada,* 7th Edition. Toronto: Between the Lines.

Long, M. and Sephton, R. (2011). Rethinking the "best interests" of the child: Voices from Aboriginal child and family welfare practitioners. *Australian Social Work,* 64(1), 96–112. https://doi.org/10.1080/0312407X.2010.535544.

Lorde, A. (2012). *Sister Outsider: Essays and Speeches*. New York: Crossing Press.
Lorde, A. and Rich, A. (1981). An interview with Audre Lorde. *Signs: Journal of Women in Culture and Society*, 6(4), 713–736.
Mehrotra, G. (2010). Toward a continuum of intersectionality theorizing for feminist social work scholarship. *Affilia*, 25(4), 417–430. https://doi.org/10.1177/0886109910384190.
Ramazanoglu, C. and Holland, J. (2002). *Feminist Methodology: Challenges and Choices*. London: Sage.
Roy, A. (2014). *Capitalism: A Ghost Story*. Chicago: Haymarket Books.
Tong, R. (1989). *Feminist Thought: A Comprehensive Introduction*. London: Routledge.
Zuffery, C. (2015). Intersectional feminism and social work responses to homelessness. In S. Wahab, B. Anderson-Nathe and C. Gringeri (Eds.), *Feminisms in Social Work Research: Promise and Possibilities for Justice Based Knowledge* (pp. 104–116). New York: Routledge.

PART ONE
ABORIGINAL PERSPECTIVES

2

Invisible from the Start: Australian Aboriginal People's Experiences of Difference and Aboriginal Community-Controlled Organisations

Sigrid Herring and Jo Spangaro

> *This chapter was written on the land of the Wallumattagal and Burramattagal people of the Dharug nation, who continue their ongoing custodianship of the land and waters. We acknowledge that we are on this land as beneficiaries of an uncompensated and unreconciled dispossession, which continues today and which was never ceded. We pay respect to Elders past, present and emerging.*

This chapter explores experiences of Aboriginal people's experience of being 'othered' in Australia, since the time of invasion/colonisation, focusing on the invisibility of their knowledges, which has continued through to invisibility and diminishment of Aboriginal community-controlled organisations. We propose some practice strategies that social workers may consider in shifting this ground. Recognising that practice changes need to go hand in hand with policy changes, nonetheless for the purposes of this chapter our focus is predominantly practice and organisational-level insights.[1] We recognise, too, the similarities between the many forms of racist and colonialist oppression in Australia, which are both multiple and intersecting (Collins and Bilge, 2016; Mattsson, 2014; Moreton-Robinson, 2004). In light of what we see as the particular invisibility of Aboriginal people's contribution *and* experiences we elected to exclusively address their experiences.

Since the occupation of Australia in 1788 Aboriginal people have experienced wholesale destruction through mass slaughter (Elder, 1988), loss of land and introduced diseases (King et al., 2009), as well as policies of assimilation, segregation and the systematic removal of Aboriginal children (McGregor, 2002). Discourses of state-directed destruction of Aboriginal cultures in Australia imply that these practices occurred only in the distant past. This denies their continuation into the late twentieth century, with Aboriginal children being removed on the basis of race until 1970 (Human Rights and Equal Opportunity Commission, 1997). Even less well known is that, until 1972, children could be excluded from a New South Wales school on the basis of Aboriginality, if any member of the school community objected to their presence (Cadzow, 2008). This othering and exclusion from Australian statutes and society continue today, resulting in a blindness on the part of white society, including social workers, to the systematic racism, which is Australian Aboriginal people's largest problem.

An example of the depth of this othering for Aboriginal people was their classification as being 'sub-human', originating from William Dampier in 1697, who described Aboriginal people as 'the miserablest ... in the world, who unlike the great variety of savages, had no houses and skin garments, sheep, poultry or fruits of the earth' (Anderson and Perrin, 2007, p. 3). This classification was continued by Charles Darwin who took a philosophical approach to the demise of Aboriginal populations explaining that 'the varieties of man seem to act on each other in the same way as different species of animals – the stronger always extirpating the weaker' (Darwin, 1989, pp. 431–436).

We come to this project as a non-Aboriginal woman (JS) and a Gomeroi Aboriginal woman (SH) who have worked together for more than ten years on research projects on Aboriginal people's experiences of abuse and racism. With profound respect for each other's thinking, SH uses joint projects as an opportunity to give voice to ideas about Aboriginal people's experiences of racism, remaining free to work in community. JS, an academic, prefers for Aboriginal women's unique experiences and responses to gendered violence to be visible in her work, welcoming the growing cohort of Aboriginal researchers leading their own projects. Our theoretical starting point is that power disparities based on gender, race and economic standing facilitate both abuse and exclusion, fostering intergenerational trauma for *most* Aboriginal people, who also face past and present tolerance towards the inhumane treatment they have experienced, being perpetually retraumatised by the embedded racism of human service systems.

Being trauma-informed is central to our work – we recognise that traumatic experiences are widespread, universally so among Aboriginal people. Drawing on the writings of Judith Herman, we recognise that trauma is both disempowering and causes disconnection, which social workers need to factor into service provision. Principles of anti-oppressive practice and intersectionality also underpin our approach, recognising that the difficulties which bring people to the attention of human service agencies are exacerbated by discrimination based on race, ethnicity, sexual orientation, gender and class.

Missing from the dominant discourse in relation to Australian Aboriginal people is recognition of their prized and continuously held knowledges and practices. As framed by Moreton-Robinson (2004), Aboriginal people are often represented as 'the known', but rarely are they represented as 'knowers' (p. 75). Previous to the 1788 invasion, Aboriginal people had determined every aspect of their lives for 65,000 years (Clarkson et al., 2017), representing 3,000 generations of people responsible for their own governance, autonomy, land management, child-rearing, law and work. An example of unrecognised Aboriginal knowledges is their extensive practices of agriculture and trade recently documented by Bruce Pascoe (2014), a Bunurong man. Awareness of this sophisticated land use was suppressed, Pascoe argues, because a dominant story of Aboriginal people as nomadic hunter-gatherers made land theft easier to justify. Aware that his thesis would be questioned, Pascoe predominantly based his argument on accounts by early white explorers, recognising that their knowledge base continues to be given greater credibility than that of Aboriginal people's own oral history. His strategy reinforces the fact that current as well as past knowledges by Aboriginal people are not recognised.

Profound understanding of Australian ecology has been documented by Aboriginal people in areas where information was considered not to be available (e.g. Burbidge et al., 1988). Aboriginal people held deep understanding of the relationship between moon phases and tides, well before this was proposed by scientists in the sixteenth century (Norris and Norris, 2007). Aboriginal understanding of the importance of autonomy and close relationships with all family members (Kruske et al., 2012) is only now being identified as central to child development. These examples are fragments of the exploding awareness of the advanced nature of Aboriginal thought and culture, which encompass spiritual and social values – principles that ensure the well-being of everyone, through interdependence, multiple attachments and relationships supported by an elaborate kinship system that sees each person, plant and animal in a reciprocal relationship (Lohoar et al., 2014). Containment of these knowledges in stories, songs, dance and art, as well as transferred orally and bodily from person to person, establishes and maintains bonds and encourages harmony and balance, ensuring interdependent relationships. The deeply held spiritual beliefs of Aboriginal people was another area of blindness for invaders, feeding into ideas of Aboriginal people as a primitive and 'decadent' form of humanity, justifying dispossession and violence (Stanner, 1979). The recent 'narrative turn' (Czarniawska, 2004), which has found recognition in Western thinking, echoes long-standing Aboriginal cultural emphasis on story, yarning and connection. Despite the depth of evidence which exists for these diverse knowledges, they remain hidden, as do collectively Aboriginal people, their culture, practices and places in Australia.

The 1788 invasion sparked 'colonisation', experienced by Aboriginal people as murder, dispossession and displacement, stripping them of agency and leaving a legacy of inequality (Australian Human Rights Commission, 1997). Since then, at least ten generations of Australian Aboriginal children have been socialised under the policies of *terra nullius*, which include extermination, exclusion and assimilation, and which have shaped their lives with messages conveying that 'you neither exist nor matter', 'you can legally be murdered' and 'you are not good enough'. Similarly, ten generations of non-Aboriginal children have been socialised to see this treatment of Aboriginal people as legitimate, reinforcing the common prejudices.

The introduction of the *Racial Discrimination Act, 1975* heralded an opportunity for Aboriginal people to once again shape their own experiences. Aboriginal community-controlled health services (ACCHSs) began to be established, although they were not recognised as legitimate parts of the health system by State and Federal governments for ten years, relying solely on donations (Bell et al., 2000). Providing important places for recovery, healing and empowerment, ACCHSs are also critical for addressing Aboriginal people's significant health disadvantages. However their contribution seems to be rarely raised in discussions about addressing Aboriginal health mortality and morbidity. The 140 ACCHSs in Australia provide primary health and other specialised care for 275,000 Aboriginal people every year (National Aboriginal Community Controlled Health Organization, 2016). Though use of these services by Aboriginal people continues to grow, and outcomes for patients improve (National Aboriginal Community Controlled Health Organization, 2016), this is not part of the dominant narrative of this important stream of services. The opposite is the case, with reports of withdrawal of funding from long-standing and valued Aboriginal services common (Alexander, 2015; Davidson, 2017; Wahlquist, 2016). These closures not only include primary care services, which communities heavily rely on, but have also been applied to whole communities in remote areas of Western Australia, which State and Federal governments have deemed 'too expensive' to support (Wahlquist, 2016). We contend that the pervasive, yet invisible, nature of white privilege means that closure of a (white) hospital would never be contemplated on the basis of governance issues, as has more than once been the case for ACCHSs.

This injustice is particularly salient given that Aboriginal people under-use mainstream (white) health services (Cunningham and Paradies, 2013; Priest et al., 2011b). Instead help is often sought only in emergencies or when situations have become serious (King et al., 2009; Shahid et al., 2009; Taylor, 2010). Indeed, accessibility of mainstream services by Aboriginal people has been identified as requiring policy redress (Wenitong et al., 2007).

Invisibility and diminishment of ACCHSs occur for three reasons, we propose. Firstly, there is systematic evidence of racism towards Aboriginal people in education, welfare, public housing, and the criminal justice system (Priest et al., 2011a). This occurs at a system as well as an individual level, with generalist Aboriginal services expected to address a multiplicity of needs for which multiple specialist agencies exist to address those same needs of white people. Secondly, we contend that the existence of services which recognise the unique needs of Aboriginal people flips the lens. These are places in which for a change, white people would experience themselves as the 'other.' For white people the existence of Aboriginal services is often seen as unnecessary, at best, and an affront at worst. In our conversations with white social workers/health practitioners about ACCHSs, a dominant view is that not all Aboriginal people want to use these services, or that many prefer to use mainstream services for issues of confidentiality. We find white health workers often view ACCHSes competitively, with defensiveness of mainstream services and criticism of ACCHSes common. A discourse of ACCHSes as valued services and the right of Aboriginal people is missing. We find in these conversations a lack of appreciation that mainstream services are white services. As has been argued elsewhere, to even notice whiteness in Australia today is often taken as a form of affront, such is the othering of black (or not-white) people and the invisibility of whiteness itself (Walter et al., 2013). Such reactions can also be understood as 'white fragility', a concept explored in Chapter 17 of this book. We suggest that this appreciation is likely to be shared by non-White individuals who are not Aboriginal.

A third reason for diminishing ACCHSs is that efforts to demonstrate the value of interventions delivered in Aboriginal community-controlled organisations are hampered by the dominant narrative about what 'evidence' comprises and its lack of fit with Aboriginal culture (Burbidge et al., 1988). 'Gold standard' medical evidence comprises randomised controlled trials, samples identified through standardised assessment and allocation to an intervention or control group. Patient willingness to answer standardised health tools, consent to research participation and accept the possibility of intervention being withheld (from control groups) are givens. None of these processes work for Aboriginal people, for whom these processes replicate the intrusion, loss of control and discrimination endured for 200 years (Sibthorpe et al., 2002). Unless culturally appropriate evidence measures are developed, the continued reliance on the 'gold standard' will render the value of ACCHSs impossible to demonstrate.

Social work in Australia has reproduced this diminishment of Aboriginal people and services in a number of ways. First, social work discourses have characterised Aboriginal people as a special population, to be managed, with social workers typically being in a role of social control, particularly in the execution of welfare policies (Bennett, 2013). Narratives of Aboriginal stories usually focus on disadvantage, bordering on depredation, with Aboriginal people seen as synonymous with social problems such as 'overcrowding'. For Aboriginal people, the social welfare system is the same sector which has been responsible for the Stolen Generation and the imposition of much of the trauma which they still carry. While Aboriginal communities are sensible of this history, most social workers seem to be unable to account for it.

Turning the lens to common practices by white social workers in engaging with Aboriginal people, we find that current practice continues to replicate the invisibility and othering of Aboriginal people in Australia. We identify six practices which we have found are common in services: (1) assuming that Aboriginal service users will trust social workers from the outset and share their personal stories and information; (2) failing to recognise cultural protocols for establishing trust; (3) concluding that if Aboriginal people do not attend mainstream health or social work services they do not need or want the service; (4) failing to appreciate the value of Aboriginal Medical Services to Aboriginal people, instead maintaining a discourse about the need for 'choice' (or need for confidentiality); (5) consulting with Aboriginal communities solely through individual high-profile workers or community members, rather than securing a range of views; (6) recruiting sole Aboriginal positions, without recognising the isolation or burdens this imposes.

We draw on interviews with Aboriginal women to understand their preferences in relation to engagement with health and human services. Undertaken as part of a study on women's decisions to disclose intimate partner violence to health providers (Spangaro et al., 2016), we explored how decisions were made more broadly to share information with health providers, and discovered the meaning of ACCHS to these 12 Aboriginal women. Recruited from three regional Aboriginal and Maternal Infant Health Services (AMIHS) at a regular clinic visit, ethical approval for the study was given by the New South Wales Aboriginal Health and Medical Research Council and agreement obtained from three local Aboriginal-controlled organisations.

While Aboriginal people have little choice but to use mainstream (white) health services in many instances, it is clear from the women's words that using such services is often stressful, bringing judgement, incomprehension and racism.

> *When you're sitting in a white fella's clinic around white people you're just sitting there – can't relax because there's no blacks there. White fellas don't really know our ways.* (R)
>
> *You get stared at or judged.* (S)

For many Aboriginal people, legacies of their own childhood experiences and those of previous generations of overt discrimination and judgement leave wariness, and a desire to protect their own children from the same treatment.

> *We'd feel like everyone was watching us all the time. That's the one thing I don't like is when my kids are playing and there's people watching them like disgusted. I don't want my kids to be put in a situation like I was back then. We're looked down upon, not all the time and you try to see stuff from their side but you just know your own history.* (U)

Being patronised in mainstream services was also commonplace for the women we spoke to, as was having stereotyped assumptions made on the basis of their colour.

> *People don't talk to you like they're on your level. They think you're not educated or whatever because of the colour of your skin. Speak down to you.* (F)

The inverse common experience for Aboriginal people, too, is having people question their Aboriginality because they have fair skin.

> *I have to explain why I'm Aboriginal – fair with blue eyes.* (N)

The women we interviewed described experiences that indicated institutional racism, not just racism on a one-off, individual basis.

> *If you are black you get accused of being a thief. If you are fair, you're not black.* (N)
>
> *At the hospital we had problems. Every time I walked in there – the Pink Ladies café – they'd yell out 'Milo – Milo chocolate'. It was really bad – to let the other workers know I was there – to watch me in case I steal something.* (R)
>
> *They assume because we are Aboriginal and because he drinks that he is abusive. They keep asking and saying, 'Are you sure ...?'* (B)

Failure to take the time to build trust and establish a relationship goes against Aboriginal protocols and has a negative impact on Aboriginal people's health care.

> *They can be quite rude to you. It feels like they do judge you because of your colour, doesn't make you feel very comfortable. It is in and out in fifteen minutes. (C)*
>
> *You see different people every time. It's sterile. You're just a number, in and out. (S)*

These accounts contrast starkly with the women's descriptions of using an ACCHS. The first element which stands out is the sense of safety and support the Aboriginal women described. Receiving a service from another Aboriginal worker contrasted with the judgement some women had experienced in mainstream services, cutting through the power differences.

> *Aboriginal workers here stay on your level. They're not racist or anything. Been there sort of thing – yeah, in your shoes. They make you feel welcome, they don't look down on you, make you feel part of the team. (F)*
>
> *The Aboriginal workers are like sisters and can sit down and have a yarn. You feel real comfortable and can open up. I'm wary though because upstairs they're white and they know a lot. (T)*

Women's accounts suggested that the Aboriginal services paid active attention to building relationships with patients, in line with cultural protocols which require getting to know people before information is shared. This practice builds cultural safety and contrasted starkly with experiences in mainstream services.

> *The service is for our people. It's lovely here. Friendly. They know everyone, know us, all one big family. (R)*
>
> *The people are nice to talk to, make sure everything's done properly, make you feel comfortable, make you laugh. (L)*
>
> *I love coming to places like this, it's like a family, you feel comfortable, culturally understood. They know your history, medical histories and family. My mother and sisters and brothers were here as well. They really do care, you can ring as many times as you want to ask questions. (C)*
>
> *The non-Aboriginal workers here are fine. They understand Aboriginal people as a community – that you don't need to be black to be Aboriginal. (B)*

The comfort of being surrounded by other Aboriginal service users was a repeated theme in the women's accounts.

> *You get to see more people you know, and you get to know more people. (S)*
>
> *We're Aboriginal so it's more comfortable, more homely, more friendly. (N)*

It is not an exaggeration to label these reactions to using Aboriginal-specific services as joy. The holistic, person-centred approach these women describe is integral to the ACCHS approach. It contrasts strongly with the dominant understanding of the role and value of ACCHSs to Aboriginal people. Valuing these services does not mean that Aboriginal people never prefer or choose to use mainstream services. Nor does it mean that Aboriginal people disregard white workers. In ACCHSs white workers are held to a different standard. Having chosen to work in an Aboriginal organisation they acculturate, adapting their practice to be culturally safe.

Support for these women's accounts is found elsewhere in the literature, with Westwood and Westwood (2010) reporting that Aboriginal communities lack confidence in mainstream services. Furthermore, the presence of other Aboriginal service users contributes to cultural safety (Spangaro et al., 2016). This is an experience that white service users take for granted but is equally desired by Aboriginal people. In Australia helping professions predominantly reflect the make-up and values of the dominant, white-Anglo culture (Walter et al., 2013), which renders culture largely invisible (Tannoch-Bland, 1998). Whiteness theory, which explores how white people's experience commonly stands in Western culture as the human or universal experience, allowing white people to be seen as individuals, while others are understood as members of racial groups, provides a useful frame for understanding these experiences (Jeyasingham, 2011). The Aboriginal women in our study understood mainstream hospitals as *white* services, a view which is missed from a position of whiteness, as is the value of Aboriginal-specific services to their users. As Walter and colleagues (2013) have observed, social work as a profession is yet to fully engage with an understanding of itself as raced.

This preference by the women we spoke with for Aboriginal services can also be understood as resistance to the prescriptions of marginalisation. Using Aboriginal services is a claim for Aboriginality. In this sense ACCHSs can be viewed as constituting sites of anti-oppressive practice, which starts with a macro-focused analysis of structural inequality (Baines, 2007), of significant relevance given the systemic discrimination Aboriginal people experience. We propose three ways white social workers can use anti-oppressive thinking in working with Aboriginal people, drawing on earlier work (Herring et al., 2013). The three elements are: (1) becoming informed; (2) taking a stance; and (3) reaching out.

First, white social workers, as others have also observed, need to *fully understand the history of Aboriginal people and their dispossession* (Bennett, 2013). Alongside this is the need for social workers to recognise the depth and extent of trauma that Aboriginal people continue to experience, coupled with the intimidation they face accessing mainstream (white) services. Service providers also need to learn about their Aboriginal communities: local history; cultural practices; cultural brokers; and spokespersons. This is work which individuals need to undertake themselves, rather than shifting responsibility for their learning to Aboriginal individuals or organisations.

Taking a stance as a social worker entails recognition that, unless the client base of your agency reflects not only the Aboriginal population but the proportion of those Aboriginal people experiencing that problem, the Aboriginal community is being discriminated against. For many social issues such as interpersonal violence and mental illness, which disproportionately affect Aboriginal people, client loads should be proportionate. In reality, Aboriginal people are invisible in most the client data of most agencies, with many non-Aboriginal service providers attributing this to preferences by Aboriginal people not to access the service. This should sound a note of warning that, rather, the service is not viewed by the Aboriginal community as welcoming or safe. Agencies cannot simply expect Aboriginal people to attend but must demonstrate their cultural safety and need to plan thoughtfully for this.

The third stage we propose, of *reaching out*, follows only after, as individuals, we have undertaken the first two steps. This is a reciprocal process in which social workers can both involve Aboriginal service users as active participants in shaping the interventions they want (Bennett, 2013) and find out how to support the local Aboriginal organisations and work to develop partnerships. Genuine offers of skills, resources and respectful, reciprocal relationships need to be at the forefront of this type of engagement, so as not to further burden already stretched Aboriginal workers. ACCHSs struggle to meet complex health and social problems on their own. In the past social workers have been too ready to see a lack of enthusiastic response by Aboriginal organisations, to any overtures, as hostile or rejecting, instead of considering the possibility these services are rightly suspicious of token consultation or, alternatively, exhausted. These three steps can provide a road map to white social workers paralysed by guilt or inertia in responding to the structural racism Aboriginal people experience.

Recasting Aboriginal people in Australia as 'knowers' who hold profound wisdom for us all changes inexorably the relationships between us. Drawing on anti-oppressive thinking, possibilities for supporting this important work and taking responsibility for one's own learning emerge for social work. Myriad opportunities exist for social workers to develop partnerships with Aboriginal organisations and to demonstrate the empathy, respect and empowering practices central to our core values to address institutional racism, provide cultural safety in mainstream services, advocate for Aboriginal communities and support rightful self-determination.

Further readings

Bennett, B. (2013). The importance of Aboriginal and Torres Strait Islander history for social work students and graduates. In B. Bennett, S. Green, S. Gilbert and D. Bessarab (Eds.), *Our Voices: Aboriginal and Torres Strait Islander Social Work*. South Yarra: Palgrave Macmillan.

Spangaro, J., Herring, S., Frail, M., Koziol-McLain, J., Rutherford, A., and Zwi, A. (2016). They aren't really black fellas but they are easy to talk to: Factors which influence Australian Aboriginal women's decision to disclose intimate partner violence during pregnancy. *Midwifery*, 41, 79–88. https://doi.org/10.1016/j.midw.2016.08.004.

Moreton-Robinson (2004), *Whitening Race: Essays in Social and Cultural Criticism*. Canberra: Aboriginal Studies Press.

References

Alexander, H. (2015). Aboriginal Medical Service to close over unpaid tax debt, *The Sydney Morning Herald*, 2 July. http://www.smh.com.au/nsw/government-closes-aboriginal-medical-service-over-unpaid-tax-debt-20150701-gi2ljo.html

Anderson, K. and Perrin, C. (2007). 'The miserablest people in the world': Race, humanism and the Australian Aborigine. *The Australian Journal of Anthropology*, 18(1), 18–39.

Australian Human Rights Commission (1997). *Bringing Them Home: Report of the National Inquiry into the Separation of Aboriginal and Torres Strait Islander Children from Their Families*. Canberra: Australian Government. https://www.humanrights.gov.au/publications/bringing-them-home-report-1997.

Baines, D. (2007). *Doing Anti-Oppressive Practice: Building Transformative Politicized Social Work*. Halifax, NS: Fernwood Publishing.

Bell, K., Couzos, S., Daniels, J., Hunter, P., Mayers, N. and Murray, R. (2000). Aboriginal community controlled health services. *General Practice in Australia*, 2000, 74–103.

Bennett, B. (2013). The importance of Aboriginal and Torres Strait Islander history for social work students and graduates. In B. Bennett, S. Green, S. Gilbert and D. Bessarab (Eds.), *Our Voices: Aboriginal and Torres Strait Islander Social Work* (pp. 11–21). South Yarra: Palgrave Macmillan.

Burbidge, A., Johnson, K., Fuller, P. and Southgate, R. (1988). Aboriginal knowledge of the mammals of the central deserts of Australia. *Australian Wildlife Research*, 15, 9–39.

Cadzow, A. (2008). A NSW Aboriginal education timeline 1788–2007. Board of Studies NSW. https://ab-ed.nesa.nsw.edu.au/go/aboriginal-studies/timeline.

Clarkson, C., Jacobs, Z., Marwick, B., Fullagar, R., Wallis, L., Smith, M. and Shulmeister, J. (2017). Human occupation of northern Australia by 65,000 years ago. *Nature*, 547(7663), 306–310.

Collins, P.H. and Bilge, S. (2016). *Intersectionality*. Newark, NJ: John Wiley & Sons.

Cunningham, J. and Paradies, Y. (2013). Patterns and correlates of self-reported racial discrimination among Australian Aboriginal and Torres Strait Islander adults, 2008–09: Analysis of national survey data. *International Journal for Equity in Health*, 12(47). https://doi.org/10.1186/1475-9276-12-47.

Czarniawska, B. (2004). *Narratives in Social Science Research*. London: Sage Publications.

Darwin, C. (1989). *The Voyage of the Beagle*. London: Penguin.

Davidson, H. (2017). Indigenous sexual health funding cut without consultation, senators told, *The Guardian Australia*, 28 March. https://www.theguardian.com/australia-news/2017/mar/07/funding-to-two-indigenous-sexual-health-programs-cut-without-consultation.

Elder, B. (1988). *Blood on the Wattle: Massacres and Maltreatment of Australian Aborigines since 1788*. New York: New Holland Publishers.

Herring, S., Spangaro, J., Lauw, M. and McNamara, L. (2013). The intersection of trauma, racism, and cultural competence in effective work with Aboriginal people: Waiting for trust. *Australian Journal of Social Work*, 66(1), 104–117.

Human Rights and Equal Opportunity Commission (1997). *Bringing Them Home: Report of the National Inquiry into the Separation of Aboriginal and Torres Strait Islander Children from Their Families*. Sydney: NSW Human Rights and Equal Opportunity Commission.

Jeyasingham, D. (2011). White noise: A critical evaluation of social work education's engagement with whiteness studies. *British Journal of Social Work*, 42(4), 669–686.

King, M., Smith, A. and Gracy, M. (2009). Indigenous health part 2: The underlying causes of the health gap. *The Lancet*, 374, 76–85.

Kruske, S., Belton, S., Wardaguga, M. and Narjic, C. (2012). Growing up our way: The first year of life in remote Aboriginal Australia. *Qualitative Health Research*, 22(6), 777–787.

Lohoar, S., Butera, N. and Kennedy, E. (2014). *Strengths of Australian Aboriginal Cultural Practices in Family Life and Child Rearing*. Melbourne: Child Family Community Australia. https://healthinfonet.ecu.edu.au/key-resources/publications/28408/?title=Strengths%20of%20Australian%20Aboriginal%20cultural%20practices%20in%20family%20life%20and%20child%20rearing.

Mattsson, T. (2014). Intersectionality as a useful tool: Anti-oppressive social work and critical reflection. *Affilia*, 29(1), 8–17.

McGregor, R. (2002). Breed out the colour; Or, the importance of being white. *Australian Historical Studies*, 33, 286–302.

Moreton-Robinson, A. (2004). Whiteness, epistemology and Indigenous representation. In A. Moreton-Robinson (Ed.), *Whitening Race: Essays in Social and Cultural Criticism*. Canberra: Aboriginal Studies Press.

National Aboriginal Community Controlled Health Organization (2016). *Healthy Futures Aboriginal Community Controlled Health Services Report Card 2016* Canberra: Australian Institute of Health and Welfare.

Norris, R. and Norris, C. (2007). *An Introduction to Australian Aboriginal Astronomy*. Sydney: Commonwealth Scientific and Industrial Research Organisation.

Pascoe, B. (2014). *Dark Emu: Black Seeds, Agriculture or Accident*. Broome, WA: Magabala Books.

Priest, N., Paradies, Y., Gunthorpe, W., Cairney, S. and Sayers, S. (2011a). Racism as a determinant of social and emotional wellbeing for Aboriginal Australian youth. *Medical Journal of Australia*, 194(10), 546–550.

Priest, N., Paradies, Y., Stewart, P. and Luke, J. (2011b). Racism and health among urban Aboriginal young people. *BioMedical Central Public Health*, 11(568). https://doi.org/2458/11/568.

Shahid, S., Finn, L.D. and Thompson, S.C. (2009). Barriers to participation of Aboriginal people in cancer care: Communication in the hospital setting. *Medical Journal of Australia*, 190(10), 574–579.

Sibthorpe, B., Bailie, R., Brady, M., Ball, S., Sumner-Dodd, P. and Hall, W. (2002). The demise of a planned randomised controlled trial in an urban Aboriginal medical service. *Medical Journal of Australia*, 176(6), 273–276.

Spangaro, J., Herring, S., Frail, M., Koziol-McLain, J., Rutherford, A. and Zwi, A. (2016). They aren't really black fellas but they are easy to talk to: Factors which influence Australian Aboriginal women's decision to disclose intimate partner violence during pregnancy. *Midwifery*, 41, 79–88. https://doi.org/10.1016/j.midw.2016.08.004.

Stanner, W.E.H. (1979). Religion, totemism and symbolism. In C.D. Rowley (Ed.), *The Destruction of Aboriginal Society*. Ringwood: Penguin.

Tannoch-Bland, J. (1998). Identifying white race privilege. In Foundation for Aboriginal and Islander Research Action (Ed.), *Bringing Australia Together: The Structure and Experience of Racism in Australia* (pp. 33–38). Brisbane: Foundation for Aboriginal and Islander Research Action.

Taylor, A. (2010). Here and now: The attendance issue in Indigenous early childhood education. *Journal of Education Policy*, 25, 677–699.

Wahlquist, C. (2016). Fears Western Australia will close remote Indigenous communities 'by stealth', *The Guardian Australia*, 14 July. https://www.theguardian.com/australia-news/2016/jul/14/fears-western-australia-will-close-remote-indigenous-communities-by-stealth.

Walter, M., Taylor, S. and Habibis, D. (2013). Australian social work is white. In B. Bennett, S. Green, S. Gilbert and D. Bessarab (Eds.), *Our Voices: Aboriginal and Torres Strait Islander Social Work*. South Yarra: Palgrave Macmillan.

Wenitong, M., Mokak, R., Councillor, H., Delaney Thiele, D. and Calma, T. (2007). Rising to the health challenge for Aboriginal and Torres Strait Islander peoples: What will it take?, *Medical Journal of Australia*, 186(10), 491–492.

Westwood, B. and Westwood, G. (2010). Aboriginal cultural awareness training: Policy v. accountability – failure in reality. *Australian Health Review*, 34, 423–429.

3
Transforming Classrooms: Developing Culturally Safe Learning Environments

Mareese Terare

My name is Mareese Terare, I am Bundjalung Minjungbal woman with ancestral ties to Goenpul country Minjerribah. I am granddaughter of slaves from Vanuatu – Tanna Island.

I pay my deepest respects to the Gadigal people of the Eora Nation whose land I write this story on. I pay my deepest respects to the Elders past and present and to Gadigal people who have maintained their tribal identity through colonisation and attempts of genocide.

Introduction

A culturally safe learning environment is where all learners believe and feel competent in talking about and promoting diversity with their cohort, and extends to within professional and personal spheres. This process is especially critical if most of the students are white (Williams, 1999). Academics (curriculum development, research and lecturing) must possess a deep understanding of issues impacting on First Nations students, their families and their communities. Privileging students' voices in the learning environment is a way forward to emancipatory education and offers self-determining learning opportunities.

Glossary

Indigenous peoples – I use the term Indigenous peoples to include original people of Australia, this includes Aboriginal peoples from the many (approximately 300) tribal areas of mainland Australia, Torres Strait Islander peoples from the Islands of

▶

the Torres Straits, and First Nations peoples. The term 'peoples' refers to the many nations of tribal peoples.

Assimilationists – Stems from early colonialists who exercised their power to stop and hinder Aboriginal people from practising their epistemology, ontology and axiology through dispossession, stolen children and oppressive policies and laws. This oppressive practice is being performed in contemporary Indigenous Australian communities.

Participants – These are adult learners and the preferred term rather than students.

Transformational learning – Participants demonstrate the capacity to learn while letting go of historical oppressive learning experiences. Oppressive experiences are where participants, as students, were treated without respect as to their individual needs, epistemology, axiology and ontology.

Interpersonal trauma – Relates to experiences of trauma that have occurred within the context of close familial relationships. This experience of trauma is also known as an adverse childhood experience, which includes sexual assault, child maltreatment and physical, emotional and psychological abuse.

Ghosts – Unresolved issues that impact on personal communication processes, including listening, trust and cognition.

Facilitators – I use the term facilitators. It is based on the assumption that all participants are equal and bring their power, knowledge and wisdom when attending learning environments. The facilitator will coordinate learning strategies to encourage the sharing of knowledge and learning.

Dilly bag – A dilly bag, or dillybag, is a traditional Australian Aboriginal bag, typically woven from the fibres of plant species of the *Pandanus* genus. It is used by women for a variety of food transportation and preparation purposes (Carew and Hughes, 1995).

Background

The very purpose of colonial Australia was penalty and correction; people were sent here for punitive measures. Punitive treatment of convicts extended to Indigenous peoples, clans and tribes and was perpetrated by colonialist governments and settlers, violating every aspect of First Nations peoples' human rights. Historical contexts have directly impacted on the capacity of educators to provide culturally safe environments, despite their stated intentions to do so. Equality and equity are well-established principles that are widely held in organisational policy but, in practice, are not consistently delivered due to historically derived cultural perceptions of race and exclusively Eurocentric worldviews.

Developing cultural safety, while considering and honouring the profound difference in realities created by politics of race and class (hooks, 1994, p. 51) in the learning environment, is essential for both Indigenous and non-Indigenous student cohorts. Through this process, transformational learning is an outcome; previous oppressive learning experiences are critiqued; and students are empowered to construct new knowledge based on new information and other worldviews.

Drawing on my professional experience with community health training, research, community development, curriculum development and higher education, I would go to the extent of saying it was an absolutely humbling experience and privilege to engage and share information with Indigenous and non-Indigenous workers about the definition, extent, prevalence, nature and characteristics of interpersonal trauma and racism. This sense of privilege is attributed to a cohort's self-determined culturally safe processes with the intent of empowering one's self and others. This is consistent with both Indigenous and non-Indigenous cohorts in their definitions of the essence of secure and safe learning environs. According to hooks, 'to educate as a practice of freedom is a way of teaching that anyone can learn' (hooks, 1994, p. 13). I would further add that part of the process of teaching for freedom is to teach for social justice. Given the opportunity, students embraced their responsibilities in making their classroom safe and secure.

Maximising students' learning is the ultimate goal and, in some situations, very challenging for facilitators. Furthermore, maximising students' learning outcomes when the topic focuses on violations of human rights, such as interpersonal trauma and cultural incompetence, can be even more challenging. The critical issue for educators is that they are competent in developing and designing learning programmes so that adult learners can maximise their learning opportunities.

Establishing safety and liberty paradigms with individual cohorts is a critical component of pedagogical praxis and is paramount for transformational learning to occur. hooks states: 'teachers who believe that our work is not merely to share information but to share in the intellectual and spiritual growth of our students' (hooks, 1994, p. 13). As teachers, we are in powerful positions that can make and shape a student. Engaging students at this level requires commitment to the ideas of reciprocity, which also relates to pedagogy and praxis of Indigenous philosophies and teaching.

Critical pedagogy of Australian colonial history is essential to establishing liberatory learning environs. The notion of Indigenous education is based on assimilationism – the continuing colonial project of 'civilising' and 'educating' Indigenous Australian peoples. Townsend-Cross refers to 'Assimilationist assumptions' as they guide the belief that 'Indigenous peoples, their knowledges and their practices were inferior to Western peoples' knowledge and practices' (Townsend-Cross, 2011, p. 68). Australian First Nations peoples' access to colonial education systems has been driven by the ideologies that the colonial education system is the way forward in ongoing colonisation and genocide which fits perfectly with maintaining the dogma of terra nullius. I concur with Townsend-Cross's summation: 'assimilationist ideology is entrenched and continues to sustain racism in Australian society' (Townsend-Cross, 2011, p. 68).

Information sharing about best practice is required to meet Indigenous peoples' health and well-being needs around critical social issues such as interpersonal trauma. The aim of education ensures that culturally safe environs are developed and presented in a way that is inviting, non-threatening, safe and secure, while taking into consideration that (given the extent of adverse childhood experiences in Australian societies) most of the cohort would have some personal experiences with interpersonal trauma and racism either directly or with a relative and/or friend.

Students usually enter learning environs with a willingness to learn, accompanied with a commitment to enhance their work prospects and the promise of a better future; they also enter with 'ghosts' as a result of previous oppressive learning experiences. The aim of establishing learning environs that support and nurture new and sometimes confronting learning irrespective of its content allows the learner to make sense of the situation and extends personal safety barriers around the new learning. Without this it is possible to trigger individual students to go into their 'default' position – they *switch off*. These default positions can hinder new learning if it is challenging. This can create a 'crisis of thinking'; it also relates to the notion of 'ghosts' – 'ghosts' that come uninvited into the learning environs. It is this phenomenon that has the capacity to challenge liberatory experiences and make learning difficult and arresting.

Teachers can make this process an enlightening and re-empowering experience. They can do this by anticipating and preparing the cohort with predictions of what learners can expect with this sort of material, while validating the learners' feelings and reactions as 'normal' responses. The facilitators would also include as part of the predictions their observations of how learners have historically managed new and often shocking information, and that this response is a normal response. It is critical to the overall learning in the classroom that this process includes the development of a cultural safety agreement.

Aboriginal historical experiences with the colonial education system and resultant current outcomes

The declaration of the myth of terra nullius over Australia, that the land was uninhabited, set the scene to ignore and dominate every aspect of First Nations peoples' survival. The precedent allowed for a terra nullius social policy supported by research that enabled the dispossession of Indigenous peoples' knowledges throughout the colonial history of this country. Martin (2009, p. 203) concurs with Hart and Whatman that 'university curriculum, teaching methodologies and research endeavors have a history of development that contributed to this dispossession' (Hart and Whatman, 1998, p. 10).

As a result of the dogma of terra nullius, Aboriginal peoples' cultural beliefs and worldviews were greatly affected by the onslaught of the colonial and hierarchical worldviews of the sovereign British empire. Barton affirms that the resultant extent of the oppressive and colonial systematic and systemic intervention has set up a scenario where Indigenous peoples 'were excluded in ways that continued the genocidal program of the British colonisers' (Barton, 2011, p. 17).

Colonial constructs maintained the deception of terra nullius in every aspect of colonising Aboriginal lands. The acculturation of Western worldviews profoundly impacted on Aboriginal tribes: dispossession of country, dispossession of belief/cultural system, indoctrination of alien beliefs, alien education systems and state-sanctioned removal of children from kinship, culture and country.

Despite the implied intent of protecting and supporting Indigenous peoples, reserves and missions were established. This allowed colonial systems to remove First Nations peoples and clans from their countries and forcibly relocate them to missions and reserves with other tribal groups. The ongoing colonisation and indoctrination continued with the introduction of Christianity to reserves and mission schools set up exclusively for Indigenous children only. Indigenous people were subjected to the most extreme forms of racism (Sykes, 1989). Missionaries maintained the ideologies of the assimilationist goal of 'civilising and Christianising' the natives. Bin Sallik summarises Indigenous peoples' experiences: 'Aboriginal people had very little formal education because the early colonial authorities were divided on whether Aborigines could be educated' (Sallik, 2003, p. 21).

The 'exclusion on demand' legislation passed by the Minister for Education in 1902 dictated access to education for Aboriginal children (Townsend-Cross, 2011). Aboriginal children were able to attend school as long as there were no complaints from the school community.

If there were complaints, the children were removed immediately, without question, from the school. This was completely up to the school public. The implications of this level of racism are felt today by Aboriginal people and carried as a historical burden and legacy of white Australians. Barton explains this as the white Australia policy, which has provided her people (white people) 'a white nation in which we flourish and part of this legacy is an inherited defensiveness, a requirement to protect my privileges, including what my people took and continue to take, resulting in continue atrocities, theft and violence' (Barton, 2011, p. 18).

The profound long-term effects of draconian laws and practices of human rights violations against First Nation peoples can be felt today. The extent of ill health, social and emotional well-being issues, rates of incarceration, high unemployment and low levels of education can be linked to the sociopolitical and historical contexts of colonisation and genocide against Indigenous people. Indigenous people carry the burden of blatant and government-sanctioned human rights violations (Atkinson, 2002). Indigenous epistemologies (ways of knowing), axiologies (ways of doing) and ontologies (ways of being) were criminalised where punitive measures were enacted on Indigenous peoples who maintained or practised their worldviews; this also included tribal language.

Atkinson, an academic and trauma specialist, is clear about the causes of family breakdown and clearly aligns this to intergenerational trauma, trauma passed down from one generation to the next (Atkinson, 2002, p. 10). Briskman affirms that Indigenous peoples' limited access to education is a common theme impacting greatly on social status (Briskman, 2007, p. 181). She further states: 'school retention is problematic and cultural ineptitude contributes to educational disadvantage' (Briskman, 2007, p. 181). Understanding the sociohistorical issues that impacted on Indigenous peoples is paramount to relating to the current educational status of Indigenous people.

Political human rights: Epistemologies, ontologies and axiologies

BC – that is, Before Cook – the education process was ongoing and lifelong where there were 'complex formal education systems, that supported and sustained Aboriginal peoples for generations and generations' (Townsend-Cross, 2011, p. 69). Indigenous tribal groups developed their strong sense of connection to country, kinship, spirituality and beliefs through yarning, ceremony and doing. This maintained a sense of reciprocity between people and country.

Australia's history of dispossession provides for culturally unsafe environments generally for Aboriginal people. The learning experiences of Aboriginal adult learners is often challenged by historical experiences with an alien colonial educational system. Townsend-Cross (2011) refers to this system as assimilationist ideology.

Indigenous worldviews or philosophies are as dimensional and diverse as our peoples and our countries. Our ways of being, knowing and doing can be located within three paradigms also known as ontology, axiology and epistemology. Wilson explains ontology as: 'ways of being and how you relate in this world, whereas your axiology considers your morals and ethics and how this informs what you know and finally epistemology relates to how you think and what informs your thinking' (Wilson, 2001, p. 175).

Indigenous students need to be supported to operate in both worlds – 'Indigenous ways (ways of knowing, doing and being) as well as non-Indigenous ("Western") ways' (Nakata, 2002, p. 9) – so that they are 'safe and secure in both domains' (Sarra, 2003 cited in Townsend-Cross, 2011, p. 65).

Adult learning theories

My practice in community and health services' industry training sector and higher education encompasses aspects of andragogy. Andragogy is defined as 'the art and science of helping adults learn' and is contrasted with pedagogy, 'the art and science of helping children learn' (Knowles, 1980, p. 43). Andragogy became a central point for those trying to define the field of adult education as separate from other areas of education. The following five assumptions underpin the ideas of andragogy:

> Has an independent self-concept and self-directive learning capacity.

> Has accumulated a reservoir of life experiences that is a rich resource for learning.

> Has learning needs closely related to changing social roles.

> Is problem-centred and interested in the immediate application of knowledge.

> Is motivated to learn by internal rather than external factors (Knowles, 1980, p. 43).

Merriam and Caffarella (cited in Hansmen, 2001, p. 44) argue that: 'Adult learning does not occur in a vacuum' (p. 22). In contrast to psychological and behavioural understandings of learning, sociocultural models posit 'learning is not something that happens, or is just inside the head, but instead is shaped by the context, culture, and tools in the learning situation' (p. 44).

It is therefore paramount that 'for educators who plan and teach, it is understanding how to plan and design programs for adult learners that will profoundly shape learning' (Hansmen, 1991, p. 44). It encompasses and incorporates the learners' developmental needs, ideas, and cultural context into the learning experience (Hansmen, 1991, p. 44).

Historical learning experiences from childhood impact greatly on how people learn as adults. Therefore, if learning was an enjoyable experience, the adult learner will be optimistic and open; however, if the experience is shrouded with failure, shame and a sense of worthlessness, oppression and harm, any new learning opportunities could be a challenge and even conflicting. It is therefore critical that we consider other variables that impact greatly on adult learners, namely adult learning theories. Most learners will have unique and profound learning needs and awareness of learning theories, and the role they have in a learner's journey is a requisite.

Considering the empowering process of hooks' work, if teachers allow their 'pedagogy' (or in this case andragogy) 'to be radically changed by our recognition of a multicultural world, we can give students the education they desire and deserve.' We can maintain the humanistic approach by a way of teaching that 'transform[s] consciousness, creating a climate of free expression that is the essence of a truly liberatory liberal arts education' (hooks, 1994, p. 45).

It is considered best practice and quality assurance that Facilitators within the Registered Training Vocational or Higher Education sectors consider every aspect of an adult learner's capacity to learn and incorporate skills and knowledge into their *'dilly bag'* of educational resources. Among these resources knowledge of adult learning theories is critical. The five schools of adult learning encompass behaviourist, humanist, constructivist, social learning and cognitivist theories.

Behaviourist learning theory consists of learning new information and essentially changing one's behaviour based on this new learning. Three key terms underpin behaviourist theory: (1) changed behaviour indicates learning; (2) learning can be determined by elements in the environment; and (3) repetition and re-enforcement of learning behaviours assist in the learning process (Marquardt and Banks, 2010, p. 87). Developing cultural safety would relate to point (2). Successful learning can be determined by elements such as culturally safe environs. Indigenous adult learners can also rest assured that learning environments are safe and secure and also consist of relevant Indigenous methodologies that actively seek processes of decolonising teaching methods.

The humanist theory applies to learners who have the capacity to self-determine their own learning. This theory works really well with most Indigenous learners. The learners apply this theory to their practice and the motivation in this instance is based on making a different life for themselves; their ways of knowing also play a role where they are wanting to make a difference to their family, community and tribe.

The constructivist learner appreciates radical change. Social justice fits within this theory. Learners apply radical changes to their behaviour and learning. Radical changes through reflective practice are key outcomes for constructivist learners.

Social learning theory focuses on the context in which people learn. Learners who fit into this category simply apply the process of interaction with their peers and mentors. Most learners are working in fields where supervision is or should be obligatory. This is a critical component to learning. Supervision can make a difference to adult learners' capacity to raise key issues that they may not feel comfortable raising in a collective learning environment.

Cognitivist learning theory also applies to learners who utilise insight and perception as a way to add meaning to current situations. This process allows learners to make sense of the impacts of their environment and the implications of this on themselves. This is a profound and transformational process when past learning experiences have been oppressive and unsafe.

Each school brings unique ways of learning and communicating. It would be considered critical practice to develop one's skills with the intent to maximise a learner's learning experiences, and facilitators should have a very good understanding of the intrinsic nature of each learning theory. This understanding extends to the curriculum, the delivery of the curriculum and assessment.

If we apply the assumptions of andragogy and underpin it with the principles of the human rights' discipline of cultural safety, the adult learning approach becomes an essence of reciprocity and self-determination.

Cultural safety

The idea of cultural safety was brought into existence by the visionary work of Ramsden (2002). Ramsden explored ways to ensure the New Zealand nursing profession broaden their knowledge and gain a deeper understanding to develop practical skills to competently respond to Maori peoples. Cultural safety in its essence is about acknowledging and understanding that we are individual cultural beings and this in fact establishes our ways of knowing, being and doing. It is based on the assumption that everyone has a culture. 'Cultural Safety became concerned with social justice' (Ramsden, 2002, p. 5) and is required to work effectively across human differences within the context of training and education within social work and policy studies.

Cultural safety extends beyond cultural awareness and cultural sensitivity. It empowers individuals and enables them to contribute to the achievement of positive outcomes. It encompasses a reflection on individual cultural identity and recognition of the impact of personal culture on professional practice; this consists of values, beliefs, privileges and power. Alternatively, unsafe cultural practices, according to Ramsden (2002, p. 9), can 'diminish, demean or dis-empower the cultural identity and well-being of an individual' (Sallik, 2003, p. 2).

The idea of cultural safety can apply across the disciplines. Cultural safety can be defined as no assault, challenge or denial of their identity, of who they are, and recognition that what they need is an environment that is absolutely safe in all of the following areas:

- Spiritually – Appreciating and welcoming differences in spirituality, religions and belief systems.
- Socially and emotionally – Acknowledging discourse and differences that may impact on one's well-being, that is, mental health or social and emotional well-being.
- Physically
    1. Identity is in the eyes of the beholder; avoid making stereotypes at all cost.
    2. Physical space needs to reflect diversity in the room.
- Self-care – Learners are informed about the potential of vicarious traumatisation. It is an obligatory component of Cultural Safe Practice to develop and implement positive self-care strategies, for example clinical/cultural supervision, body work and so on.
- Reflexivity – The nature of reflexivity allows for educators and students alike to consider and reflect on self and difference. It also applies to decolonising praxis. Martin articulates that: 'Reflexivity challenges us to claim our shortcomings, misunderstandings, oversights and mistakes, to re-claim our lives and make strong changes to our current realities – reflexive practice ensures we do not compromise our identity [while learning]' (Martin, 2009, p. 213).

This allows an empowering exchange of humility, trust and respect. The implementation of a culturally safe group agreement ensures that all learners develop their learning environs to encompass their learning needs as suggested by Bin Sallik: 'an environment that is spiritually, socially and emotionally safe, as well as physically safe for people; where there is no assault, challenge or denial of their identity, of who they are and what they need. It is about shared respect, shared meaning, shared knowledge and experience of learning together' (Sallik, 2003, p. 9).

Cultural vitality must be the outcome for participants where emotional strengths and pride in their culture underpin their ways of knowing, being and doing. Eckermann defines cultural vitality as: 'the emotional strength, the spirit, the essence of people who strive and struggle to maintain strong identity and adapt to new and challenging environments, while they value and pass on distinctive cultural beliefs, practices and life ways' (Eckermann, Dowd et al., 2010). Rigney reinforces that cultural safety and cultural respect are critical when applying the three principles to Indigenous research, namely emancipatory imperative; political integrity; and privileging Indigenous voices, which must also be applied to teaching both Indigenous and non-Indigenous groups about Indigenous epistemologies, ontologies and axiologies (Rigney, 1999).

Reflections

It is critical that we consider and capture the variables that have impacted on learner needs where their learning becomes more than they had hoped for. Pedagogy must include an opportunity to discuss difference and how this affects the learning environment. In thinking about creating cultural safety, the following questions need to be considered:

- How are you developing an understanding of past and contemporary experiences of Indigenous Australians?
- How do you examine Indigenous Australian history and the social, economic and health disadvantages that challenge Indigenous communities in your teaching?
- How do you assist social work students in expanding their understanding of Indigenous ways of being, doing and knowing and gaining the knowledge to provide culturally safe practice to determine their own learning around issues of human rights violations within the context of white privilege?

Conclusion

The cultural interface between Indigenous and non-Indigenous students within classrooms provides challenges and opportunity for change (Nakata, 2002). The educator's role and responsibility are to examine rank and power and whether the dynamics are explicit for the whole group (Mindell, 1995).

Within social work, human rights are key to our work and therefore must underpin our teachings to ensure learners reinvigorate and maintain their individual *cultural vitality*. We cannot despair when there is conflict. Our solidarity must be affirmed by a shared belief in the spirit of intellectual openness that celebrates diversity, welcomes dissent and rejoices in the collective dedication to truth (hooks, 1994, p. 33).

Further readings

Martin, K. (2009). Ways of knowing, being and doing: A theoretical framework and methods for indigenous and Indigenist research. *Australian Studies*, 26(27). https://doi.org/10.1080/14443050309387838

Nakata, M. (2002). Indigenous knowledge and the cultural interface: Underlying issues at the intersection of knowledge and information systems. *International Federation of Library Associations and Institutions Journal*, 28(5/6), 281–291.

Sallik, M. A. B. (2003). Cultural safety: Let's name it!. *The Australian Journal of Indigenous Education*, 32, 21–28.

References

Atkinson, J. (2002). *Trauma Trails, Recreating Song Lines: The Transgenerational Effects of Trauma in Indigenous Australia*, North Melbourne: Spinifex Press.

Barton, A. (2011). Going white: Claiming a racialised identity through the White Australia Policy. *Indigenous Law Bulletin*, 7(23), 16–19.

Briskman, L. (2007). *Social Work with Indigenous Communities*, 1st Edition, Sydney: Federation Press.

Carew, M. and Hughes, A. (1995). *Maningrida: The Language of Weaving*, Melbourne: Australian Exhibitions Touring Agency.

Eckermann, A.-K., Dowd, T., Chong, E., Nixon, L., Gray, R. and Johnson, S. (2010). *Binan Goonj: Bridging Cultures in Aboriginal Health*, 3rd Edition, Chatswood, NSW: Churchill Livingstone.

Griffin, F.J. and Rowell, C.H. (1999). An interview with Farah Jasmine Griffin. *Callaloo*, 22(4), 872–892.

Hansmen, C.A. (2001). Context-based adult learning. *New Directions for Adult and Continuing Education*, 2001, 43–52. https://doi.org/10.1002/ace.7

Hart, V.G. and Whatman, S.L. (1998). Decolonising the concept of knowledge. Paper presented at the HERDSA: Annual International Conference, Auckland, NZ.

hooks, b. (1994). *Teaching to Transgress: Education as the Practice of Freedom*, New York: Routledge.

Knowles, M.S. (1980). *The Modern Practice of Adult Education: From Pedagogy to Andragogy*. Englewood Cliffs, NJ: Cambridge Adult Education.

Marquardt, M. and Banks, S. (2010). Theory to practice: Action learning. *Advances in Developing Human Resources*, 12(2), 159–162.

Martin, K. (2009). Ways of knowing, being and doing: A theoretical framework and methods for Indigenous and Indigenist research. *Australian Studies*, 27(76), 203–214. https://doi.org/10.1080/14443050309387838.

Mindell, A. (1995). *Sitting in the Fire: Large Group Transformation Using Conflict and Diversity*, 2nd Edition, California USA: Deep Democracy Exchange.

Nakata, M. (2002). Indigenous knowledge and the cultural interface: Underlying issues at the intersection of knowledge and information systems. *International Federation of Library Associations and Institutions Journal*, 28(5/6), 281–291.

Ramsden, I. (2002). Cultural safety and nursing education in Aotearoa and Te Waipounamu, Doctoral dissertation, Victoria University of Wellington.

Rigney, L.-I. (1999). Internationalization of an Indigenous anticolonial cultural critique of research methodologies: A guide to Indigenist research methodology and its principles. *Wicazo Sa Review, Emergent Ideas in Native American Studies*, 14(2), 109–121.

Sallik, M.A.B. (2003). Cultural safety: Let's name it!. *The Australian Journal of Indigenous Education*, 32, 21–28.

Sarra, C. (2003). *Young, Black and Deadly: Strategies for Improving Outcomes for Indigenous Students*, Deakin West: Australian College of Educators.

Sykes, B. (1989). *Black Majority*. Hawthorn, VIC: Hudson Publishing.

Townsend-Cross, M. (2011). Indigenous education and Indigenous studies in the Australian Academy: Assimilationism, critical pedagogy, dominant culture learners and Indigenous knowledges. In G. J. Sefa Dei (Ed.), *Indigenous Philosophies and Critical Education: A Reader* (pp. 68–79). New York: Peter Lang.

Williams, R. (1999). Cultural safety: What does it mean for our work practice? *Australian and New Zealand Journal of Public Health*, 23, 213–214. https://doi.org/10.1111.1467-842X.

Wilson, S. (2001). What is indigenous research methodology? *Canadian Journal of Native Education*, 25(2), 175–179.

4

Ownership and Protection of Aboriginal Knowledge: Academic Response and Responsibility

Bindi Bennett

> *I acknowledge the Traditional Custodians of the land I live in, the Jinibara people and the Elders past, present and emerging.*

The normative pronoun 'she' is used throughout this chapter but many of the comments and ideas refer to both male and female Aboriginal people. The chapter is written from a cisgendered Aboriginal woman's viewpoint.

The analogy

Aboriginal people think and speak in stories to teach lessons. In order to keep decolonising the way we write and present information, this chapter will use a story.

It begins with the question which came first – the chicken or the egg?

The chicken

The chicken in this story is the Aboriginal people, holder of vast amounts of cultural knowledge, dating back to the creation of the Earth. She holds this knowledge both consciously and unconsciously, has learnt much by listening, watching and doing, and has a unique world view.

Aboriginal elders have recorded their wisdom and knowledge through song, pictorial and performance art and stories. The ability to interpret this knowledge has been passed down from cultural knowledge holders through the generations, providing Aboriginal people with an unwritten history and rules of life (Calma, 2009a). Aboriginal cultural knowledge has been defined as:

> accumulated knowledge which encompasses spiritual relationships, relationships with the natural environment and sustainable use of natural resources, and relationships between people, which are reflected in language, narratives, social organisation, values, beliefs, and cultural laws and customs. (Andrews, Daylight, Hunt, 2006, p. 3)

Cultural knowledge holders is a term used to describe individuals, family groups or communities that hold and maintain specific details and aspects of cultural knowledge (NSW Government, 2010). Aboriginal people are connected traditionally and historically to their land and peoples. This gives them the right and ability to create and receive ideas passed down from generations of Ancestors. This knowledge is entrusted to her and built on by her teachings and learnings and life experience. This, now well-developed, idea belongs to her and all other Aboriginal peoples.

Colonisation policies have marginalised and oppressed Aboriginal peoples (Bennett, 2013). Many Aboriginal peoples have not received the same opportunities and access to education as others. Aboriginal knowledge is primarily an oral tradition and, therefore, the 'chicken' (Aboriginal academic) may not have the skills or knowledge to make the idea into something larger, bigger, better, influential or permanent. Therefore, she decides to get some help – usually from a non-Indigenous academic or researcher to translate her ideas into a journal article, conference presentation or a grant application.

The egg

The egg in this analogy is the idea, for example an article, presentation or book. In the academic world once an idea has been formally presented it becomes public property and once it has been published it becomes something to be discussed, debated, argued about and developed by others. What occurs in this process is that the Aboriginal voice, governance and ownership often gets lost or diluted. Sometimes other academics start to cite the work and then it may become incorrectly attributed to the individual who cites the work. Often non-Indigenous peoples continue to be seen as leaders in the space and there are numerous examples of Aboriginal-themed books by non-Aboriginal 'experts' that are not authored or even edited by Aboriginal people. Inevitably, some of these publications misrepresent Aboriginal people and their knowledge.

In academia many research supervisors take credit for the prolonged efforts of their PhD students and become senior/corresponding authors of papers that contain topics they have little idea about. Many universities also have guidelines around this type of authorship. This is evidence of the Western thinking around knowledge and ownership of knowledge being tenuous at best.

It is then important to look to raising Aboriginal people into the spaces, privileging voices in a truly collaborative, culturally respectful and meaningful way. In this way we avoid the idea becoming colonised, assimilated or culturally appropriated.

The 'collaborative' omelette

When making something with the egg it is best if the process is collaborative and equal – both chefs add an equal amount of knowledge and skills into the ingredients. Sometimes, though, one chef adds more than the other, especially when it is about Aboriginal cultural knowledge. However, there are times when the process can go wrong, creating if you will scrambled eggs. This can occur in many ways:

The contributions and identity of the Aboriginal person are at risk of not being recognised in the process of writing and academic publishing. This occurs when the Aboriginal person is not given recognition for the production of the idea or the resulting product.

An important question is: Who gets ownership and control of Aboriginal cultural knowledge? Should it be the Aboriginal academic or cultural owner of the knowledge, the Indigenous or non-Indigenous academic who translates the knowledge into academic content, or the academic who integrates the academic content in publications? And should the idea become public property at some point? These are complex issues because, in the academic world, once an idea has been presented, although the copyright remains with the publishers, it becomes public property and, as such, open to discussion, debate and development. Should Aboriginal people somehow keep control of certain topics, ideas or content? It would be hard to argue this is a time of increasing open access but there might be a better way of respecting Aboriginal history and heritage. The important question is: How can Aboriginal views, perspectives and ideas be respected, fully represented and incorporated into Western academia? How do we make sure that Aboriginal people keep control of certain topics, ideas or content? The Australian Association of Social Workers (AASW) is the professional representative body of social workers in Australia. What role does the AASW play in this debate? (Are they the stove, whereby all the cooking around this – for example, principles, protocols – occurs?)

When does the use of Aboriginal knowledge in academia become cultural appropriation?

> But you can't even imagine what it is to live in a culture ... Imagine rethinking all your language and all your exchanges and encounters, all your greetings ... And above all imagine having to do this, in the face of the arrogance of a culture which has not only ruled much of the world but also finds it inconceivable that a culture formally its subject and slave might possess anything even resembling knowledge, let alone wisdom. (Sivaramakrishnan, 1989, p. 6)

Cultural appropriation is the misuse of a group's culture by someone with power to redefine it. In the process of doing this they disassociate it from the people who originally created the idea. While this process often elevates the non-Aboriginal person involved and gives them status and privilege, it can also be interpreted as an inadvertent extension of historical oppression and colonialism (Oluo, 2017). Cultural appropriation is a symptom of the oppressive society in which many Aboriginal peoples live. By defining the ground rules for acceptable cultural appropriation we may enable a situation in which white privilege continues. There are many individuals and institutions that, even when informed of the issues, will continue to manipulate the system for their sole benefit and maintain the status quo. It is essential that Aboriginal governance groups, cultural consultants and Aboriginal academic/researchers are involved in designing and developing equality in universities.

Another way that Aboriginal knowledge/contributions to academic publications is made invisible is the established editorial convention of using 'et al.', whereby only the first author of a reference is identified in the text, although they may be in the reference list. We adopt this practice although its origins are related to the costs of printing and number of pages and words required by journals. It could be argued that the principal researcher, team leader or the person with the most ideas leads the publication. My argument is that without the Aboriginal cultural knowledge the idea could not have progressed and would not have been published. Is there a way to balance this? Nowadays, when most papers are published online and word counts are not as important, there is no need for this restriction. Maybe a small resistance is to never use 'et al.', regardless of the number of authors, or even inventing a new form of in-text referencing specifically to deal with this invisibilising and reconfirming of 'lead' authorship as a taken-for-granted practice. If there were no Aboriginal authors on a paper that was about Indigenous knowledge, perhaps a Governance Group could be cited as lead authors instead to acknowledge the 'chickens' in academia, as long as this group were accepting of the content.

The dangers of cultural appropriation need to be recognised by all researchers and potential authors, and the cultural appropriation of information recognised and acknowledged (Olou, 2017). All parties involved in a product's creation should have rights shared equally according to their contributions and Aboriginal peoples should be fully and appropriately identified. The development of a collaborative relationship between Indigenous and non-Indigenous peoples facilitates the sharing of knowledge and, most significantly, the creation of new intellectual ideas (McGregor, 2014).

How these changes can be achieved is currently the focus of exploration and debate in universities in Australia where the new professional requirement of increasing Aboriginal and Torres Strait Islander content of undergraduate and postgraduate courses is challenging educators (AASW, 2010).

What is intellectual property?

Intellectual property is a generic term for the various rights which the law defines for the protection of creative effort and, in particular, the economic and creative investment made by individuals, groups and institutions. Australian intellectual property regimes are established and governed primarily through Commonwealth legislation (Law Reform Commission of Western Australia, 2006). The World Intellectual Property Organization (WIPO) Intergovernmental Committee on Intellectual Property and Genetic Resources, Traditional Knowledge and Folklore argues that the recognition and protection of Indigenous traditional knowledge has largely taken place within the parameters of intellectual property law (United Nations, 2007). However, WIPO recognises that compliance has been limited due to the Western constructs of intellectual property laws and their failure to accommodate the vastly different requirements for the protection of Indigenous traditional knowledge (United Nations Permanent Forum on Indigenous Issues, 2007).

Article 31, paragraph 1 of the United Nations Declaration on the Rights of Indigenous Peoples provides the most explicit recognition internationally of Indigenous peoples' rights to their traditional knowledge (United Nations, 2008). It states that Indigenous peoples have the right to maintain, control, protect and develop their cultural heritage, traditional knowledge and traditional cultural expressions. Aboriginal peoples also have the right to maintain, control, protect and develop their intellectual property, cultural heritage, traditional knowledge and traditional cultural expressions (United Nations, 2008).

Article 8(j) of the Declaration specifically gives recognition to the traditional knowledge, innovations and practices of Indigenous peoples and local communities while expressing the importance of its protection, preservation and maintenance (United Nations, 2008). Article 8(j) also provides that the use of Indigenous traditional knowledge, innovations and practices should only occur with the approval and involvement of the Indigenous or local community and that any benefits that arise from its use are to be shared with the people or community from which that knowledge originated (Fourmile-Marrie and Kelly, 2000).

However, the United Nations Convention on Biological Diversity (2010) is the only detailed international standard that highlights the importance of traditional knowledge and practices to be protected, preserved and maintained and the need for approval and involvement of the Indigenous person or community responsible for the knowledge when drawing upon Indigenous knowledge systems.

Janke (1998) discusses a suite of areas of rights concerning Indigenous cultural knowledge. She found Indigenous people wanted to own, control and define. We also want to be recognised as the primary guardians and interpreters of our cultures. We ask non-Indigenous peoples to gain prior informed consent for access, use and application of Indigenous cultural knowledge. Lastly, Indigenous peoples want to control the dissemination of our ideas and innovations.

The study by Janke (1998) discusses the rights that Indigenous people have over their cultural and intellectual property and was an important paper when published. However, it does not specifically address knowledge held by universities and social work researchers and how they should interact with these rights. There is no legal obligation for university administrators or academics to adhere to these requests, nor any repercussions if they are ignored or abused. There is a need for research and application in this area. There is limited literature that focuses on the ownership of Indigenous knowledge in regard to social work, or how Australian academics and researchers can remain responsible and respectful. Therefore, the current intellectual property and copyright laws that are enforced to protect and maintain Indigenous knowledge in Australia remain both inadequate and inappropriate (Australia Human Rights Commission, 2008; Calma, 2009a; Smallacombe, 2000).

What is Indigenous knowledge?

I believe that our ability to use our knowledges to secure sustainable futures for our people and our communities, is crucial to our self-determination. (Calma, 2009b, n.p.)

Australian Aboriginal people are the oldest living cultural history in the world (Australian Human Rights Commission, 2008). Indigenous knowledge is based on the social, physical and spiritual understandings that have formed distinct systems of knowledge, innovation and practices (International Council for Science and Traditional Knowledge, 2002). Aboriginal peoples taught successive generations what was important for them to know in order to maintain and care for the land, protect and feed their families and continue to survive (Zubrzycki et al., 2014).

Aboriginal societies are based on an oral rather than literary culture. Nakata (2007) views the differences between Indigenous and Western scientific knowledge systems as 'so disparate as to be incommensurable or reconcilable on cosmological, epistemological and ontological grounds' (p. 8). Eurocentric scholars seeking to understand the Aboriginal cognitive system often interpret it as oppositional to the established Western methods of sharing knowledge (Battiste, 2002, pp. 1–69). 'Indigenous knowledge systems and western knowledge systems work off different theories of knowledge frame who can be the knower, what can be known, what constitutes knowledge, sources of evidence for constructing knowledge and how truth is to be verified' (Nakata, 2007, p. 8). Indigenous knowledge is the information base for a society, which facilitates communication and decision making. Indigenous information systems are also dynamic and continually influenced by internal creativity and experimentation as well as by contact with external influences (Flavier et al., 1995).

Within the academic literature, traditional knowledge is often referred to as intellectual property (Smallacombe, 2000) but the idea that these terms are synonymous is incorrect. The term intellectual property implies that all knowledge is 'property' and an owner may use intellectual rights for economic gain (Daes, 1993; Smallacombe, 2000). Indigenous people do not adopt this Western view of their knowledge as property but regard it as collectively owned by the Indigenous community (Australian Human Rights Commission, 2008; Daes, 1993; Smallacombe, 2000). Therefore, Aboriginal traditional knowledge is conceptualised as held, managed and transmitted based on the rights and interests of the community rather than economic gain. Protection of Indigenous intellectual property is a challenge, as current intellectual property laws in Australia provide individual protection not communal protection (Australian Human Rights Commission, 2008). Additionally, copyright law does not apply to the many Indigenous oral stories. It is important to note that the current intellectual property and copyright laws enforced to protect and maintain Indigenous knowledge have remained inadequate and inappropriate within Australia (Australian Human Rights Commission, 2008; Calma, 2009a; Smallacombe, 2000).

Indigenous peoples claim that their rights as traditional holders and custodians of their knowledge are not adequately recognised or protected (Calma, 2009a). They demand not only recognition and protection of this knowledge but also the right to share equitably in benefits derived from its uses (Davis, 1988). It is necessary to consider who is responsible for embedding Aboriginal content in university education and the part that both Indigenous and non-Indigenous staff in the academy have in delivering the curricular content to students (Zubrzycki et al., 2014).

So what?

When Indigenising university curricula non-Indigenous academics must be aware of any inaccurate preconceptions and distorted interpretations of Indigenous knowledge (Nakata, 2004). To overcome these problems Nakata (2004) identified the need to recognise the cultural interface, where the negotiation of Indigenous knowledges and Western knowledges are interpreted. In order to do this it is essential that academics have some understanding of the major differences between the Aboriginal knowledge systems and those of non-Indigenous peoples (Nakata, 2007).

Integral to change is the direct consultation with Aboriginal peoples regarding their customary law, and it is essential to seek consent for the access and use of any Aboriginal traditional knowledge from the custodians of that knowledge. It is also necessary to ensure ethical conduct during any consultation and data collection and to establish mutually agreed terms for all parts of the process. Finally, it is incumbent on the researcher to subscribe to equitable benefit-sharing arrangements and acknowledge the contribution of Aboriginal peoples (Australian Human Rights Commission, 2009).

A good foundation for the protection of Indigenous knowledge is to accept that Aboriginal people have the right to maintain, control, protect and develop their intellectual property as it relates to their cultural heritage, traditional knowledge and cultural expressions (Janke and Lacovino, 2012). Indigenous peoples have the right to teach their cultural 'ways of knowing' within universities. Some Aboriginal holders of cultural knowledge have the equivalent level of knowledge required for a PhD and this level of achievement should be acknowledged by academic institutions (McGloin et al., 2009). Lastly, non-Indigenous people must acknowledge their history of privilege in order to develop true collaborative relationships that ensure respectful, culturally responsive, and socially just and human rights-based interactions (Young et al., 2013).

Case studies

1. An Indigenous and a non-Indigenous colleague co-author an article. The non-Indigenous colleague does most of the writing and the Indigenous colleague makes a major contribution to cultural ideas. The non-Indigenous colleague now uses this jointly compiled information in a book chapter with another non-Indigenous author with no mention of the Indigenous colleague. Subsequently, a review of the book is published and the chapter is discussed along with the original ideas. The review is now two stages removed from the original publication and, inevitably, referenced as belonging to the non-Indigenous author. The review uses 'built upon' knowledge and has evolved, but it has lost the Aboriginal voice and the Aboriginal author receives no credit for the original ideas. *Is this an example of cultural appropriation?*

2. Universities are teaching Aboriginal content in many degree programmes such as Social Work, Indigenous Studies and Sociology. One could argue that without authentic contributions from Aboriginal peoples these subjects cannot be taught correctly. Once the units are up on a website, the knowledge will be owned by the university. In this instance, *who is acknowledged as the specialist, and who should own the knowledge? How should this ownership be identified and what protocols should be developed to make sure Aboriginal voices are acknowledged?*

3. A book is being written on a topic. The editors contact the Indigenous academic and invite her to contribute a chapter on an Indigenous subject. In this case the non-Indigenous editors 'own' the egg as they will receive money and kudos for the book. The author's chapter will be 'donated' for free. No one non-Indigenous author can write the Indigenous chapter and so they are in fact hiring expert knowledge. *Is this abuse of power and privilege?*

4. An Aboriginal and non-Aboriginal academic discuss the need for more Aboriginal and Torres Strait Islander students to enter the Social Work degree. The Aboriginal academic makes a suggestion with regard to how to encourage students to apply to the course. The non-Indigenous academic applies for and receives funding to run the project. During the first year the workers share the workload of organising, presenting and establishing the course but thereafter the non-Indigenous member of staff carries on with the course for several years in partnership with other academics and the local Aboriginal and Torres Strait Islander community. Both the local Aboriginal community and students are now participants in this project and become co-consultants in it.

One of the successful features of this project was the adoption of a community development approach to workshop planning. This included: (1) inviting input and participation from current and graduated Aboriginal and Torres Strait Islander students; (2) working with a range of local Aboriginal and Torres Strait Islander agencies; (3) forming a partnership with the Aboriginal unit on campus; (4) using the workshop to provide information about the social work profession, course content, employment opportunities and student support resources; (5) meeting the academic and support staff; (6) engaging with past and present Aboriginal and Torres Strait Islander students and learning about their experiences of university and its social work; (7) sharing experiences of difficulties and successes with key social work academics; and (8) touring the campus to be able to envisage themselves and the university (Zubrzycki et al., 2014, p. 62). All these involvements contribute to a genuine and productive partnership and have the potential to role-model true governance and Aboriginal ownership. *Is this a partnership?*

Reflective questions

When can the non-Indigenous individual understand and develop the Aboriginal knowledge?

How should the academic acknowledge the source of his/her information?

Who should teach Aboriginal content?

When should non-Indigenous academics seek collaboration with Indigenous people?

Whose voice am I privileging here?

How can a non-Indigenous academic ensure that he/she is not assumed to be the sole expert in reports and publications?

Further readings

Janke, T. and Lacovino, L. (2012). Keeping cultures alive: Archives and Indigenous cultural and intellectual property rights. *Archival Science*, 12(2), 151–171.

Oluo, I. (2017). When we talk about cultural appropriation we're missing the point. *The Establishment*, https://theestablishment.co/when-we-talk-about-cultural-appropriation-were-missing-the-point-abe853ff3376.

Smallacombe, S. (2000). On display for its aesthetic beauty: How western institutions fabricate knowledge about Aboriginal cultural heritage. In D. Ivison, P. Patton and W. Sanders, *Political Theory and the Rights of Indigenous Peoples* (pp.152–162). Cambridge: Cambridge University Press.

References

AASW (Australian Association of Social Workers) (2010). *Code of Ethics.* https://www.aasw.asn.au/document/item/1201.

Andrews G, Daylight C, Hunt J. 2006, *Aboriginal cultural heritage landscape mapping of coastal NSW*, prepared for the Comprehensive Coastal Assessment by the NSW Department of Natural Resources, Sydney, NSW.

Australian Human Rights Commission (2008). *Face the Facts. Questions about Aboriginal and Torres Strait Islander peoples.* www.humanrights.gov.au/publications/2008-face-the-facts-chapter-1.

Australian Human Rights Commission (2009). *Native Title Report.* https://www.humanrights.gov.au/sites/default/files/content/social_justice/nt_report/ntreport08/pdf/ntr2008.pdf.

Battiste, M. (2002). *Indigenous Knowledge and Pedagogy in First Nations Education: A Literature Review with Recommendations.* Ottawa: National Working Group on Education.

Bennett, B. (2013). Why is the history of Aboriginal and Torres Strait Islander people important for social work students and graduates? In B. Bennett, S. Green, S. Gilbert and D. Bessarab (Eds.), *Our Voices: Aboriginal and Torres Strait Islander Social Work* (pp. 1–25). Melbourne: Palgrave Macmillan.

Calma, T. (2009a). *2008 Social Justice Report*, Aboriginal and Torres Strait Islander Social Justice Commissioner. Sydney: Human Rights and Equal Opportunity Commission.

Calma, T. (2009b) *Our Right to Protect our Knowledge in Australian Human Rights Commission Launch of the Aboriginal Knowledge and Intellectual Property Protocol Community Guide*, Canberra: Parliament House. https://www.humanrights.gov.au/news/speeches/our-right-protect-our-knowledge.

Daes, E.I.A. (1993). Some considerations on the right of Indigenous peoples to self-determination. *Transnational Law and Contemporary Problems*, 3(1).

Davis, W. A. (1988). Knowledge, acceptance, and belief. *The Southern Journal of Philosophy*, 26(2), 169–178.

Flavier, J.M., Jesus, A.D., Navarro, C.S. and Warren, D.M. (1995). The regional program for the promotion of Indigenous knowledge in Asia. In D.M. Warren, L.J. Slikkerveer and D. Brokensha (Eds.), *The Cultural Dimension of Development: Indigenous Knowledge Systems* (pp. 479–487). London: Intermediate Technology Publications.

Fourmile-Marrie, H. and Kelly, G. (2000). *The Convention on Biological Diversity and Indigenous People: Information Concerning the Implementation of Decisions of the Conference of the Parties under the Convention on Biological Diversity.* Sydney: Centre for Indigenous History and the Arts, University of Western Sydney.

International Council for Science, Science and Traditional Knowledge (2002). Report from the ICSU Study Group on Science and Traditional Knowledge. Paper delivered at the 27th General Assembly of ICSU, Rio De Janeiro, Brazil, 24–27 February.

Janke, T. (1998). *Our Culture, Our Future: Report on Australian Indigenous Cultural and Intellectual Property*. Surry Hills, NSW: Michael Frankel, Solicitors.

Janke, T. and Lacovino, L. (2012). Keeping cultures alive: Archives and Indigenous cultural and intellectual property rights. *Archival Science*, 12(2), 151–171.

Law Reform Commission of Western Australia (2006). *Aboriginal Customary Laws, Final Report – The interaction of Western Australian law with Aboriginal law and culture*. Project 92, September, Government of Western Australia.

McGloin, C., Marshall, A. and Adams, M. (2009). Leading the way: Indigenous knowledge and collaboration at the Woolyungah Indigenous Centre. *Journal of University Teaching and Learning Practice*, 6(2).

McGregor, D. (2014). Traditional knowledge and water governance: The ethic of responsibility. *AlterNative: An International Journal of Indigenous Peoples*, 10(5), 493–507.

Nakata, M. (2004). Indigenous Australian studies and higher education. *The Wentworth Lectures*.

Nakata, M. (2007). The cultural interface [online]. In M. Nakata (Ed.), *Disciplining the Savages: Savaging the Disciplines* (pp. 195–212). Canberra, A.C.T: Aboriginal Studies Press.

NSW Government (2010). *What is Aboriginal cultural knowledge? Office of Environment, Climate Change & Water*. Fact sheet 1. www.environment.nsw.gov.au/resources/cultureheritage/commconsultation/09782factsheet1.pdf.

Oluo, I. (2017). When we talk about cultural appropriation. We're missing the point. *The Establishment*. https://theeestablishment.co/when-we-talk-about-cultural-appropriation-were-missing-the-point-abe853ff3376.

Sivaramakrishnan, A. (1989). The Slave With Two Hearts: The Asymmetry of Cultural Assimilation, *Third Text*, 3(7), 3–10.

Smallacombe, S. (2000). On display for its aesthetic beauty: How western institutions fabricate knowledge about Aboriginal cultural heritage. In D. Ivison, P. Patton and W. Sanders, *Political Theory and the Rights of Indigenous Peoples* (pp. 152–162). Cambridge: Cambridge University Press.

United Nations (2008). Declaration on the Rights of Indigenous Peoples. http://www.un.org/esa/socdev/unpfii/documents/DRIPS_en.pdf.

United Nations (2010). Convention on Biological Diversity. https://www.cbd.int/undb/media/factsheets/undb-factsheets-en-web.pdf.

United Nations Permanent Forum on Indigenous Issues (2007). *Report of the Secretariat on Indigenous traditional knowledge*, UN Document No. E/C.19/2007/10. http://daccessdds.un.org/doc/UNDOC/GEN/N07/277/15/PDF/N0727715.pdf?OpenElement.

Young, S., Zubrzycki, J., Green, S., Jones, V., Stratton, K. and Bessarab, D.C. (2013). 'Getting it right: Creating partnerships for change': Developing a framework for integrating Aboriginal and Torres Strait Islander Knowledges in Australian Social Work Education. *Journal of Ethnic and Cultural Diversity in Social Work*, 22(3–4), 179–197. https://doi.org/10.1080/15313204.2013.843120.

Zubrzycki, J., Green, S., Jones, V., Stratton, K., Young, S. and Bessarab, D. (2014). Getting it right: Creating partnerships for change. Integrating Aboriginal and Torres Strait Islander knowledges in social work education and practice. http://www.acu.edu.au/__data/assets/pdf_file/0010/655804/Getting_It_Right_June_2014.pdf.

PART TWO
CRITICAL PERSPECTIVES ON CULTURAL DIFFERENCE

5
Islamophobia and Social Work Collusion

Lobna Yassine and Linda Briskman

> We acknowledge the Australian Aboriginal and Torres Strait Islander peoples of this nation. Australia was and always will be Aboriginal land.

Introduction

In Australia anti-Muslim sentiment, commonly known as Islamophobia, has taken hold, driven by a convergence of actors in political, public and media spheres. Thinly disguised strategies of 'social cohesion' laws, particularly 'anti-terrorism' laws, are incrementally put in place, justified on the grounds of 'national security' and compounded by policies that align with national security perspectives. Australia's anti-terror laws were enacted as a response to attacks in the United States on September 11, 2001 and subsequent attacks in Europe. Academic lawyer George Williams states (2011, p. 1137) that the laws were cast as a temporary, emergency reaction. However, he argues that Australia's anti-terror laws can no longer be cast as a transient, short-term response. This reflects the assessment of the Australian government and its agencies that terrorism remains a persistent threat.

This chapter examines the incremental entry of anti-Muslim policies that build on legal codification and shifting social relations. Our attention focuses on the Australian government's Countering Violent Extremism (CVE) policy, which we posit is anti-Muslim and entrenched in Islamophobic ideas and beliefs.

We examine social work complicity in Islamophobia in two ways: first, the scant attention given by social work to the 'wicked problem' of Islamophobia and, second, complicity by the Australian Association of Social Workers (AASW, 2017) through adopting CVE policies. By not naming social work collusion, we allow harmful policies and practices to flourish.

Islamophobia in Australia

Islamophobia is a global 'movement', manifest in many countries through legislation targeting Muslims, the rise of right-wing extremist groups, media complicity and attacks on Muslims. Although it is beyond the scope of this chapter to provide detail of the Islamophobia context in Australia, all of the above factors converge to enable the growth of what Lean (2012) refers to as the Islamophobia industry, a phenomenon that is not accidental but is knowingly designed. Consequences of anti-Muslim sentiment are apparent in surveys revealing that more than 20% of the Australian population have negative feelings about Muslims; attacks on women wearing hijabs; and alienation of young people (Akbarzadeh and Conduit, 2016). A report on Islamophobia in Australia documented findings from the Islamophobia Register non-governmental organisation (Briskman et al., 2017), confirming 243 reported incidents between September 2014 and December 2015, a figure believed to be 'the tip of the iceberg', and with women disproportionately featuring as victims of Islamophobic incidents.

For social work, Islamophobia has not garnered professional interest. This is surprising for a profession that purportedly stands up for social justice and human rights and promotes anti-racist constructs. Although there is no empirical data available, it is highly likely that, in their daily practice, many social workers encounter Muslims and bear witness to accounts from them of discrimination and racism, both individual and institutional. What is more surprising than mere silence is that social work is not only participating in the 'Islamophobia Industry' through CVE programs but in doing so is gaining both political and financial profit.

The participation by the AASW in CVE programs has forced us to question the role of social work in Australia and its shaping within a professional discourse. Is social work at risk of aligning itself with injustice, inequality and racism? How does the whiteness and mainstream political affiliation of Australian social work make it vulnerable to being co-opted into governmental apparatuses of social control? Should we focus less on 'difference' as a justification for ill-treatment (such as in Islamophobia) and begin to focus more on 'sameness' (or white fragility; see Baines and Waugh, Chapter 17, in this volume)?

Locating ourselves

Lobna

I am a Muslim woman of Lebanese descent who was born in Australia. I am by extension a settler who lives on, and benefits from, stolen land. I write in the context of the ongoing colonisation of First Australians.

Anti-Muslim rhetoric and Islamophobia have impacted me and others around me directly, both materially and discursively. I do not state this with the purpose of contributing more value to my words, but rather to highlight where I speak from. I speak from a personal, political and academic standpoint. As a Muslim woman living in Australia, I am hyper-vigilant to the rhetoric surrounding the 'War on Terror'. Shakira Hussein (2016) has discussed the shift in the thinking about Muslim women in Australia, from being positioned as 'victims' to being positioned as 'suspects' who are potentially protecting their 'radical' male relatives. As a result, families (read 'women') are encouraged to keep a watchful eye on their sons and husbands. For example, in 2015 the Foreign Affairs minister, Julie Bishop, addressed Australia's Regional Summit on Countering Violent Extremism, highlighting women as 'key players' in the role of 'challenging terrorist propaganda'. In the name of 'empowering women' she stated:

> The ability of women and families to act as champions of counter-radicalisation means we must do more to engage women and families and empower them in this role. This means including women and families in the whole process – in the design, implementation, monitoring and evaluation of our Countering Violent Extremism efforts. (Bishop, 2015)

The 'soft policing' of Muslim people in Australia, and young Muslim people in particular, has become a dominant form of governing since 2008. For example, the general public may not be aware of the fact that in the state of New South Wales (NSW) there is a policy that instructs public schools to record and 'audit' the names of Muslim students who wish to perform afternoon prayers (NSW Government Media Release, 2015). The NSW government has not made it clear why this information is required, or what it is used for. This means that my 15-year-old nephew, who attends a public high school that is mainly populated by Muslim students, is required to record his name whenever he attends afternoon prayer in the school hall. Via counter-terrorism policies, my nephew is being constructed as somehow inherently prone, or 'vulnerable', to radicalisation.

My interest in this area is also due to my work with young Muslims in the community. 'Youth work' in Muslim communities has increasingly become an additional form of monitoring and surveillance, with the bulk of CVE funds being directed to 'youth' in Australia. Through youth-orientated activities, consultant-contractors are 'cashing in' on the fears surrounding the radicalisation of 'home grown' terrorism.

Linda

I am a white, social work academic. I position myself as an academic human rights activist, confronting political and social structures that cause harm, and drawing on minority group voices and collaborations to do so.

My activities in the sphere of Islamophobia are personal and political. I am a Jewish woman, who is acutely aware of the consequences of hatred, bigotry, stereotyping and complicity. I am also conscious of how easy it is for social work to slide into complicity, for example colluding with decrees within Nazi Germany (Schnurr, 1997). To my consciousness is the Jewish edict Tikkun Olam, or repair the world, as well as the unfulfilled refrain that arose from the Holocaust of 'never again'.

I spend considerable time in the Muslim majority country of Iran, a nation that is subjected to stereotyping by the West to reinforce 'superiority' of Western thinking and which causes harms to society and to the humanity of those living within the country. In Australia over recent years I have seen the rise of Islamophobia and have been witness to accounts of Muslim colleagues, students and friends on the receiving end of harmful anti-Muslim discourses and practices. I observe the revival of the alarmist clash of civilisations discourse (Huntingdon, 1996) that is manifest in political statements and media opinion and am conscious of how, by not being critical readers of text or news, complicity takes hold. One example of collusion pertains to the 'rescue phenomenon' that privileges the 'oppressed' Muslim woman homily, which proclaims Western 'virtues' and denies agency. Such an approach is inconsistent with anti-colonialist and anti-racist theorising of social work.

What is Islamophobia?

Although Islamophobia is theoretically and ideologically manifest in a variety of ways, including as a subset of racism, we take as our starting point the conceptualisation of Massoumi and colleagues (2017, p. 3), by focusing on political practices. This turns our gaze to directly examining institutions, policies and practices that disproportionality impact Muslims. Although our focus is the social work profession, to set the scene we begin by examining the wider context in which social work operates. Through this it becomes possible to understand the ways in which Islamophobia has become normalised, and how constructs and practices of white privilege have entered the profession.

As Susan Carland (2017, p. 5) says, Islam is arguably the most discussed religion in the West in both media and society. The negativity of this discussion is emphasised by Muslim writer and activist Yassmin Abdel-Magied, who states that: 'People of colour are considered "conditionally" Australian and the moment they step out of line, the country explodes with outrage' (cited in The Australian 2017). Muslim voices are silenced in the public domain or misinterpreted by celebrity commentators such as Ayaan Hirsi Ali, a former Muslim and now outspoken critic of Islam, backed up by powerful resources and people (Briskman and Latham, 2017, p. 109).

Amal Awad (2017, p. 7) expresses the problem succinctly:

> the women in these discourses are so often exoticised or minimised; or the complexity of life in a different country, which enjoys a rich and diverse culture, is buried under the assumption that the Western way is superior.

Pervasive fear has led to what can be defined as 'Islamophobia creep' (Briskman, 2015) in Australia. This gradual progression has resulted in a largely uncritical public (and professional) response to 'raids' on Muslim households that were prompted by the rise of what has become known as 'Islamic extremism' abroad and the criminal acts of a minority. Pervasive fear has had a profound effect on the everyday lives of Muslims, who are seen to be lacking the capacity to 'integrate' into Australian society. These tropes are often promoted by government spokespeople, right-wing extremist groups and sections of the media. It has enabled the flourishing of hate speech, disguised as the right to free speech.

The politics of Countering Violent Extremism (CVE) policies and programs

We analyse CVE policies through a 'governmentality' approach to policy, where 'government' is understood in the Foucauldian sense as the 'conduct of conduct' (Gordon, 1991, p. 2). Bacchi and Goodwin (2016) explain:

> In this broader understanding, government refers to any form of activity that aims to shape, guide, or affect the conduct of people. Government can concern how people monitor or regulate their own conduct, how interpersonal relations are guided and controlled, as well as the state-generated rules, regulations, provisions, and punishments we usually associate with the term.

The following discussion on the policies and practices governing Muslim people in Australia is guided by Bacchi's 'what's the problem represented to be?' (WPR) approach to policy, which encourages 'An explicit challenge to the conventional view that policies address problems' (Bacchi and Goodwin, 2016, p. 6). The WPR approach instead 'approaches policies as problematizations that produce "problems" as particular types of problems' (Bacchi and Goodwin, 2016, p. 6).

Problematising Countering Violent Extremism (CVE) policies and programs

On 27 September 2017, in its 'National e-Bulletin', the AASW invited members to apply for an 'expression of interest' for those that were experienced in conducting training, to develop a professional development program for social work, mental health and welfare professionals on the theme of 'building resilience and preventing radicalisation to violent extremism – an awareness-raising workshop'. The initial stage of the project was to involve 16 trainers across four states, with payment of $800 per day for trainers, a not insubstantial amount of money. More importantly, this call for expressions of interest signified the AASW's embrace of the CVE program. In order to understand why we argue that participation in this particular program is problematic, we provide an overview and critique, from the literature and our perspectives, of the trajectory of government responses to what is presented to the public as 'Muslim terror risks'.

CVE policies have become the new way to respond to terrorism, globally. These policies take on different forms across different countries. In Australia CVE policies consist of both 'preventative' and 'interventionist' forms. For example, intervention policies are aimed at 'de-radicalising' people once they have been found guilty of planning or engaging in terrorist activities. At the other end of the spectrum CVE policies include approaches that are preventative in nature, aimed at *pre*-venting radicalisation, via the community. CVE policies include initiatives such as training professionals about violent extremism (for example, social workers, psychologists, health professionals and teachers), as well as more general youth work and community-based programs, that aim to build 'social cohesion', 'build resilience' and educate people about violent extremism. The latter kind of approaches are a more recent development that tie together 'community relations' with 'national security'.

CVE policies in Western nations have already been widely criticised in the literature (Coppock and McGovern, 2014; Monaghan, 2014) and in public debate. Although similar policies in the United Kingdom and elsewhere (Oliver-Dee, 2018; Thomas, 2010; Vermeulen, 2014) may be considered significantly more overtly oppressive and intrusive than Australia's CVE policies, they are all underpinned by the same principles that inform its approach.

Control through 'community' and 'Australian-ness'

CVE is a policy approach that is coupled with national security. In the Australian context what is central to CVE policies and programs is the presupposition that 'community' is where extremism 'happens', and therefore 'community' is where extremism is combated. We question what, and who, is actually being protected by these policies? Martin (2014) argues that 'community cohesion' is a technology of government, that (re)establishes an ideal vision of 'Britishness'. Similarly, in Australia 'asserting Australian identity' is at the heart of CVE programs. But what is 'Australian-ness'? What is an 'Australian identity'? And how has extremism become tangled with 'Australian-ness' and 'Australian identity'? We also question what is meant by the concept of 'community', and how 'community' has been used to attribute collective responsibility for social problems, as well as who is afforded individuality, and therefore an absence of collective responsibility for 'community'. Despite the slippery and contentious concept of 'community', the cause of, and the solution to, extremism largely lies in 'community'.

The co-option of 'communities', and in particular of Muslim organisations and individuals in the design and facilitation of CVE policies and programs, causes Muslims themselves to participate and contribute to a system that has historically excluded them. Under the guise of 'building community resilience and cohesion' CVE policies and programs have produced Muslim communities as 'suspicious communities' (see Cherney and Murphy, 2016).

It is when Muslim communities come to see themselves as 'vulnerable' and requiring 'intervention' that CVE policies are perhaps considered most 'successful'. CVE policies consequently have Muslim communities begin to partake in self-governing activities, take up harmful subject positions and voluntarily participate, engage, invite and actively pursue CVE funding and programs. CVE policies effectively get Muslim communities to 'self-police' and 'conduct' themselves more 'effectively'.

The concern by Muslim 'communities' for 'its youth' is a very powerful tool for the dispersion and strengthening of CVE policies. The 'community' desperately tries to understand the actions of what has now become 'their youth', gathering at community forums and events to try and get a grasp on the 'radicalisation problem', this problem that is so distant from their 'peaceful ordinary' Australian lives. Their demands for answers, especially from youth and 'radicalisation experts', who range from academics, psychologists, social workers, teachers, youth workers, mental health workers, national security experts, religious leaders, lawyers and politicians, are mostly derived from their desire to distance themselves as much as possible from the 'radicalisation problem'. This desire for distance is understandably appealing to a community that has been consistently under attack and blamed for the actions of their 'troubled, at-risk, undisciplined' children. The uptake of CVE policies by 'communities' only strengthens the 'problem', and is in fact seen as a sign of an 'effective' policy.

Fixing dangerous minds

The central targets of CVE interventions are overwhelmingly young Muslim men, who are not only 'suspect' but also in need of being 'saved' from extremism. The rhetoric of 'vulnerability' to extremism has given open-ended access to every domain of the young Muslim's life, especially their school life.

CVE initiatives are undeniably linked to surveillance, identification and monitoring. Although it is beyond the scope of this chapter to expand on the security/CVE/education nexus (see more on this by Novelli, 2017), a few key points are salutary. Underpinning the problem representations in CVE policies and programs is the presupposition that being 'radical' leads to 'extremism' which leads to 'violence', and that 'violent extremism' has a clear causal 'pathway'. These taken-for-granted terms are beginning to be used almost interchangeably and vaguely, lacking clear definitions. Coppock and McGovern (2014) state:

> Such open-ended vagueness may not, however, be entirely unintentional, allowing as it does for the re-construction, re-interpretation and re-articulation of what constitutes 'radicalisation' and the potential widening of a net of applicability to various individuals, groups, attitudes and actions ... As with the idea of 'radicalisation', 'extremism' is a vague concept that is easily exploited to demonise anyone whose opinions are radically different ... it is a definition in which no reference to advocating or using violence is felt necessary to count someone as 'radical'. (p. 245)

A young Muslim questioning and voicing injustice, or the racism of their own governments, for example, could easily be reframed as 'oppositional' and 'dangerous', every word or action considered a possible 'trigger' for criminal charges. Coppock and McGovern (2014) discuss this in more depth suggesting that young Muslim men in particular are perceived to be outside of 'normal childhood', and are not afforded the luxury of the rationales for behaviour that are otherwise often attributed to the 'youth' life stage, such as 'rebellion', searching for 'identity', searching for 'belonging' and the general privilege of a questioning disposition. The young Muslim who speaks politically is thus cast outside Western developmental norms, distanced from understandings of 'normal childhood' and understood to be *too* political, *too* critical, *too* engaged in foreign policies. For young Muslims, there are limited spaces for resistance, counter-conduct or for subversive forms of knowledge production.

CVE policy is shaping educational institutions more than it should, and we fear that CVE policy is another form of what Foucault (1975) refers to as 'disciplinary power', a type of power that ensures subjects, in this case young Muslims, are always monitored. As Foucault stated, 'It is the fact of being constantly seen, of being able always to be seen, that maintains the disciplined individual in his subjection' (p. 187). CVE policy ensures that the power to 'see' the young Muslim is vastly expanded, shaping not only individuals, families and communities but also our educational institutions.

The Countering Violent Extremism (CVE) industry

The particular approach to social policies in this chapter also requires us to question and to position knowledges, including scholarly and university-based research, as producing the subjects they aim to 'correct'. For as long as there has been a 'War on Terror' there have been professionals, systems and institutions produced to do the work of 'fighting', 'countering' and 'preventing' terrorism. As we have shown, this 'workforce' extends well beyond armies, police forces and intelligence agencies. Taking this further, we understand 'knowledge production' itself as a technique of government, and as a way to govern populations *through* knowledge. 'The Muslim' is an object of knowledge, and is the subject of power. 'Knowledge' about 'terrorism' has justified the dissection of every part of the Muslim's life, from their socioeconomic status, to what they wear, to what they eat, right through to the very personal act of prayer.

Entire industries, and individuals, are now benefiting (economically, socially, politically and academically) from the production of the 'dangerous Muslim' subject. The race to 'win' CVE tenders and contracts through competitive processes is particularly disturbing. The net effects of these actors and institutions are producing a system for the manufacturing of 'The dangerous Muslim'.

From this perspective, the example at the heart of this chapter, whereby the AASW is a 'winner' in the current CVE policy process, provides a serious cause to question the place of social work in this 'industry'. Relevant to social workers, the dominant literature on radicalisation and CVE has focused on the 'causes' of radicalisation, and the 'outcomes/effectiveness' of policies and programs. What goes unquestioned are racialised assumptions and presuppositions that shape CVE policies. For example, violent extremism has been linked to a variety of social factors such as 'political alienation', 'miseducation' and the 'socioeconomic marginalisation' of Muslims in Australia (see Akbarzadeh, 2013). It is imperative that social workers are aware of the implications of relating socioeconomic marginalisation to the risk of radicalisation. How do these types of knowledges reframe and replace social justice matters, to criminal national security matters?

As critical social workers, we (Lobna and Linda) remain aware of our own complicity in the writing and publication of this very chapter, and acknowledge that we are not 'outside' of the knowledge-making process. We will both benefit from its publication, as do the 'experts' on 'radicalisation' and 'youth' who have researched Muslims, and continue to do so, right through to the AASW trainers who 'trained' front-line social workers. Needless to say it continues to be the case that often the very people we claim to advocate for are rarely the producers of the types of 'knowledges' that we have come to privilege, disseminate and value.

Colour-blind policies and the State as 'neutral'

Although there are CVE programs in Australia that directly and explicitly target young 'vulnerable' Muslims (see the examples given in Akbarzadeh, 2013), other CVE programs are much more open-ended; they do not present as targeting Muslims directly, and invite people of 'all' backgrounds to participate. We could see how CVE supporters would argue that these policies are not in fact racialised, because they apply to 'anybody', 'even non-Muslims'. (As Sara Ahmed (2017, p. 72) points out, the *even* in this attestation is racism. The *even* functions purely to reassure the white person that they have been distanced from anything that could be described as racist.) In contrast, we approach the ostensibly 'colour-blind'/'race-neutral' stance with scepticism due to the empirical fact that the people who have been mostly affected by CVE policies are Australian Muslims specifically. We argue, for example, that the deployment of CVE programs only in schools that have a large number of Muslim students undermines the policy rhetoric that the programs are suitable/available to 'all' schools.

We would also like to alert readers to the fact that CVE programs are in fact being deployed in very specific communities, that is, locations that consist of a high number of Muslims. For example, the Australian government has explained that CVE prevention strategies will focus on geographical locations deemed to have populations who are at 'higher risk' of radicalisation. The Assistant Secretary from the Commonwealth Attorney-General's Department stated that CVE programs are 'quite geographically focused … by virtue of living in an area of social exclusion, we are interested in them' (Commonwealth of Australia, 2015).

What this means 'on the ground' is that when applying for a CVE grant an applicant is more likely to be successful if justification is based on geographical locations that have high rates of Muslims. Yet CVE policies in Australia are still sold as 'colour-blind' policies, and 'neutral' in their approaches.

This 'colour-blind' approach, somewhat naively, also assumes that the state is a 'neutral', 'objective' body, outside of a history of colonisation, genocide, unjust foreign wars and the ongoing inhumane treatment of those seeking asylum. A similar issue is taking place in Australia's penal system, where there is insistence that the 'justice' system is 'fair', 'neutral' and 'colour-blind', despite the fact that Indigenous Australians are currently the most over-represented imprisoned people on earth. Yet it is almost impossible to argue that the penal system is a racist one.

The decision to support CVE policies is disconnected from the reality that these policies and programs have isolated and hurt Australian Muslims, and will continue to so. The expansion of these policies, we believe, is 'whiteness at work'. Here, definitions of what the 'problem' is, what the 'solutions' are, as well as whose knowledges are valued, and counted, over others maintain and reproduce the dominance of white power. This power even shapes the internal narratives of the Other, where the Other can only understand themselves through a white lens, and a white vocabulary, and only in reference to whiteness. If a marginalised group themselves believes that social policies are particularly and directly harmful to them, whiteness discounts their knowledge and their experiences, insists that they are not harmful and not racist, and then continues to partake in these policies. The expertise of the dominant group is privileged, and actioned.

A critical social work perspective

The response of the AASW is not isolated to Australian social work. On a global scale the Islamophobia industry directs its scrutiny to illegal (but uncommon) practices wrongly designated as Islamic, which become overblown in the public domain. One example is that of female genital cutting (FGC) in the United Kingdom. Similar to the distress felt by families in Australia whose children are singled out as at risk of radical extremism, British families suspected of having undergone FGC were targeted and their children subjected to lengthy periods of time in foster care waiting to have their genitals checked. Exposing the collusion of 'care' professionals in this hysteria, combined with lack of evidence, revealed that the removal of children by child protection authorities was mere scaremongering and collusion with an incontestable narrative (Hehr, 2017).

It is due time that the profession seriously considers the incorporation of 'intersectionality', a concept developed by Crenshaw (1989) to bring attention to forms of power and oppression based on multiple and overlapping socially constructed identities. Deploying this concept requires social workers to question how social work (re)produces racialising gendered subjects (young Muslim men), and also how an all-women board, like that of the AASW, has not explicitly advocated for Muslim women in Australia, despite the fact that they are most often the victims of Islamophobic attacks. Deploying the concept of 'intersectionality' makes it possible to position and challenge whiteness as an invisible social category, not often framed as 'intersectional' (Carbado, 2013).

With rare exceptions, social workers have not tackled questions of rising Islamophobia and the forms which it takes. In a climate of populism, fear, racism and conflation of Islam with terrorism, social workers have a particular responsibility to challenge racism, through its values and ethics base as well as understanding what exclusion means for those who experience not only hurtful stereotypes but also vilification and harmful practices. Challenging Islamophobia may seem a thorny area and one in which social workers may be hesitant. Social workers like other professionals are not necessarily immune to experiencing the fear propagated by carefully crafted propaganda. And social work is a site of struggle itself with neoliberal dictates trumping the quest for justice, with risk, metrics, surveillance and control dominating practice frameworks, and the quest for professionalisation rather than liberation prevailing. We concur with the views of Olson (2008) who sees the social justice project and professionalisation as discourses in conflict. Should not social work be reinventing itself as a profession where politics are at its core, a profession of resistance that can challenge societal wrongs, bearing in mind that much of social work knowledge derives from practice experience and bearing witness?

Through bearing witness, responsibilities and obligations of social workers are self-evident. In the practice of social work we directly encounter injustices, and our code of ethics calls on us to challenge these – and the code is by no means a radical document. Rather than being courageous ethnographers – speaking out about what is witnessed (Briskman, 2013) – social workers and those who educate them may unwittingly be agents of the State, as this chapter suggests.

Standing back from received wisdom, enshrined in social work texts and dictums, it is time to move further on critical social work endeavours, that have served us well, to a reinvention that enables us to see more clearly the prospects for minimisation of paradigms that are antithetical to our long-established value base. The whiteness of social work has been increasingly interrogated but needs to be centre stage, rather than being one of a series of constructs that relegate it to an add-on.

One new way of thinking that is emerging is to challenge the 'rational, evidence-based project' of modernity that has captured social work in its grip and to engage with a politics of emotion, of moral outrage (Briskman, 2015). Individually and collectively social workers can develop a collective garnering of emotion, combining critical reflection with personal subjectivities and values arising from social work and other encounters. By re-visioning our work through emotion, we have a basis for contesting notions of rationality that are devoid of feeling and in which feature ideas of tools, prescription, risk.

We can also delve more deeply into ethics and how to grow 'virtuous practitioners' as expressed by Pawar and colleagues (2017, p. 2), who see virtues as 'qualities, character, good habits or attributes of practitioners that help them to achieve excellence in their practice' (p. 5).

As social workers we need to interrogate the dual loyalty paradigm that is largely absent in social work analysis. By doing so we can centre-stage where our loyalties rest, to employing agencies and their funders or to those we are tasked with assisting.

There is a social work duty to guard against ideological co-option and to prevent social workers from being unwittingly captive to world views antithetical to the profession.

Conclusion

By adopting policies of the right-wing state, the AASW has positioned itself within the ideology and processes of that state and outside the realm of defending marginalised voices and championing social justice. Purposely minimised voices can be purposely maximised through what social work professes to do: listening, countering racism and challenging. Stories that currently sit at the margins, such as those expressed by Lobna at the beginning of this chapter, can help to dislodge the repressive narratives of those with power, privilege and prejudice and reignite engagement not only with voices unheard but with the hurt felt by those who are effectively shunned in the public domain.

In mounting these challenges we again turn to 'whiteness'. In 2011 the entrapment of social work within a whiteness paradigm was argued by Walter and colleagues (2011) in relation to social work's engagement with Indigenous peoples. Their argument on the whiteness of social work is adaptable to the sphere of Islamophobia and the need to do what these authors suggest, to decentre whiteness and the assumptions so deeply embedded by those who hold them.

The statement by the Director of the Centre for Islamic Studies and Civilisation, Mehmet Ozalp (2017), is one which Australian social work can heed:

> A very important aspect of Australian liberal democracy is the protection of its minorities. Minorities do not always have a voice in politics or media and can

often find themselves overwhelmed by negative perception and antagonism. We would do disservice to the betterment of Australia if the problem of Islamophobia is ignored or played down. It only serves to entrench the problem deeper. (p. v)

There is unfinished business in social work to robustly challenge the dominance of Western world views, deconstruct current education programs and practice norms, and listen to voices of groups that are depicted as marginal. And, more urgently, to challenge the participation of our professional association when state policies are oppressive and produce inequities. Social work identity can be a source of pride when it promotes social justice but can just as easily be a source of shame when it does the opposite.

Further readings

Briskman, L., Iner, D., Krayem, G., Latham, S., Matthews, Z., Pearson, C., Poynting, S., Vargani, M., Yasmeen, S. and Zayied, I. (2017). *Islamophobia in Australia 2014–2016*. Sydney: Centre for Islamic Studies and Civilisation, Charles Sturt University. https://researchdirect.westernsydney.edu.au/islandora/object/uws:46351

Crabtree, S.A., Husain, F. and Spalek, B. (2017). *Islam and Social Work: Culturally Sensitive Practice in a Diverse World*. Bristol: Policy Press.

Fawzi, S. (2015). Social and political Islamophobia: Stereotyping, surveillance and silencing. In R. Tottoli (Ed.), *Routledge Handbook of Islam in the West* (pp. 229–243). Abingdon: Routledge.

References

Ahmed, S. (2017). *Living a Feminist Life*, Durham, NC: Duke University Press.

Akbarzadeh, S. (2013). Investing in mentoring and educational initiatives: The limits of de-radicalisation programmes in Australia. *Journal of Muslim Minority Affairs*, 33(4), 451–463.

Akbarzadeh, S. and Conduit, D. (2016). The Syrian refugee crisis. *Ethos*, 24(2), 8.

Australian Association of Social Workers (2017). 'Wanted: Countering violent extremism CPD trainers', National Bulletin, 27 September.

Awad, A. (2017). *Beyond Veiled Cliches: The Real Lives of Arab Women*, Sydney: Vintage Books.

Bacchi, C. and Goodwin, S. (2016). *Poststructural Policy Analysis: A Guide to Practice*, Basingstoke: Springer.

Bishop, J. (2015). Address to Regional Summit to Counter Violent Extremism. Panel on key players – the role of women and families in challenging terrorist propaganda. 11 June. https://foreignminister.gov.au/speeches/Pages/2015/jb_sp_150611.aspx

Briskman, L. (2013). Courageous ethnographers or agents of the state: Challenges for social work. *Critical and Radical Social Work*, 1(1), 51–66.
Briskman, L. (2015). The creeping blight of Islamophobia in Australia. *International Journal for Crime, Justice and Social Democracy*, 4(3), 112–121.
Briskman, L., Iner, D., Krayem, G., Latham, S., Matthews, Z., Pearson, C., Poynting, S., Vargani, M., Yasmeen, S. and Zayied, I. (2017). *Islamophobia in Australia 2014–2016*. Sydney: Centre for Islamic Studies and Civilisation, Charles Sturt University. https://researchdirect.westernsydney.edu.au/islandora/object/uws:46351
Briskman, L. and Latham, S. (2017). Refugees Islamophobia and Ayaan Hirsi Ali: Challenging social work co-option. *Affilia*, 32(1), 108–111.
Carbado, D.W. (2013). Colorblind intersectionality. *Signs: Journal of Women in Culture and Society*, 38(4), 811–845.
Carland, S. (2017). *Fighting Hislam*, Carlton: Melbourne University Press.
Cherney, A. and Murphy, K. (2016). Being a 'suspect community' in a post 9/11 world: The impact of the war on terror on Muslim communities in Australia. *Australian & New Zealand Journal of Criminology*, 49(4), 480–496.
Commonwelath of Australia (2015). *How to Counter Extreme Terrorism: A quck Guide*. Parliament of Australia. https://www.aph.gov.au/About_Parliament/Parliamentary_Departments/Parliamentary_Library/pubs/rp/rp1415/Quick_Guides/Extremism
Coppock, V. and McGovern, M. (2014). 'Dangerous minds'? Deconstructing counter-terrorism discourse, radicalisation and the 'psychological vulnerability' of Muslim children and young people in Britain. *Children and Society*, 28(3), 242–256.
Crenshaw, K. (1989). Demarginalizing the intersection of race and sex: A black feminist critique of antidiscrimination doctrine, feminist theory, and antiracist politics. *University of Chicago Legal Forum*, 1989, 139–167.
Foucault, M. (1975). *Discipline and Punish: The Birth of the Prison*, trans A. Sheridan. London: Penguin Books.
Gordon, C. (1991). Governmental rationality: An introduction. In G. Burchell, C. Gordon and P. Miller (Eds.), *The Foucault Effect: Studies in Governmentality* (pp. 1–51). Hemel Hampstead: Harvester Wheatsheaf.
Hehr, B. (2017). Questioning the basis for the UK FGM industry, *Shifting Sands*, 25 September. http://www.shiftingsands.org.uk/questioning-the-basis-for-the-uk-fgm-industry/
Huntingdon, S. (1996). *The Clash of Civilizations and the Remaking of World Order*. New York: Simon & Schuster.
Hussein, S. (2016). *From Victims to Suspects: Muslim Women since 9/11*, Sydney: New South Wales Books.
Lean, N. (2012). *The Islamophobia Industry: How the Right Manufactures Fear of Muslims*. London: Pluto Press.
Martin, T. (2014). Governing an unknowable future: The politics of Britain's prevent policy. *Critical Studies on Terrorism*, 7(1), 62–78.
Massoumi, N., Mills, T. and Miller, D. (2017). Islamophobia, social movements and the state': For a movement-centred approach. In N. Massoumi, T. Mills and D. Miller (Eds.), *What Is Islamophobia: Racism, Social Movements and the State* (pp. 3–32). London: Pluto Press.

Monaghan, J. (2014). Security traps and discourses of radicalization: Examining surveillance practices targeting Muslims in Canada. *Surveillance & Society*, 12(4), 485.

Novelli, M. (2017). Education and countering violent extremism: Western logics from south to north?. *Compare: A Journal of Comparative and International Education*, 47(6), 835–851.

NSW Government Media Release (2015). *Countering Violent Extremism in Public Schools*. https://www.nsw.gov.au/your-government/the-premier/media-releases-from-the-premier/countering-extremism-in-public-schools/

Oliver-Dee, S. (2018). Started but contested: Analyzing US and British counter-extremism strategies. *The Review of Faith and International Affairs*, 16(2), 71–83.

Olson, J. (2008). Social work's professional and social justice projects. *Journal of Progressive Human Services*, 18(1), 45–69.

Ozalp, M. (2017). For a more harmonious and cohesive Australia. In D. Iner (Ed.), *Islamophobia in Australia 2014–2016*. Sydney: Charles Sturt University.

Pawar, M., Hugman, R., Alexandra, A. and Anscombe, A.W. (2017). Introduction: The Role of Virtues in Social Work Practice. In M. Pawar, R. Hugman, A. Alexandra and A.W. Anscombe (Eds.), *Empowering Social Workers: Virtuous Practitioners* (pp. 1–16). Singapore: Springer.

Schnurr, S. (1997). Why did social workers accept the new world order. In N. Germany, H. Sunker and H.U. Otto (Eds.), *Education and Fascism: Political Identity as Social Education* (pp. 121–143). Washington: Falmer Press.

Thomas, P. (2010). Failed and friendless: The UK's 'preventing violent extremism' programme. *The British Journal of Politics and International Relations*, 12(3), 442–458.

Vermeulen, F. (2014). Suspect communities – Targeting violent extremism at the local level: Policies of engagement in Amsterdam, Berlin, and London. *Terrorism and Political Violence*, 26(2), 286–306.

Walter, M., Taylor, S. and Habibis, D. (2011). How white is social work in Australia. *Australian Social Work*, 64(1), 6–19.

Williams, G. (2011). A decade of Australian anti-terror laws. *Melbourne University Law Review*, 35(3), 1136–1176.

6

Pushing Back Against Stereotypes: Muslim Immigrant Women's Experiences of Domestic Violence

Nafiseh Ghafournia

I acknowledge the Traditional Custodians of the land on which I work and live, and recognise their continuing connection to land, water and community. I pay respect to Elders past, present and emerging.

Introduction

Violence against women has pervasive and traumatic effects on all women's lives. For victims from immigrant backgrounds, the situation can often be more complex. Despite this complexity, there has been little effort until recently to address domestic violence within the immigrant communities in Australia (Australian Bureau of Statistics, 2013). Studies examining the experiences of abused Muslim immigrant women in Australia are especially limited, despite Muslim Australians being one of the fastest growing minority groups in the country.

Even though the Australian government supports immigration and multiculturalism, the contemporary climate for Muslims in Australia has become increasingly volatile and attitudes towards Muslim immigrants are directed by anti-Muslim sentiments (Sohrabi and Farquharson, 2016). This political climate has become amplified since September 2001 and more recently with the emergence of the so-called 'Islamic State' (ISIS). In Australia events such as the so-called 'Lebanese gang rapes' in August 2000; the 2002 and 2005 Bali bombings; the 2005 Cronulla riots; controversial comments made by some Muslim religious figures; and, more recently, the 2014 Sydney Lindt Café siege have led to more unfavourable media coverage for Muslims (Levy and Visenten, 2014). These have all contributed to the increased marginalisation of

Muslims and subjected them to racism, humiliation and injustice (Johns et al., 2015).

Following September 11, 2001 and subsequent events mentioned above, Muslim women increasingly became the target of discrimination and, in some cases, of public violence. In particular, those wearing Hijab have been more vulnerable to racism and Islamophobia. They have been portrayed as oppressed, passive, submissive victims of Islamic fundamentalism who need to be rescued (Aly, 2007; Navarro, 2010). In this climate of anti-Muslim sentiment, Muslim immigrant women have been further deterred from seeking help in the case of domestic violence, as they fear it may provoke political harassment and cause a backlash against them and their family members (Poynting and Noble, 2004).

Domestic violence among immigrant and refugee women

While research on domestic violence among immigrant women is limited, a number of heterogeneous studies have been conducted in this area. Despite some differences in their sample populations, the regions of the studies and the methodologies used, recurring themes are identified in these works. For example, the literature suggests that immigrant and refugee women have broad understandings of domestic violence. However, some prefer other terms such as family problem or family conflict (Fisher, 2009). In some studies, CALD (culturally and linguistically diverse) women understood domestic or family violence as physical assault (Ogunsiji et al., 2011) whereas others mentioned emotional, financial, economic and social violence (Easteal, 1996; Rees and Pease, 2007), as well as immigration-related, spiritual and in-law abuse (Colucci et al., 2014). According to the literature, women from CALD backgrounds are less likely to report cases of domestic violence due to immigration, cultural or other structural challenges and barriers (Fisher, 2013; Zannettino, 2012). Abused women usually prefer to seek informal help such as talking to family members and friends (Taylor and Putt, 2007).

In addition, gender inequality is one of the central considerations for many of the studies. Fixed gender roles lead to different responsibilities for men and women in family life. Within the family it is usually women who have a role in keeping the family together in ways that prevent women from seeking help for domestic violence. Radical changes to men's traditional roles as husbands and fathers after immigration have been identified as a significant contributing factor in marital conflict and domestic violence (Colucci et al., 2014; Zannettino, 2012).

In line with some international studies most of the literature in the Australian context reported that immigration-related factors increase women's vulnerability to domestic violence. The literature underlines how immigration has a negative impact on women's experiences of violence by setting up barriers to seeking help (Colucci et al., 2014; Zannettino, 2012). Isolation, lack of knowledge of services, language barriers, fear of deportation, experience of racism and discrimination, and fear of police were among the most important barriers for abused immigrant women in seeking help. Furthermore, some studies explored the role of cultural beliefs in immigrant women's experience of domestic violence. These studies mainly focus on cultural belief as a barrier for seeking help (Fisher, 2013; Rees and Pease, 2007; Zannettino, 2012). These challenges faced by immigrant women highlight the particular vulnerability of immigrant women experiencing domestic violence.

Theoretical framework

Feminist theories prioritise gender as the main determinant of women's oppression and disadvantage. They challenge male privilege as well as the traditional notion that domestic violence is a private family matter (McPhail et al., 2007). In these approaches there is an implicit perception that domestic violence affects every person equally, across race, class, nationality and religion.

However, in this universalising approach it has been argued that the experiences of all abused women are generalised from white, middle-class, heterosexual perspectives. It has been argued that the one-size-fits-all approach is not capable of describing the experiences and needs of diverse groups of abused women (Collins, 2000; Crenshaw, 1994). The essentialism in feminist theory and domestic violence theorisation has been questioned by postmodern feminism, postcolonial feminism, black feminism, feminists of colour and intersectional feminism. These feminisms challenge the radical white feminism that assumes gender is the main determinant of women's destiny and that women are a homogeneous group sharing the same life experience. Feminist intersectionality has thus developed to explain the intersection of gender with other social categories (Sokoloff and Pratt, 2005). This approach is based on the assumption that each social group has unique qualities influenced by interactions between different social identities such as race, gender and class (2005).

Researchers drawing on feminist intersectional perspective (Crenshaw, 1994; Sokoloff and Pratt, 2005) argue that battered women's oppression is often multiplied by their location at the intersections of particular race, ethnic, class, gender, sexual orientation and immigration systems or regimes. In an intersectional approach no factor alone can be the explanation for domestic violence (Shields, 2008). Intersectional perspectives, in particular, have contributed to understandings of domestic violence among different immigrant communities.

Method

This chapter draws on qualitative interview data collected for a doctoral thesis. In total, 14 in-depth, semi-structured interviews were completed with women who self-identified as Muslim. Interviews were audio recorded, transcribed and analysed using NVivo, a computer-based qualitative data analysis package. The University of Sydney's Human Ethics Committee provided approval for the study. A pseudonym was chosen for each interviewee. Following the interviews a debriefing session took place. Most of the women reported that giving voice to their experience of domestic violence and sharing their stories was a relief. Thematic analysis was employed to analyse the accounts of the participants.

Findings

Data analysis revealed five major themes. These themes included (1) how domestic violence is understood; (2) women's responses to domestic violence; (3) immigration; (4) culture; and (5) religion. In each of these major themes some sub-themes emerged.

How domestic violence is understood

The participants defined domestic violence in similar ways. All of the women were aware of different kinds of abuse. They talked about domestic violence *not* being limited to physical abuse.

> Every woman who is the target of domination or misuse is the victim of domestic violence. It's not just hitting or swearing, if a woman is under control of a man, it is domestic violence. (Shadi, 32, Iran)

In general, the women's attitude towards domestic violence was very negative. They all condemned it and none of the respondents considered any forms of partner abuse as the right of a man. In addition, no informant justified abuse towards women or blamed women for partner abuse. In this way the research participants' perception of abuse was similar to mainstream women in the Australian context (VicHealth, 2014). In addition, the participants' definitions of domestic violence and their attitudes towards it challenge the common belief that domestic violence is normal and acceptable among immigrant communities (Pedersen and Hartley, 2012; Volpp, 2011) and particularly among Muslims.

Response to domestic violence

According to most of the respondents, bearing their partners' abuse was difficult. Even from the first incident of domestic violence they all wanted the abuse to stop. They each used different strategies to respond to their situation. The common strategies were silence, being nice to the abuser, ignoring the abuser and trying not to be around him, distracting themselves with other things like reading and singing, relying on various forms of spirituality, advising the partner to see a counsellor, psychologist or attend anger management courses, talking to friends and family members.

> I tried to go for walk early in the morning and mixing with a lot of people. I tried to keep my mind busy ... and just redirect my mind to birds and blue sky and other things that took me away from there from getting upset. Sometimes I read books. (Maryam, 62, Iran)

The women's narratives all clearly show their resilience and strength in dealing with the abuse, even those who were still living with their partners. Some forms of resistance that the women utilised while in abusive relationships were hiding their money, passports and other documents and developing escape plans; keeping the domestic violence hotline number with them at all times; looking for GPs and/or psychologists in their own community and asking for interpreters in order to provide opportunities to break the silence about their abuse.

> I had everything ready in case I wanted to escape, my small savings, my passport, my jewellery and some clothes. (Azar, 44, Iran)

> I wanted to go to English class but my husband and his mother said you are not allowed. So I taught myself. I turned the radio on while I was cleaning and cooking and tried to remember words. At night I asked my children. (Farah, 26, Lebanon)

According to the women, one of the most helpful and accessible first points of contact were teachers in English classes and at Training and

Further Education (TAFE) who then referred them to counsellors. For those women who were kept socially isolated by their abusers, the only way to get out of the house was English classes or TAFE. For the majority of the women in the study, formal external help was very useful and the experience of using these services was very positive. Other sources of help for the women were social workers in hospitals and Centrelink, psychologists, GPs and nurses, and community workers in Migrant Resource Centres and other organisations.

Contrary to the common stereotype of immigrant women, especially Muslim women, being unwilling to approach relevant formal services, most of the participants reached for external formal help, despite the significant barriers they faced in doing so. In addition, the women's response to abuse was similar to the mainstream population, as most of the women reached out for formal help after trying other informal help such as talking to family and friends (Mouzos and Makkai, 2004).

Immigration

In this study the connection of immigration to the experience of domestic violence emerged as a key theme. For example, the women in the study talked about the stresses associated with immigration. Consistent with numerous studies, the experience of immigration for almost all of the women in the sample was a challenging one. Moreover, the intersection of immigration and abuse was manifested in a number of different ways. For most of the women, immigration had an adverse effect on men's level of violence.

Moreover, there are aspects of the experience of domestic violence that participants highlighted as being specifically related to being an immigrant, rather than to other social categories such as gender, culture or religion. It is notable that these factors usually interact and do not affect immigrant women independently. First, most of the women in the study have left their entire social support system behind in their home country, which furthered their emotional, social and psychological reliance on their partners.

> Back home he abused me too but at least my parents and brothers talked to him and I left him for a while and stayed with my parents. He was behaving better. (Tasnim, 45, Bangladesh)

Second, for many of the participants, language was a major barrier. It further exacerbated the women's isolation and resulted in their not having access to services, being financially dependent on the abuser and having low self-esteem and confidence. The women, especially those who were recent arrivals in Australia, had little access to relevant information or knowledge of where to go for advice.

> Well, I was really frustrated, and I had no family members and no friends. I was on my own ... no English at all, no job ... I used to cry for months and months and months. (Vesna, 60, Bosnia)

> When my husband hit me I went out. I slept in the park ... I didn't know where to go. (Zella, 31, Somalia)

Third, the threat of being deported affected women in terms of increasing their stress and sense of insecurity.

> He was telling me that both my daughter and he is Australian not me and my visa will finished in some time. If I leave or divorce he will take my daughter and I go to my country. (Amal, 35, Syria)

Fourth, women's socioeconomic status was another challenge, which affected women's experience of abuse in different ways.

> I had three children and in a small unit; if I left him where would I go? I didn't have money, no job; I was dependent on him. (Ziba, 62, Iran)

Fifth, women's vulnerability has been exacerbated by gender-biased immigration policies and laws, as there are still some limitations in these policies.

> I found out later that he was in jail four times. He broke his girlfriend's nose once; it was not fair. How the government let him who has criminal record to sponsor his wife. (Shadi, 32, Iran)

> While I was in a refuge I didn't have any money as I was not permanent resident. (Farah, 26, Lebanon)

Finally, there were a few cases of discrimination from service providers which delayed women's response to the abuse.

> Some of staffs treated me badly. For example, the first day I went to a refuge I had some Halal food with me the food from my country that I like. They didn't let me to bring the food with me. (Zeinab, 26, Iraq)

> When I was in a refuge I didn't have any money as I was not permanent resident. I asked for nappy for my daughter they gave me one or two. It was hard for me to ask every day. It was an Australian girl who always got boxes of nappies. I felt so bad. (Amal, 35, Syria)

Culture

In the study references to culture and community arose repeatedly throughout the interviews. The terms 'my community' or 'our community' and culture were used interchangeably. Almost all of the women in the study were aware of the effect of their culture on their experience of abuse. Despite being from different ethnic backgrounds, the women talked about some common cultural beliefs and values such as the sanctity of family and women's role in keeping the family together, women's role in the husband's abuse, and the stigma attached to divorce. For most of the women in the study, these cultural values were part of the challenges they faced while dealing with their experience of domestic violence.

> They [my community] would say look she has been married for so many years and then if I go to court and get separated it's a shame and my children will be embarrassed they can't get married. (Sakina, 40, Afghanistan)

While it is important to recognise that cultural values and practices contribute to the pressure not to seek help and instead to endure domestic violence, they also need to be viewed as sources of strength for many abused women in responding to violence and coping with related challenges (Runner et al., 2009, p. 47). In this study some women focused on positive aspects of their culture. For most of the women, emotional support, when provided by their family, friends or sometimes their community, was very empowering. Their extended families, particularly brothers and fathers – even when they were back home – usually got involved in stopping the abuse in different ways such as confronting the abuser, supporting the woman's decision to leave and providing other emotional and financial help.

> Because I was far from my family, I did not tell them at first. But if I told them they would have supported me definitely. (Maryam, 62, Iran)

Religion

The women in this study mostly relied on spirituality rather than religion. Most, even the non-practising Muslims, relied heavily on their belief in God or some divine power. They repeatedly talked about God as a significant refuge in their life, particularly when facing their partner's abuse.

> I pray when he hit me after that I go to pray and I pray to my Allah then I feel better and be stronger. (Tasnim, 45, Bangladesh)

In the women's narratives the positive role of religion was mentioned mainly as a source of empowerment, resistance towards abuse and even towards the mainstream culture, a support for mental and emotional well-being, and a great coping strategy.

Religion also played a negative role in women's experience of domestic violence, primarily in the guise of religious leaders. This has been mentioned as typically hindering women's response to the abuse (Kulwicki et al., 2010). The negative role of religious leaders has been identified by some studies among different religious groups such as Christianity, Judaism and Hinduism (Mathur, 2008; Nason-Clark, 2004). Most of the leaders encouraged women to stay in abusive relationships and to be patient.

> I went to Imam in the mosque; he just advised me to go back to my husband. I didn't go there anymore. (Shakila, 35, Pakistan)

Consistent with the women's stories, there were different views on the role of religion in their experience of domestic violence. Few believed that if their partners were religious they would never abuse them. Some believed that Islam is a religion of peace and equality but men or religious leaders interpret it according to their wishes and take advantage of religion to abuse women.

> Our men take advantage of our religion. We have in our religion that men should treat women as something dear and valuable, but in practice none of them do that. Some Muslim men don't follow these religious rules. (Tasnim, 45, Bangladesh)

One woman even explained that according to her religion she should have left the abuser many years ago and it was her religious duty to stop the abuse.

> Although I am saying I am religious but in this particular case I think I should have religiously spoken about this behaviour and got help many years ago but I didn't. (Ziba, 62, Iran)

Furthermore, the women in the study were aware of the relationship between culture and religion. They stated that culture influences religion and clearly differentiated between Islamic values and cultural beliefs. They believed that it was mainly the cultural values and expectations that delayed their responses to the abuse.

Discussion

Based on the intersectional approach employed, and in accordance with the women's stories, there are five major findings of this study.

First, structural factors, particularly immigration-related aspects of the women's lives, act as stressors in exacerbating the abuse. Based on the women's stories, being an immigrant had a huge impact on their experience of and responses to the violence. These structural inequalities resulted in the shaping of new tactics of abuse by abusive partners and led to more control of women, making them more vulnerable.

Second, the women in the study identified 'culture' as a key factor in their experience of abuse. Despite coming from different ethnic backgrounds, most of the women talked about some common cultural beliefs and values as main barriers to responding to partner abuse. However, according to the findings of this research, it is essential to bear in mind that cultural specificity in the case of domestic violence cannot be denied. One clear example is in-law abuse, a common type of abuse experienced within the sample. This form of abuse is usually reinforced by social structures such as cultural expectations of daughters-in-law, which create conflict that can facilitate the abuse. This abuse is more common in the context of joint family systems and in collectivist societies in general (Raj et al., 2011, p. 709).

Third, according to the study findings, gender role expectations are still exploited by abusive partners to control the participants. Almost all of the women implicitly or explicitly talked about unequal gender roles as one of the main factors in their experience of abuse. Regardless of whether gender-related factors are based on culture or other structural factors, they exist in the women's narrative of domestic violence.

Fourth, consistent with the women's stories, the role of spirituality and religious belief was more empowering than it was a barrier. However, in Islam, like other religions, common cultural beliefs are based on patriarchal ideologies. These beliefs are justified in the name of religion and sometimes even replace religious rules and values. So, it was not the patriarchal nature of religion but the patriarchal interpretation that facilitated the abuse.

Finally, the relevance of an intersectional approach, and its application in different social contexts, has been identified. Various categories intersect to shape women's experience of domestic violence. In other words, in particular historical and social contexts some social divisions or categories are more important than others (Anthias, 2013). Based on the findings of this study, some factors have more weight in shaping the women's experience of abuse. However, the hierarchy of different structural and cultural factors and the essence of the intersection may be different in another sample of immigrant women.

Implications for social work practice and policy

The findings of this study shed light on some issues of relevance to service providers and policy makers, which need to be addressed in the areas of practice, education and policy. First, a reflection on the important role of social workers, counsellors and ESL (English as a Second Language) teachers in this area is a fundamental consideration. The findings indicate that these sources were the very first formal resource for most of the participants in disclosing their experience of abuse. This suggests a need to equip this group of service providers with relevant information and training, as well as enough funds and the authority to refer abused immigrant women to more relevant domestic violence services.

Second, one of the major findings of the study is the important role of religion and spirituality in empowering women to deal with the abuse. Religious institutions can be a great source of support and information for both immigrant abused women and their abusers. Providing domestic violence training for religious leaders can be the first step to familiarising them with the issue and appropriate responses.

Third, cultural beliefs that were identified in the study commonly acted as barriers to responding to the abuse. However, the support of family, friends and communities were mentioned as sources of empowerment for other women. Multicultural domestic violence education initiatives could increase immigrant communities' awareness of abuse and empower them to respond to it.

Fourth, in the study the role of immigration-related factors emerged as a dynamic that perpetuates discrimination and acts as a barrier for immigrant women. The role of structural inequalities is often overshadowed by the focus on immigrant culture. However, the existing literature confirms that difficulties faced by abused immigrant women coexist with the challenges they face as immigrants. Providing material resources such as independent housing, job training, childcare and bridging courses to recognise overseas qualifications are some of the structural interventions which could empower marginalised immigrant women to deal with their abuse. Settlement services should also provide immigrants with information about domestic violence legislation soon after their arrival in Australia. Provision of compulsory and adequate interpreting services is also essential. Fifth, immigration and domestic violence provision (DVP) policy needs to be modified to fill the existing gaps. For example, the DVP does not cover some visa subclasses such as student visas and some other temporary visa holders. These visa holders do not have access to crisis services and accommodation in the case of domestic violence. There is also a need to monitor the eligibility of spouse sponsors to prevent serial sponsorship by those citizens who already have a history of perpetrating domestic violence against their partners (Ghafournia, 2011).

Finally, domestic violence services should create more opportunities for their front-line workers to attend cultural competency workshops and training. The need for this is seen in the examples of misunderstanding and discrimination towards the immigrant women among the service providers. Domestic violence services can utilise abused immigrant women's experience in service delivery. Hearing their voice is an essential step in combating marginalisation of CALD women.

Conclusion

To sum up, this research has been a necessary stepping stone to future research of other abused immigrant women's experiences of domestic violence. It is also a beginning point in attempting to fill a gap in the field of domestic violence research among CALD women in Australia, a much under-researched area. The results have clearly indicated that Muslim immigrant women in this research have a unique and complex experience of abuse, while sharing some commonalities with mainstream women and other immigrant groups. It is argued that intersectionality is a useful framework for exploring Muslim immigrant women's experience of domestic violence because it renders visible factors that are otherwise played down. The study tried to go beyond a simple portrayal of the women as one-dimensional individuals and has alternatively demonstrated them as women with a diverse range of backgrounds, histories, beliefs, opinions and resources.

Further readings

Sokoloff, N.J. and Pratt, C. (2005). *Domestic Violence at the Margins: Readings on Race, Class, Gender and Culture.* New Brunswick, NJ: Rutgers University Press.

Vaughan, C., Davis, E., Murdolo, A., Chen, J., Murray, L., Block, K., Quiazon, R. and Warr, D. (2015). Promoting Community-led Responses to Violence against Immigrant and Refugee Women in Metropolitan and Regional Australia: The ASPIRE Project: State of Knowledge Paper. *ANROWS Landscapes*, Australia's National Research Organisation for Women's Safety (ANROWS).

Wendt, S. and Zannettino, L. (2014). *Domestic Violence in Diverse Contexts: A Re-examination of Gender.* New York: Taylor & Francis.

References

Aly, A. (2007). Australian Muslim responses to the discourse on terrorism in the Australian popular media. *Australian Journal of Social Issues*, 42(1), 27–40.

Anthias, F. (2013). Intersectional what? Social divisions, intersectionality and levels of analysis. *Ethnicities*, 13(1), 3–19.

Australian Bureau of Statistics (2013). *Defining the data challenge for family, domestic and sexual violence: A conceptual data framework*. Canberra: Australian Bureau of Statistics.

Collins, P.H. (2000). *Black Feminism Thought: Knowledge, Consciousness and the Politics of Empowerment*. New York: Routledge.

Colucci, E., O'Connor, M., Field, K., Baroni, A., Pryor, R. and Minas, E.H. (2014). Nature of domestic/family violence and barriers to using services among Indian immigrant women. *Alterstice – Revue Internationale de la Recherche Interculturelle*, 3(2), 9–26.

Crenshaw, W.K. (1994). Mapping the margins: Intersectionality, identity politics and violence against women of color. In M.A. Fineman and R. Mykitiuk (Eds.), *The Public Nature of Private Violence: The Discovery of Domestic Abuse* (pp. 93–118). New York: Routledge.

Easteal, P. (1996). Double jeopardy: Violence against immigrant women in the home. *Family Matters*, 45, 26–30.

Fisher, C. (2009). *The exploration of the nature and understanding of family and domestic violence within the Sudanese, Somalian, Ethiopian, Liberian and Sierra Leonean communities and its impact on individuals family relations, the community and settlement*. Perth: Association for Services to Torture and Trauma Survivors.

Fisher, C. (2013). Changed and changing gender and family roles and domestic violence in African refugee background communities post-settlement in Perth, Australia. *Violence against Women*, 19(7), 833–847.

Ghafournia, N. (2011). Battered at home, played down in policy: Migrant women and domestic violence in Australia. *Aggression and Violent Behavior*, 16, 207–213.

Johns, A., Mansouri, F. and Lobo, M. (2015). Religiosity, citizenship and belonging: The everyday experiences of young Australian Muslims. *Journal of Muslim Minority Affairs*, 35(2), 171–190.

Kulwicki, A., Aswad, B., Carmona, T. and Ballout, S. (2010). Barriers in the utilization of domestic violence services among Arab immigrant women: Perceptions of professionals, service providers and community leaders. *Journal of Family Violence*, 25(8), 727–735.

Levy, M. and Visenten, L. (2014). The siege ends, two hostages, gunmen dead, *The Age*, 16 December.

Mathur, K. (2008). Body as site, body as space: Bodily integrity and women's empowerment in India. *Economic and Political Weekly*, 43(17), 54–63.

McPhail, A.B., Busch, N.B., Kulkarni, S. and Rice, G. (2007). An integrative feminist model: The evolving feminist perspective on intimate partner violence. *Violence against Women*, 13(8), 817–841.

Mouzos, J. and Makkai, T. (2004). *Women's Experiences of Male Violence: Findings from the Australian Component of the International Violence against Women Survey (Ivaws)*. Canberra: Australian Institute of Criminology.

Nason-Clark, N. (2004). When terror strikes at home: The interface between religion and domestic violence. *Journal for the Scientific Study of Religion*, 43(3), 303–310.

Navarro, L. (2010). Islamophobia and sexism: Muslim women in the western mass media. *Human Architecture*, 8(2), 95–114.

Ogunsiji, O., Wilkes, L., Jackson, D. and Peters, K. (2011). Suffering and smiling: West African immigrant women's experience of intimate partner violence. *Journal of Clinical Nursing*, 21(11–12), 1659–1665.

Pedersen, A. and Hartley, L.K. (2012). Prejudice against Muslim Australians: The role of values, gender and consensus. *Journal of Community and Applied Social Psychology*, 22, 239–255.

Poynting, S. and Noble, G. (2004). Living with racism: The experience and reporting by Arab and Muslim Australians of discrimination, abuse and violence since 11 September 2001. http://www.uws.edu.au/ccr.

Raj, A., Sabarwal, S., Decke, M.R., Nair, S., Jethva, M., Krishnan, S., Donta, B., Saggurti, N. and Silverman, J.G. (2011). Abuse from in-laws during pregnancy and post-partum: Qualitative and quantitative findings from low-income mothers of infants in Mumbai, India. *Maternal Child Health Journal*, 15(6), 700–712.

Rees, S. and Pease, B. (2007). Domestic violence in refugee families in Australia. *Journal of Immigrant and Refugee Studies*, 5(2), 1–19.

Runner, M., Yoshihama, M. and Novick, S. (2009). *Intimate partner violence in immigrant and refugee communities: Challenges, promising practices and recommendations*. http://www.endabuse.org/userfiles/file/ImmigrantWomen/IPV_Report_March_2009.pdf.

Shields, S.A. (2008). Gender: An intersectionality perspective. *Sex Roles*, 59(5), 301–311.

Sohrabi, H. and Farquharson, K. (2016). Social integration of Australian Muslims: A dramaturgical perspective. *Journal of Sociology*, 52(2), 387–402.

Sokoloff, N.J. and Pratt, C. (Eds.) (2005). *Domestic Violence at the Margins*. New Brunswick, NJ: Rutgers University Press.

Taylor, N. and Putt, J. (2007). Adult sexual violence in indigenous and culturally and linguistically diverse communities in Australia. *Trends and Issues in Crime and Criminal Justice*, 345, 1–6.

VicHealth. (2014). Australians' attitudes to violence against women: Findings from the 2013 National Community Attitudes towards Violence against Women Survey (NCAS). https://www.vichealth.vic.gov.au/~/media/.../ncas/ncas-stakeholderreport_2014.ashx.

Volpp, L. (2011). Framing cultural difference: Immigrant women and discourses of tradition. *Journal of Feminist Cultural Studies*, 22(1), 90–110.

Zannettino, L. (2012). 'There is no war here; it is only the relationship that makes us scared': Factors having an impact on domestic violence in Liberian refugee communities in South Australia. *Violence Against Women*, 18(7), 807–828.

7
Working with Cultural Differences: Teaching First-Year Undergraduate Students to Unpack Unjust Power

Jioji Ravulo

As part of my genuine commitment, personally and professionally, I acknowledge the Traditional Custodians of the land in which this chapter was written, the Bidjigal people of the Eora nation and the Cabrogal people of the Darug nation. I also pay my ongoing respects to Elders past and present, and have hope that future leaders will arise from the strength that is found in their Indigenous ways of knowing and doing, being and becoming. Everyone, Indigenous and non-Indigenous, is responsible for ensuring such approaches are upheld; with a spirit to collaborate and include Aboriginal and Torres Strait Islanders in decision making across every aspect of Australian society.

Introduction

Society is complex – made up of complex individuals, families and communities. The way in which society is structured is shaped, in part, by the way that we collectively draw meaning to objects that, in turn, prescribe our values, beliefs, ideals and practices. How we interpret and place meaning on certain activities can also be complicated by the diverse relations of social life that pervade and construct our sense of belonging and purpose. This includes perceived differences based on gender, religion, sexuality, language, ability, class, ethnicity and other diverse categories, situations and circumstances. How do we then, as a society, create fair and just communities that support such diversity and differences for individuals and families to feel like they belong? And how is this contrasted against dominant discourses that continue to uphold hegemonic values and belief systems that suppress difference, ignore inequity and devalue critical discourse social work practice, policy and research? This chapter will explore the possibilities to shift the way that social work educators can better assist tertiary students to develop a greater insight and understanding of their own position on working with cultural differences, while simultaneously challenging sites of ignorance and unjust power. It is hoped that the practices discussed here can also be helpful to those working in community development or providing workshops and presentations on diversity and social justice. This content will also be useful to front-line practitioners in terms of providing a language and concepts and activities that will be useful in addressing difference and inequity in ways that engage communities, students, service users and educators in generating more socially just practices. Key theories such as deconstructionism are highlighted, as well as the need to create transformational learning environments that promote social justice education. An innovative approach to promoting undergraduate engagement will be presented and unpacked in order to provide an example of transformative education. This engagement strategy includes the use of a social media platform to encourage students to be more mindful of their own positionality, while encouraging wider engagement with fellow learners within face-to-face teaching.

Theory and approaches

The literature explored in the chapter ranges from key concepts associated with philosophical thought from thinkers such as Derrida and Foucault, as well as looking at the ways that some people position themselves in ignorance. Other literature will examine the importance of creating learning environments that promote social justice, and may also promote levels of transformational outcomes and outputs. The aim of such a broad scope is to encourage first-year undergraduate students to question and challenge their preconceived understanding of self and others, with a view to recreate a personal stance that may lead to the development of a professional identity embedded with social justice insights and understanding.

Deconstructionism and différance

The notion that society is fixed and static, set up with institutions and organisations that prescribe a set structure of right and wrong, has been greatly challenged by philosophers like Jacques Derrida. A key figure in the poststructuralist movement, Derrida questioned the role of writing in an evolving society, placing more and more meaning on the literal, and the way spoken language was replacing the previous importance placed on written text (Guillemette and Cossette, 2006).

Deconstructionism challenges the status quo by questioning why this is seen as accepted, while looking at the possibility of other perspectives. At the same time, Derrida acknowledged that oppositional binaries limit the way in which people understand or seek to explore beyond such static positions. Rather, the notion of différance creates an opportunity to re-shift existing perceptions, while seeking to understand the possible greys that exist beyond the binaries. Through Derrida's work one is challenged to sit uncomfortably with the idea that Western society cannot be simply explained through a single line of thought or theory, but through complex reasoning that reshapes the meaning of how one constructs self and others within this concept of reality. Therefore, people are encouraged to constantly challenge the position they sit within, and to deconstruct and/or question this while being content to sit within the infinite possibility that exists across society, and the way it is constructed. By not challenging such ideals, individuals, community and society are bound to a set of discourses that privilege one over the other, while creating discourses that uphold dominant positions of power and knowledge.

Power/discourse/marginalisation

The godfather of the power and knowledge conundrum, Michel Foucault, provided a greater understanding of the relationship society places on discourse as an expression of power (Foucault cited in Nola, 1998, p. 112). Understanding the complexities of human society and the role of power, as well as the way in which society may favour or uphold certain discourses, can also demonstrate this notion of power and knowledge, as 'there is no power relation without the correlative constitution of a field of knowledge, nor any knowledge that does not presuppose and constitute at the same time power relations' (Foucault cited in Nola, 1998, p. 113). In saying this, as members of modern-day Australia, there is a need to esteem formal education that provides scope for learners to understand the realities of how society upholds certain values, beliefs and perspectives; which then shape the society in which people are positioned. Knowledge consumption and production should be characterised by and through a critical lens, and a commitment on the part of the individual to create a better understanding of why powerlessness may occur, and more so, how this may be overcome through the acquisition and use of knowledge.

Stuart Hall, the eminent cultural studies scholar, saw language as a means to communicate and as a way to uphold dominant rhetoric and discourse. The value in being able to have a shared understanding and interpretation of the world reflects the notion of a 'circuit of culture', where identity, production, consumption and regulation have an interconnecting relationship and influence. Language is an underlying 'representational system ... whether they are sounds, written words, electronically produced images, musical notes, even objects – to stand for or represent to other people our concepts, ideas and feelings' (Hall, 1997, p. 1). The way in which a culture is upheld or challenged can be discerned by the value and meaning people express within this circuit. A plethora of diverse cultural identities are also formed against this backdrop, which may be developed from influences like nationalism, alongside an array of differences based on language, ethnicity and religion.

Marginality can also be seen, and known, as a place of resistance, and an opportunity to create a counter position to the idea of the centre constantly and consistently shaping the voice of the margins, and relegating those as the 'other' (Chambon, 2013). According to the ever-challenging bell hooks,

> it was this marginality that I was naming as a central location for the production of a counter hegemonic discourse that is not just found in words but in habits of being and the way one lives. As such I was not speaking of a marginality one wishes to lose, to give up or surrender as part of moving into the centre, but rather as a site one stays in, clings to even, because it nourishes one's capacity to resist. It offers the possibility of radical perspectives from which to see and create, to imagine alternatives, new worlds. (hooks, 1990, p. 341)

Allowing those that are characterised in the margins to have a valid voice can also assist in those in the centre to further understand the true realities associated with such positions, while also striving to move beyond such ignorance. The need to also encourage those in the centre to also actively contribute in the margins as a fellow 'liberator' (hooks, 1990, p. 343) is another important part of resistance, where a meaningful exchange can occur, and be utilised in moving beyond sites of ignorance and unequal power.

Within Western countries that have opened their borders to migration 'the strengthening of local identities can be seen in the strong defensive reaction of those members of dominant ethnic groups who feel threatened by the presence of other cultures ... sometimes matched by a strategic retreat to more defensive identities amongst the minority communities themselves in response to the experience of cultural racism and exclusion' (Hall, 1992, p. 308). How do undergraduate students position themselves in such identities, and how can this create positions that also perpetuate a lack of insight and understanding into how such difference may manifest over time? The next theory looks deeper into challenging such perspectives.

Epistemologies of ignorance

According to the work undertaken by Linda Martín Alcoff (2007), epistemologies of ignorance are based on three types, where ignorance occurs through (1) an individual's situatedness and their knowledge; (2) group association and identities; and (3) oppressive systems (Alcoff, 2007, p. 40). Unpacking this further is the idea that people are and can be limited by their own lack of understanding and insight into their own ignorance; which is further perpetuated by other influences in and around them – including access to new ways of thinking and how this is embedded into identity. This can be further perpetuated by systemic inequalities and attributes that privilege certain voices, while marginalising others without fully appreciating the negative impact this has as a whole.

Exploring this concept further in the context of education, and the process of learning through educational processes, epistemologies of ignorance strive to also challenge the way dominant discourses and perspectives pervade positive learning attitudes and outcomes. Rather than uphold practices that gear students towards a goal where they increase their capacity to cater for new and innovative perspectives of the world in and around them, educators should further promote environments that unpack why levels of ignorance around ways of knowing, doing and believing occur. That is, 'instead of a linear sense of development, epistemologies of ignorance work in difference that intentionally holds together disjunctive lines of thought in the search to map the variety and divergence of contemporary knowledge production in education' (Malewski and Jaramillo, 2011, p. 3). More so, 'epistemologies of ignorance also centre the "subject" – woman, man, child, teacher, student – not as objects of knowledge production, but as sensuous beings who affectively live out the contradictions embedded within ignorance' (Malewski and Jaramillo, 2011, p. 5). Therefore, such an approach is striving to encourage a reshaping of the position in which one holds their knowledge base, and to subsequently re-examine the space in which knowledge is produced and utilised.

How do the above three theoretical perspectives also create scope for undergraduate social work students to engage in this process of learning, while developing skills and perspectives that create a professional identity worthy of the profession? The next two areas explored in this chapter highlight the importance of practically developing this academic and educational approach, through the notions of social justice education and transformational learning.

Social justice education

Teaching and learning practices are not free from bias or discrimination. Curricula are traditionally created with a view to engage students in a process of learning that will ensure intended learning outcomes are achieved. The way in which knowledge is taught tends to be premised on a pedagogical framing that is influenced by the educator. This raises concerns around the subjective nature of creating value-free environments that may in turn force students to comply and enforce meaning, rather than co-create knowledge that challenges varying positions of ignorance and unjust power. Therefore, the role of social justice education becomes one where both educator and student are encouraged to examine their own social positionality as part of this process of change. The spirit of 'social justice education challenges traditional education through applying principles of social justice to both explicit and hidden curriculum to expose unequal power relations that privilege some whilst disadvantaging other at individual, institutional, and societal levels' (Adams, 2016, p. 28).

With this in mind, professional courses like social work fall into the realm of social justice education as they strive to promote scope for students to develop skills, attributes and attitudes oriented to making a difference. In alignment with the Australian Social Work Education and Accreditation Standards created by the Australian Association of Social Workers (AASW), 'three core values of professional social work practice – respect, social justice and professional integrity – must be practiced in social work education' (Australian Association of Social Workers, 2015, p. 10). All Australian universities must receive some form of accreditation from the AASW to officiate the running of social work education, who ensure through these standards the ability to have students complete their course who can demonstrate nine prescribed graduate attributes. Such rigour requires tertiary institutions to structure undergraduate and postgraduate qualifying social work courses that exemplify such standards, while investing resources that are commensurate with these professional learning outcomes.

Social work education should encourage participants to become more aware of their own biases and judgements by challenging them to critically reflect and review such positions. Optimally, social work courses 'are cognitively challenging, emotionally charged, and personally unsettling. They can also be transformative, as participants develop greater personal awareness, expand knowledge that counters dominant narratives, and commit to making changes in themselves and their environments' (Bell et al., 2016, p. 55). Individual units that are part of social work programs should then endeavour to scaffold and bolster learning; where students transform their position from ignorance to embracing differences.

Transformational learning

Jack Mezirow (1997) talked extensively about the importance of the individual learning to transform their perspective through an adult education environment that encourages critical reflection. Such reflection may occur by challenging currently held positions and through the examination of discourses and assumptions. He believes there are four processes of learning which may enable a transformation to occur by encouraging learners to: (1) 'elaborate on existing points of view'; (2) 'establish new points of view'; (3) 'transform our point of view' by experiencing another culture; and (4) 'becoming aware and critically reflective of our generalised bias in the way we view groups other than our own' (Mezirow, 1997, p. 3). This kind of learning environment is one where a shared appreciation for diversity and difference may occur, as people become more willing to question their own assumptions, while exploring and examining the possibilities of others. An onus is also placed on the facilitator of adult learning and their personal commitment to transformational learning, 'to create norms that accept order, justice and civility in the classroom and respect and responsibility for helping each other learn, to welcome diversity; to foster peer collaboration, and to provide equal opportunity for participation' (Mezirow, 1997, p. 3).

Apart from encouraging the educator to be a responsible facilitator, Mezirow also developed a concept called Andragogy, were students are encouraged to be self-directed learners through their process of engagement in adult education. A listing of 12 goals was developed through his seminal work (Mezirow, 1981) which prompted a platform for learners to be perceived in a new and exciting way. This included encouraging learners to be less dependent on the educator; helping learners utilise resources to develop further learning; creating a deeper insight for the learner to understand their learning needs; promoting a level of responsibility in learning; assisting learners to prioritise their learning in the context of personal issues; support students in being willing to take on viewpoints of others; improving self-reflexive opportunities; enhancing self-correction and further reflection; encouraging learners to pose problems and start conversations about possible solutions; highlighting the importance of being a learner of learning and fostering the ability to express opinions; and providing a range of activities that engage differing learning styles, including experiential, and exploring all options and possibilities before making a definite choice (Mezirow, 1991, pp. 199–200).

Case study: Working with cultural differences

With the above literature in mind, the following case study will explore the undergraduate first-year unit I previously co-ordinated during my tenure at Western Sydney University, Working with Cultural Differences (WWCD). The unit draws on the above-mentioned theories. The course is also informed by a pedagogical framing that fosters social justice education and transformational learning. Social justice is actively discussed throughout the semester with students, as it helps students to deconstruct their personal perspectives before enhancing their own positions away from ignorance and upholding notions of unjust power in their burgeoning development of a professional identity. The unit is scaffolded within various undergraduate degrees, including Social Work within the School of Social Sciences and Psychology at Western Sydney University.

History and context of the Working with Cultural Differences (WWCD) unit

Western Sydney University (WSU), previously known as the University of Western Sydney, was established in 1989 with a vision to be a university of the people. The growing economic and population corridor of greater Western Sydney, the demography of students across its programs are reflective of the rich diversity represented in the region. According to the *Securing Success 2015–2020 Strategic Plan* (Western Sydney University, 2015), of the 45,383 students: 89.4% are domestic students, 54.9% are female, 80.6% are undergraduate, 24.5% are from a low socioeconomic status (SES) (which is the largest in the sector), 1.4% are Aboriginal and/or Torres Strait Islander, and 64.3% are first in family (p. 14). Overall, 76% of domestic students come from the greater Western Sydney region; where 35% of the population are born overseas, 39% speak language other than English, and only 27% have a university qualification (compared with 45% evident in the rest of Sydney) (p. 13). In addition, the most popular field of education taken by students is Society and Culture, with 12,000 enrolled across various WSU programs.

WWCD was developed as one of the initial core units offered in the discipline of social sciences in the late 1990s. Dr Jane Durie, a sociologist, saw the opportunity to further celebrate and capture such diversity in the classroom, with the view to teach theories of power, knowledge and marginalisation to students who traditionally experienced such issues and otherness themselves due to socioeconomic barriers and factors evident in being the first in their family to study at university.

And this is still a key feature of the unit – the ability to provide opportunities for students from an array of diversity and difference to contribute to each other's learning; through face-to-face tutorial classes enhanced with collaborative learning opportunities, further supported by lecture material and assessments designed to challenge positions of ignorance and unjust power. Generally, the unit is taken as a core first-year, second-semester unit for social sciences and social work, and as an elective for many other degrees under the School, including Policing and Anthropology. The unit also has enrolments from other Schools across the university, ranging from business to law. In total, around 400 students enrol each semester it is offered. I took on the Unit Coordination and overall responsibility of delivery from 2015 to the end of 2017, with the view to further enhance and streamline previous outcomes, while further refining the way in which social justice education principles and transformational learning practices overtly occur via the student experience.

As per Table 7.1, the respective seven learning outcomes have also remained consistent since the inception of the unit, with the view that students are encouraged to critically review and unpack what traditionally is perceived as macro concepts not previously discussed before coming to tertiary studies.

Table 7.1 WWCD Learning outcomes

1	Articulate current theories and concepts of culture, identity, difference and power; and the interrelationships among them
2	Identify the historical and social contexts of cultural differences and power relations in Australia through personal narratives and readings
3	Explain the concept of whiteness as a structure of authority and as a location of identity
4	Discuss the history of Indigenous/non-Indigenous relations in Australia since 1788 and its impacts for Aboriginal and Torres Strait Islanders today
5	Evaluate different discourses and practices of multiculturalism in recent Australian history
6	Describe and analyse intersecting markers of difference such as class, gender, race, location and sexuality in the Australian context
7	Evaluate research, policy and practice skills in working with cultural differences within professional contexts

Teaching content (lecture and tutes)

Weekly topics are arranged to promote clear scaffolding (as per Table 7.2) – with theoretical topics taught initially, and then pragmatically approached through utilising clear examples of diversity, and its difference, in following weeks. The final two weeks consolidate the learning, with the last week acting as a key reflection on reiterating the concept of *intersectionality* as developed by Kimberlè Crenshaw (Hancock, 2016) and the notion of *assemblage* postulated by Manuel DeLanda (Price-Robertson and Duff, 2016). Weekly readings are mapped to weekly topic areas, and are chosen to create an insight into the concepts associated with cultural differences.

Table 7.2 WWCD Weekly topics

Week	Topic	Key Themes
1	What Is Culture?	• Definitions of culture • Evolving nature & modern perspectives • Culture as fixed or dynamic
2	Culture & Identity	• Cultural terminology • Cultural objects & producing meaning • Cultural change and development • Enculturation & Acculturation
3	Discourse/Power/Knowledge	• Discourse – Michel Foucault • Power & Knowledge • Centres & Margins • Language & Power • Oppositional Binaries & Difference – Derrida
4	Whiteness (Part 1): Theorising Whiteness	• Emergence & intention of Whiteness studies • Defining whiteness • Language, power and whiteness • White Privilege and its manifestation
5	Whiteness (Part 2): Whiteness, Identity & Racism	• Australia's black history • White Australia policy • Indigenous protection & assimilation policy including the use of eugenics • Stolen Generation • Other Whiteness movement in Australia
6	Indigenous Australia: Aboriginal and Torres Strait Islanders	• Shared history – positions of ignorance and situatedness • Indigenous Australia – current issues • Influences from the past – discourse/power/knowledge/marginality • Reframing issues within Indigenous perspectives

Week	Topic	Key Themes
7	Multicultural Australia (Part 1): Immigration	• Early waves of migration before & after settlement • Multicultural Australia before Federation • Immigration – post-WWII • Whitlam Era – multiculturalism as policy • Regression through the Howard period
8	Multicultural Australia (Part 2): Policy, Practice & Current Issues	• Multiculturalism as policy & practice • Racism & Power relationships • Islamophobia in Australia • Refugees vs. Boat People • Current campaigns and trends
9	Gender & Feminism	• Gender & Diversity • Feminism, gender and language • Oppositional binaries and power discourse • Evolving nature of gender & society • Male privilege and toxic masculinity
10	Sexuality	• Relationship between gender & sexuality • Compulsory heterosexuality • Heteronormativity • Institution of marriage and level of power • Marriage equality and inequality
11	Class	• Marx and Engels • Tensions in capitalist democracies • Measure of class & definitions – Habitus (Bourdieu) • Class as a process and educational achievements • Privileging class
12	Intersectionality & Assemblages	• Intersectionality: theory & perspectives (Crenshaw) • Intersecting axes of privilege, domination and oppression (Morgan) • Intersecting identity (Audre Lorde) • Assemblage (DeLanda)

As mentioned, the ongoing diversity within the classroom assists in developing the learning environment. This influences the way in which classroom discussions are undertaken, with students' personal experiences influencing their social positions, and views. Tutors strive to encourage a culturally safe space to allow students to voice their respective opinions in a diplomatic manner.

As displayed in Table 7.3, class time is equally broken into 3 × 20 minute sections; where students are encouraged to (1) reflect, (2) review and (3) refocus. Each section allows in-depth reflection of a reflexive question, which is further explored in a class activity. As also shown in Table 7.3, this has been mapped against Bloom and Krathwohl's (1956) work on systematic learning; where cognitive, affective and kinaesthetic activities – when undertaken simultaneously – promote and enhance meaningful learning opportunities and outcomes (Bell et al., 2016, p. 65).

Section 1 reviews the weekly reading students are asked to read before class, and tutors actively reflect on the key themes within. Section 2 is a broader class discussion on the topic, with tangible examples discussed, further highlighting and creating a more relational conversation among students. Each of the weekly topics listed in Table 7.2 is generally evident and profiled across various media platforms on a regular basis, including social media and TV, thus the learning process is further enhanced by asking students to bring in examples they may have seen. Section 3 asks students to further discuss the possibilities around current or new research, policy and practice that could provide change. For example, in looking at Week 8 topics, students are asked to consider what could promote better engagement with newly arrived communities, and what services in the community could help with settlement issues. This may also spur conversations around appropriate policy recommendations for funding, and the need for research that highlights social and welfare needs.

Staffing composition and facilitation are important components of ensuring students are provided with a learning environment that yields

Table 7.3 Three domains of learning via Reflect/Review/Refocus

Domain Bloom & Krathwohl (1956)	Section	Reflexive Question	In-Class Activity
Cognitive (intellectual)	(1) REFLECT	What's my position?	Tutor to facilitate conversation on key points within prescribed weekly reading
Affective (social – emotional)	(2) REVIEW	What do we need to consider?	Students review practical examples, e.g. social media, videos, new articles
Kinaesthetic (skills and behaviours)	(3) REFOCUS	How can we change?	Discussion of current/new research, policy and practice that could impact topic area

the expected anticipated learning outcomes. This includes ensuring staff understanding the sensitive nature of the material being presented, and how this may cause some discomfort for students. Nonetheless, tutors are encouraged to utilise their facilitation skills in a professional and diplomatic manner; encouraging a shared and open learning space, while also creating a framework for rigorous debate and critical conversations.

Embrace differences (social media inclusion and Facebook page)

Material cited is from a wide array of sources, including traditional newspaper websites, social media news sites and YouTube videos posted by various professional and personal channels. This active Facebook page is utilised by all tutors across the teaching team to post relevant material for students to further reflect on and utilise during class-time discussion. Check out the very active page located at: www.facebook.com/EmbraceDiffer. The page also promotes a relevant hashtag to further reiterate the underlying learning process of #ReflectReviewRefocus.

Areas of development and possible future direction

Our experience with this course over the years shows that it is important that tutors are given opportunity to debrief and share from each other's experience with engaging students on such topics, especially early career academics.

We have also found that it is important to encourage facilitators to be aware of how resistance in the group can also be addressed. This is particularly important if the facilitators are from a diversity group. Students from the dominant group may see such dissonance as very challenging, and respond in ways that are not constructive or open to learning. This has occurred across the teaching team, for example when presenting on the topic of Whiteness. When I have lectured on this area, as a person of colour, I have felt the need to provide a 'disclaimer' before the start of this lecture – reinforcing to students that this topic is taught within the context of power and language. We provide this sociological concept to help students better understand society and to give them a way to grapple with confronting feelings and ideas. Interestingly, I suspect that if the person leading the lecture on Whiteness were not a person of colour, or physically appeared to be part of the dominant group, then such a disclaimer would not need to be given. This ongoing tension we encounter in our teaching highlights how important race studies are in Australian institutions, and also underscores the need to have more diversity represented in academia.

Conclusion

Creating opportunities across our communities to be more inclusive and aware of cultural differences will support positive outcomes. Rather than seeing this as an attempt to promote political correctness, or as a token gesture of good will, we are able to mould societies that are more positive for all when we genuinely challenge our own individual viewpoints, and unpack the way in which we place power on such perspectives. In turn we may see the ability to collectively create happier, healthier communities that support social cohesion and mobility. Positioning diversity as a positive attribute, instead of a barrier, is the key message here – embracing differences as a source of strength within the reality of our diverse communities across a multifaceted and multicultural Australia. Social work can play a big part in promoting such approaches through responsive education, practice, policies and research further underpinned by the tenets of social justice.

Further readings

Adams, M. and Bell, L. A. (2016). *Teaching for Diversity and Social Justice*. New York: Routledge.

Hage, G. (2000). *White Nation Fantasies of White Supremacy in a Multicultural Society: Radical Writing*. Annandale, NSW: Pluto Press.

Sue, D.W., Rasheed, M.N. and Rasheed, J.C. (2016). *Multicultural Social Work Practice: A Competency-Based Approach to Diversity and Social Justice*, 2nd Edition. Hoboken, NJ: Jossey-Bass.

References

Adams, M. (2016). Pedagogical foundations for social justice education. In M. Adams and L.A. Bell (Eds.), *Teaching for Diversity and Social Justice*, 3rd Edition (pp. 27–54). New York: Routledge.

Alcoff, L.M. (2007). Epistemologies of ignorance – Three types. In S. Sullivan and N. Tuana (Eds.), *Race and Epistemologies of Ignorance* (pp. 39–58). Albany: State University of New York Press.

Australian Association of Social Workers (2015). *Australian Social Work Education and Accreditation Standards*. Canberra: AASW. https://www.aasw.asn.au/document/item/3550.

Bell, L.A., Goodman, D.J. and Ouellett, M.L. (2016). Design and facilitation. In M. Adams and L.A. Bell (Eds.), *Teaching for Diversity and Social Justice*, 3rd Edition (pp. 55–94). New York: Routledge.

Bloom, B.S. and Krathwohl, D.R. (1956). *Taxonomy of Educational Objectives: The Classification of Educational Goals, by a Committee of College and University Examiners. Handbook 1: Cognitive Domain*. New York: Longman, Green.

Chambon, A. (2013). Recognising the Other, understanding the Other: A brief history of social work and Otherness. *Nordic Social Work Research*, 3(2), 120–129. https://doi.org/10.1080/2156857X.2013.835137.

Guillemette, L. and Cossette, J. (2006). Deconstruction and differance. In L. Hebert (Ed.), *Signo* (pp. 1–5). Rimouski [Online]. http://www.signosemio.com/derrida/deconstruction-and-differance.asp.

Hall, S. (1992). The question of cultural identity. In T. McGrew, S. Hall and D. Held (Eds.), *Modernity and Its Futures* (pp. 274–325). Cambridge: Polity Press and the Open University.

Hall, S. (1997). The work of representation. In S. Hall (Ed.), *Representation: Cultural Representations and Signifying Practices* (pp. 41–64). London: Sage Publications.

Hancock, A.M. (2016). *Intersectionality: An Intellectual History*. New York: Oxford University Press.

hooks, b. (1990). Marginality as site of resistance. In R. Ferguson and T. Minh-ha (Eds.), *Out There: Marginalization and Contemporary Cultures* (pp. 341–343). New York: MIT Press.

Malewski, E. and Jaramillo, N.E. (2011). *Epistemologies of Ignorance in Education*. Charlotte, NC: Information Age Publishing.

Mezirow, J. (1981). A critical theory of adult learning and education. *Adult Education*, 32(1), 3–24. https://doi.org/10.1177/074171368103200101.

Mezirow, J. (1991). *Transformative Dimensions of Adult Learning*, 1st Edition. San Francisco: Jossey-Bass.

Mezirow, J. (1997). Transformative learning: Theory to practice. *New Directions for Adult and Continuing Education*, 74, 5–12. https://doi.org/10.1002/ace.7401.

Nola, R. (1998). Knowledge, discourse, power and genealogy in Foucault. *Critical Review of International Social and Political Philosophy*, 1(2), 109–154. https://doi.org/10.1080/13698239808403240.

Price-Robertson, R. and Duff, C. (2016). Realism, materialism, and the assemblage: Thinking psychologically with Manuel DeLanda. *Theory and Psychology*, 26(1), 58–76. https://doi.org/10.1177/0959354315622570.

Western Sydney University (2015). *Securing Success 2015–2020 Strategic Plan*. Sydney: Western Sydney University. https://www.westernsydney.edu.au/__data/assets/pdf_file/0007/1097710/4.Securing_Success_Strategic_Plan.pdf.

PART THREE
CRITICAL PERSPECTIVES ON GENDER DIFFERENCE

8

Allyship and Social Justice: Men as Allies in Challenging Men's Violence and Discrimination Against Women

Alankaar Sharma

> *I acknowledge the Aboriginal and Torres Strait Islander peoples as the Traditional Custodians of the land and waters of Australia. I pay respect to Elders – past, present and future – and appreciate their cultures, knowledge and resilience.*

Confronting and ending oppression against marginalised and minoritised peoples is at the heart of social justice-oriented social work practice. Developing a critical understanding of power and oppression and enacting social change aimed at challenging structural factors that contribute to oppression are integral to the core mandates of the social work profession (International Federation of Social Workers, 2014). Different ways of challenging oppression are therefore of significant interest to social workers. The allyship model of social justice offers social workers a meaningful way of engaging with anti-oppressive practices that help address privilege and interrupt oppression. In this chapter I will introduce the idea of allyship from a social justice perspective and illustrate it through the example of men allies working with a profeminist framework to challenge men's violence and discrimination against women (MVDAW). I have chosen this example because this is a political position I am committed to, and because of my experiences of working against sexual and gender-based violence. Social workers can apply the core ideas of allyship to diverse contexts. I will occasionally discuss illustrative examples drawn from my personal and professional experiences. My purpose in doing so is not to communicate that my understanding of feminist issues is wholesome or that my politics is perfect. On the contrary, I hope the imperfect and evolving nature of my politics will become apparent in my sharing of these examples. I will discuss some of the salient aspects of allyship in this context, and argue that politicisation of allyship practices is important to meaningfully serve a feminist agenda. I should add that gender-based violence is a broad subject, and in this chapter I only focus on men – cisgender men, in particular – in addressing discrimination and violence against women. Men perpetrate violence and discrimination against women as well as against people of diverse gender identities including transgender and genderqueer. I acknowledge that efforts to prevent and address gender-based violence have historically been led by women and people of diverse gender identities who have had to unfairly and disproportionately shoulder the weight of experiencing such violence and discrimination, educating others about it, and working to end it.

Allyship and social justice

Allies, from a social justice perspective, are persons 'from a privileged group who make intentional choices to support or work for the rights of those from the oppressed group' and are 'committed to eliminating a form of oppression from which they benefit' (Goodman, 2011, p. 157). As allies, members of dominant or oppressor groups (e.g. white people, men, cisgender people, non-disabled people) are invested in critically inspecting their unearned privilege in relation to members of the marginalised or oppressed groups (e.g. people of colour, women, transgender people, people with disability) and working towards diminishing this privilege in order to create a more just and equitable society. To be a social justice ally is to engage in the practice of allyship, which can be understood as 'intentional, overt, consistent activity that challenges prevailing patterns of oppression, makes privileges that are so often invisible visible, and facilitates the empowerment of persons targeted by oppression' (Ayvazian, 2010, p. 625). Allyship requires that members of the dominant group approach examination of their power and privilege as not simply a one-time activity but as a continuous process of critical self-reflection, becoming aware of the toxic effects of oppression in the lives of marginalised communities, and unceasingly attending to the power dynamics between themselves and targets of oppression with whom they seek to build alliances. Since people occupy multiple social identities at once, it is possible for most people to be members of both dominant and oppressed groups (Gibson, 2014). For example, cisgender immigrant men of colour living in predominantly white societies are members of dominant groups because of their gender identity but are also members of oppressed groups based on their racialised identity and migrant status. Since privilege is located along multiple axes of power, it is important to develop an intersectionality-oriented understanding of privilege when looking at dominant or marginalised identities. Intersectionality refers to the idea that the different factors determining power such as race, class, sexual orientation, gender, age and so on operate not in mutual isolation but as 'reciprocally constructing phenomena that in turn shape complex social inequalities' (Collins, 2015, p. 2). Moreover, sometimes people may belong to what Adams and Zúñiga (2016) call 'border identities' (p. 109), that is, identities 'that border but do not fully fit' (p. 109) the binary of dominant and oppressed groups. Examples of border identities can be children of colour adopted and raised by white parents, or mixed-race people with one white parent; people with membership to such border identities experience unique and specific lived experiences of power and oppression (Adams and Zúñiga, 2016).

Historically the allyship model has its roots in anti-racist work (Gibson, 2014) and a substantial part of contemporary scholarship on allyship continues to focus on race and racism (e.g. Case, 2012; Reason et al., 2005; Spanierman and Smith, 2017). However, it has also now been applied to a wide range of social justice research and practice areas such as LGBTQ rights (e.g. Broido, 2000b; Duhigg et al., 2010; Pinto, 2014), violence against women (e.g. Casey, 2010; Fabiano et al., 2003), education (e.g. Boutte and Jackson, 2014; Edwards, 2006; Patton and Bondi, 2015), Islamophobia (e.g. Bhattacharyya et al., 2014), workplace discrimination (e.g. Sabat et al., 2013), and disability rights (e.g. Evans et al., 2005). There is no singular model of allyship in social justice and different authors have proposed different models (e.g. Bishop, 2002; Broido, 2000a; Edwards, 2006; Getz & Kirkley, 2003; Reason et al., 2005; Waters, 2010).

Men as allies

There is a significant and growing body of scholarship on the possibility and politics of men as allies in challenging MVDAW. The reason why men should be involved in efforts to prevent and address MVDAW is simple: it is primarily men who perpetrate it and benefit from it. Men allies' engagement with challenging MVDAW can take place at three levels: personal, interpersonal and systemic. At the personal level, the goal is to become aware of one's own acceptance of patriarchal norms and values, and confront one's own participation in sexist and misogynistic practices. At the interpersonal level, the goal is to identify and challenge patriarchal attitudes and practices of other men, and hold them accountable for their perpetration of MVDAW. At the systemic level, the objective is to expose and indict structural sexism, such as sexual objectification of girls and women, normalisation of violence against women, and gender unequal and inequitable policies and practices in institutions, workplaces, laws and cultural customs. Of course, men's participation as allies in ending

MVDAW is not an apolitical or straightforward enterprise. As Flood (2003) notes, 'men's collective and profeminist mobilizations on gender issues are a delicate form of political activity' (p. 458). Some feminist women are suspicious of men's involvement with feminism work and have problematised it (Bailey, 2015; Linder and Johnson, 2015; Williams, 1990). The concerns they have raised are important; some of the dangers of men's involvement in feminism include weakening of a feminist agenda, discounting women's work and leadership, and taking financial and other resources away from women who have experienced men's violence (Flood, 2011a). At the same time, some other feminist women support men's engagement and remain hopeful that men's participation can meaningfully contribute to feminist efforts to end MVDAW (hooks, 2000; Messner et al., 2015; Precopio and Ramsey, 2017).

An important idea at the core of men's engagement with feminist efforts to end MVDAW is that this work requires men's commitment to challenging their own gender privilege. The 'contradictory position' (Bailey, 2015, p. 443) of not just coming face-to-face with but also actively undercutting their own power and privilege is a slippery terrain, a 'situation that is replete with struggles and pitfalls' (p. 443). Although all men do not enjoy patriarchal privilege equally because their gender identity might possibly intersect with other marginalising identities in relation to race or ethnicity, religion, class, disability, sexual orientation and so on, all men inevitably benefit from the 'patriarchal dividend' (Connell, 1997, p. 64) based on unequal social structures vis-à-vis gender. 'Fighting patriarchy', therefore, for men, 'means fighting themselves' (Kahane, 1998, p. 213). Thus, when men participate in feminist efforts to end MVDAW, their motives and practices cannot be considered beyond suspicion. When men try to convince others through their 'confessional writing' (Williams, 1990, p. 64) – admittedly this chapter is partly an example of such writing – that they have 'laid down their arms' (p. 64), there are few reasons for feminists to accept them at face value.

There also are several arguments for encouraging men's engagement with feminist efforts to end MVDAW. As I have argued earlier, men have a role in addressing MVDAW because they are the primary offenders and beneficiaries of these oppressive practices and it is only fair to expect them to 'clean up their act'. This, however, is not the only reason why men could be interested in challenging MVDAW. Some men recognise that patriarchy costs men dearly in relation to their emotional, social and physical health (Pease, 2001; Scott-Samuel and Crawshaw, 2015; Sharma, 2015), and therefore participating in feminist struggles to undermine patriarchy can help them lead healthier and more fulfilling lives. Flood (2007) lists several arguments for involving men in fostering gender equality, including that men as gendered individuals participate in gender relations in society and are therefore *'unavoidably involved in gender issues'* (p. 9, italics in original), that many men's attitudes and behaviours need to change in order to achieve gender equality, that men can possibly be productive stakeholders in building gender equality through realising that inequality and injustice are not merely women's concerns, and that excluding men from gender justice work can hurt such efforts by antagonising men.

If men want to engage with women in feminist movements, how might they go about it? In the following sections, I will discuss what I consider some important aspects of men's allyship practices towards challenging MVDAW.

Relationship with feminism and feminist women

I mentioned earlier that this chapter is, in part, confessional writing. Here is a confession: I used to identify as feminist but I no longer lay claim to this identity. I learnt about feminism when studying social work and immediately found it profoundly meaningful at personal and professional levels. It helped me understand and articulate the injustices around me that I witnessed, experienced and perpetrated. It gave me a peg on which to hang my own experiences of facing gender-based bullying in adolescence, while simultaneously forcing me to come face-to-face with my own patriarchal privilege. It enriched my friendships with people of diverse genders, and allowed me life-changing opportunities to learn from and work with women in feminist settings on challenging MVDAW. In many ways, feminism anchored my lived gendered experiences of being a man, and my evolving professional awareness as a social worker. Feminism and I had found each other, and I believed that I was a feminist. So, what happened?

I found profeminism, eventually. But before that I attended a 'Take Back the Night' march in the USA. A small group of young white men led the march, followed by a much larger group primarily comprised of women. 'What do we want', the leading men chanted. 'Safe streets', women chanted back. 'When do we want them?', asked the men. 'Now', was the response. The alignment of men's and women's experiences through the use of 'we' was bewildering. If streets were unsafe for a group of young, non-disabled, college-educated, cisgender white men in the American Midwest, then for whom were they safe?

Through this experience and many others, I realised that unless men become reflexive and conscientious about their position within feminism, they will continue to dilute and hurt feminist efforts regardless of their intentions. Men's ways of dominance and appropriation are, in Audre

Lorde's (1983) words, the 'master's tools' (p. 94) that cannot be used to dismantle patriarchy (or, as Lorde might say, the master cannot be trusted to use his tools to dismantle his own house). Therefore, men allies need to figure out their relationship with feminism.

Feminism is not about men, particularly cisgender men. Cisgender men do not, and cannot, fully comprehend the burden of patriarchy simply because of their patriarchal privilege and on account of the fact that they do not have to deal with the challenges of MVDAW. When people occupy positions of privilege, their disproportionate social power diminishes their ability to notice and understand the damaging effects of oppression for marginalised groups. Just like white people living in white supremacist societies cannot fully understand the brutality of racism for people of colour, cisgender men in a patriarchal society cannot fully understand women's experiences of sexism and violence. I now believe that my previous understanding of myself as feminist was a naïve, uncritical position. When cisgender men seldom experience the full extent of patriarchy's wrath and while they remain agents of patriarchal oppression, it is not productive for them to lay claim to the feminist identity.

This does not mean that feminism has nothing to offer for men. On the contrary, it carries immense promise and potentialities for men. It allows men to imagine and work towards an equal and just world for everyone, including themselves, beyond the narrow and rigid boundaries of social constructs vis-à-vis gender. It lets men see and confront the toxicity of patriarchy in their own lives; for example, it helps them see how hegemonic masculinity marginalises other kinds of masculinities (Connell, 2005) and puts restrictions on fundamental things in their lives such as how they express their emotions, how they relate to women and how they should behave sexually. Feminism helps men become aware of the damage patriarchy causes in the lives of women and people of other genders, many of whom they may care for, and how their sexism, microaggressions and violence hurt these peoples. It offers men perspectives on developing nurturing, intimate and violence-free relationships with their children, romantic and sexual partners, parents, and friends, in contrast with relationships modelled after patriarchal values and practices. It gives men language to label and articulate their own challenges and struggles rooted in personal and societal expectations about being a man in a patriarchal society. Therefore men can, in fact they must, have a stake in feminist futures and possibilities (Brod, 1998).

How, then, do men stay invested in feminism without claiming to be feminists? Profeminism offers a constructive space for men allies to engage with feminism. Brod (1998) defines profeminism as the 'developing feminist politics of, by, and for men' (p. 208). He draws an important distinction between 'profeminism' and 'pro-feminism' through arguing that the latter concept refers to men supporting feminism from the outside 'without a *position from which* to be either radical or activist' (p. 207, italics in original). Describing profeminism, Brod (1998) argues:

> Profeminism of course includes pro-feminism as its primary principle, but it also includes much more. It is a call from and to men to develop feminist and pro-feminist personal and political principles and actions. It insists that men must recognize their own stake in the transformations advanced by feminism, *not* because men should put their needs ahead of others, but because this recognition is part and parcel of being able to fully commit oneself to the liberation of others. Thus, along with its pro-feminism, profeminism articulates men's contributions to and benefits from feminism. (p. 208, italics in original)

The profeminist identity offers men allies a standpoint from which to understand their own subjective location in relation to feminism, as well as develop a critical and nuanced relationship with feminism. Identifying as profeminist can serve men allies as a personal reminder of two things: one, that their own emancipation as gendered individuals is invariably linked to a feminist agenda, and two, that their role and place within feminism is not of co-opting and appropriating women's work but to invest in it following women's leadership.

Relationship between members of dominant and oppressed groups is of crucial importance in the context of allyship. Men allies need to cultivate respectful and productive alliances with feminist women. Here is another confessional story. Several years ago, I came across a feminist blog on the internet that I enjoyed and appreciated. At the time, I used to sporadically write for a blog on feminist issues in India. I discovered this new blog and wanted to explore the possibility of contributing to it. I emailed blog admins with some ideas. I received a polite but firm response saying that the blog was a women-only platform and they were not interested in men's contributions. I had no choice except to begrudgingly accept their decision, but I had a bit of sulk about it. I was 'one of the good guys', I thought, and resented that I had not been allowed to contribute when all I wanted to do was 'make a difference'. This is what unproductive and negative ally behaviour looks like. I did not accept that women-exclusive spaces are not only important but also necessary, expected the women running the blog to just agree with me instead of accepting their leadership, and failed to notice the stark contrast between my one small lack of opportunity to contribute to this blog and the overwhelming lack of opportunity women frequently face in every sphere of their social and professional lives. I also assumed that I could enter this space just because I wanted to be there, which reflects how routinely and unreflexively men colonise women's spaces. I am thankful I was eventually able to view this experience as an educational moment, but I utterly failed to do so at the time it happened.

Bishop (2002) recommends a list of meaningful ally behaviours. Men allies can benefit from these ideas when building and maintaining alliances with women to challenge MVDAW. These include but are not limited to listening and reflecting, being honest and authentic, educating yourself on oppression, speaking up against examples of oppression at work, not assuming the role of leading members of the marginalised group, refusing to act as a spokesperson for the oppressed group, not putting the responsibility of educating yourself on oppressed group members, and not expecting oppressed group members to provide emotional support to dominant group members.

At the core of men's ally behaviours has to be the idea of accountability to women (Pease, 2017). A woman participant in Macomber's (2018) study on male privilege in domestic violence work described accountability in this way: 'Accountability was about men realizing that being involved was not enough. It's *how* they got involved that really mattered. Are you following women's leadership and expertise? Are you responsive to women's criticisms to your work?' (p. 16, italics in original). Profeminist men can use this advice to guide their allyship practices.

Relationship with self

Relationship with oneself is crucial for an ally. Focusing on personal values, experiences and practices is integral to critical reflexivity in allyship. I will discuss two areas where men allies can face significant challenges with regard to exploring their relationship to self as allies challenging MVDAW: guilt, and positivity towards self.

Guilt

Experiencing guilt is often a significant step on the journey to becoming an ally. As dominant group members begin to learn about oppression and its impact on the oppressed group, they begin to realise that contrary to popular belief that the 'problem' lies with the members of the oppressed group (e.g. 'people living in poverty are poor because they are lazy', 'immigrants are a burden on the economy'), it relates to the oppression perpetuated by members of the dominant group instead (Broido, 2000b). They start to examine their own role in perpetuating oppression and notice how they have been personally complicit. This upheaval in the way they understand the world can often result in feelings of guilt and shame (Broido, 2000b).

I experienced guilt when working with women experiencing domestic violence in India. Many of these women had experienced months or years of physical, emotional or sexual violence perpetrated by their husbands. When I heard their stories and saw their injuries, I often felt embarrassed and guilty about being a man myself. Sometimes the intervention included working with men perpetrators whose wives had approached the agency for help. When they came in through the office door, I could observe some of them relax when they noticed that the social worker was a man. Occasionally these men would give me a look as if to say, 'You should understand my perspective because you too are a man.' Being considered 'on the same team' by my clients' violent partners, even if I only ever felt it in my gut, sickened me and sent my guilt soaring; I felt ashamed and anxious. Through supervision and mentorship of some feminist women, and critical reflexivity, I came to the understanding that my ideas and actions around my privilege guilt were not helpful. My clients did not need me to wallow in my own guilt and self-pity; they needed me to be the social worker who would help them challenge the violence they had been experiencing. When men perpetrators insinuated that I was one of them, my clients did not need me to ride my guilt horse into the sunset; they needed me to stand by them and send a clear message to the men who hurt them that violence and sexism were not okay. In other words, they needed me to be their ally, and I could not be one while I focused my energy on my guilt.

Being vulnerable is integral to being an ally. It is crucial for men allies to confront their unearned privilege and power. It is not only natural but also important to feel stung by the unfairness of the situation. Feeling contrition about one's sexist or violent attitudes and behaviours is important too. As allies, we must be reflexive, and critically so. We must also commit to personal change to align ourselves with feminist values. However, this should not result in descending into guilt if we wish to stay productive and contribute meaningfully.

Guilt, Kaufman (1994) suggests, 'is a profoundly conservative, demobilizing, and disempowering emotion' (p. 158). Men as members of the oppressor group may react to their privilege guilt in a wide range of ways. They may feel that they should not be feeling guilt for the actions of other men who perpetrate violence; they may feel overwhelmed or debilitated by emotions of guilt and may feel that the problem of patriarchy is too big for them to do anything about; they may avoid discussing or reflecting on patriarchy in others' and their own lives; they may feel cornered and defensive, and consequently refuse to be self-critical;

or they may focus their energy on themselves and their emotions of guilt and shame as opposed to utilising this energy to support the rights of women and focusing on women's issues. None of these responses to guilt is healthy or helpful.

It would be unwise to be entirely dismissive of guilt because it is often a part of the process of becoming an ally. Most allies will experience some guilt on their allyship journeys. The challenge is to channel that energy towards accountability. While men allies need not feel personal guilt over the violent actions of other men, they must feel personal accountability towards challenging MVDAW. While violence can be pinned to the specific men who perpetrate it, the benefits of patriarchy as a system accrue to all men, whether or not they display violent behaviours themselves. MVDAW is an essential component of patriarchy. Men collectively receive a 'patriarchal dividend' (Connell, 1997, p. 64) just for being men. All men share – unequally, but nonetheless share – among themselves the plunders of patriarchy. From this vantage point, it becomes easy to see how some men's violent actions benefit *all* men. While men allies need not feel guilty or remorseful for certain men's specific actions, the moral imperative for them is to accept personal accountability for benefiting from MVDAW, and the only way they can address it is by rejecting and diminishing their patriarchal privilege.

Positivity towards self

An important attribute of an ally is to '[feel] good about own social group membership and [be] comfortable and proud of own identity' (Wijeyesinghe et al., 1997, as cited in Gibson, 2014, p. 202). It is therefore important for men allies to maintain a positive and affirming stance towards themselves as men. This may sound somewhat contradictory to the idea of allyship because men in patriarchal societies are not typically known for their low opinion of themselves. If anything, the patriarchal entitlement that men enjoy and often enact is part of the problem. How does the idea of allyship, then, align with a self-positive and self-affirming position? Brod (1998) argues that male-positivity is necessary for profeminist politics to keep it sustainable. He further argues that the idea that profeminist men should not see themselves as male-positive is based on the popular but incorrect notion that feminism is anti-male. When profeminist men allies take on male-positive stances with regard to themselves, they disrupt the normative ideas regarding masculinity. Therefore men allies can adopt male-affirmative approaches – critical approaches that reject the idea that men are innately or inevitably violent, and perceive men as 'beings who must be challenged to change and whose change must be facilitated' (Brod, 1998, p. 201). From this standpoint, Brod (1998) argues, profeminism 'is not only compatible with, but requires, the firmest male affirmative stance' (p. 205).

A note of caution is warranted here. It is important to differentiate between self-positive attitude and self-congratulatory behaviour. Men's anti-sexist and anti-violence behaviours tend to garner a disproportionate amount of praise, including and especially from women, which is yet another sign of their patriarchal privilege (Flood, 2014; Linder and Johnson, 2015; Macomber, 2018). Men allies need to recognise that the bar for men is too low and the rewards are disproportionately high. They may receive praise for saying something that feminist women have been saying for years or decades, and may be extolled for simply showing up. There are many examples where men's attempts to support women are hypervalued. Such disproportionate rewards for being a 'good man' can shore up patriarchal social structures instead of undermining or dismantling them. It is therefore contingent on men allies to redirect that attention back to feminist leaders and feminist issues. Bishop (2002) points out that, as an ally, it is important to 'never take public attention or credit for an oppressed group's process of liberation' (p. 117). Self-aggrandising behaviours are tantamount to this flaw in men's allyship practices.

Relationship with other (profeminist) men

Profeminist men allies' relationships to men in general, and other profeminist men in particular, are significant in several ways. Bishop (2002) asks allies to recognise that the members of the dominant group are often more willing to listen to other members of their own group as opposed to members of the oppressed group. Men allies can use their patriarchal privilege to amplify women's voices so that other men can hear them loud and clear, and in this way help 'break through others' ignorance of the oppression' (Bishop, 2002, p. 118). Profeminist men can take on leadership roles when working with other men on challenging MVDAW. While taking on leadership roles with women is emblematic of men's domineering and appropriating tendencies, their leadership with other men is acutely needed. Men allies can expose and indict patriarchy in the lives of other men, and help them see how patriarchy causes damage in men's experiences and relationships too.

Men allies also need to prepare to challenge MVDAW when they see it. This is not always easy, but is important nevertheless. Flood (2011b) makes some useful recommendations that men can use to intervene as bystanders in situations where they see other men being violent towards women, such as calling the police, being a witness, intervening verbally, creating a distraction, expressing rejection of their behaviour and so on. Men allies can also resist other men's microaggressions against women, such as sexist jokes. Men can do this by not making sexist jokes themselves, and by letting others know that they don't appreciate sexist humour.

Men allies' alliances with other men allies are fundamental to profeminist politics because these can potentially be critical, constructive and creative spaces of educating each other about oppression and anti-oppressive ideas and practices, and unlearning oppressive attitudes and behaviours. Men allies can provide emotional support to one another as they understand oppression and its ravages in the world around them, examine the impact of patriarchy in their own lives, and come to terms with emotions such as shame and guilt. They can also allow for warm, intimate and rewarding friendships to organically grow among men. Crucially, men allies can hold other men allies accountable to a feminist agenda. Flood (2014) suggests that 'it should not surprise us that some men involved in the counter-hegemonic project of ending men's violence against women also are complicit in patriarchal masculinities' (p. 47). One can readily find several examples of such men allies in academic institutions or non-government organisations (NGOs). Linder and Johnson (2015) share the example of a university-based program for men to engage as allies to end violence against women where men participating in the program sexually assaulted two woman students. An ex-colleague of mine who worked on sexual violence and frequently waxed lyrical about reforming patriarchal masculinities also nonchalantly discussed his practice of buying and exchanging pornographic videos – of the kind that clearly objectified women – among his friends; they would compete over who could bring videos featuring largest breasts. These are not necessarily examples of 'men allies gone bad' but instead an illustration of the fact that profeminist men are not immune to patriarchal privilege and practices (Flood, 2014).

Besides engaging in blatant sexism and violence, men allies can also move away from effective allyship practices. Holding each other accountable to principles of feminism and to high standards of allyship and calling each other out when allies co-opt or dominate women's struggles instead of following their leadership emerge as important roles for men allies.

Politicising MVDAW and resisting depoliticisation

Politicised approaches are essential to anti-oppressive social work practice (Baines, 2011). Sometimes anti-MVDAW campaigns adopt a conciliatory tone towards men to become more acceptable to them. Such mainstreaming of these campaigns marks a shift away from social movement politics of explicitly considering feminist analyses of MVDAW as key to fostering change (Pease, 2017). Depoliticised approaches to challenging MVDAW can look like campaigns that appeal to men through stereotypical notions about masculinity, for example campaigns which propose that men who sexually assault women fall short as 'real men'. These may also look like tokenistic campaigns such as 'Walk a Mile in Her Shoes' in which men march for a mile while wearing feminine-identified high-heeled shoes in order to bring attention to violence against women (Bridges, 2010); these campaigns engage with MVDAW only superficially and may even symbolically reproduce gender inequality (Bridges, 2010). Focusing solely on men's behaviour without attending to the structural factors that create and maintain gender inequities depoliticises anti-violence efforts. For example, batterer intervention programs that approach social work practice with men perpetrators of violence from a largely clinical perspective and focus on behavioural approaches such as anger management will remain limited in their effectiveness on account of their constrained or depoliticised view of the problem. Therefore, profeminist men allies can politicise MVDAW and resist its depoliticisation wherever possible. Politicising MVDAW requires men allies to ensure that a 'feminist analysis remains as the central underpinning of violence prevention' (Pease, 2008, p. 13).

Conclusion

The allyship model of social justice offers a meaningful approach for social workers to address oppression through building respectful and conscientious alliances between members of different dominant and oppressed groups. In this chapter I have illustrated some aspects of allyship through the example of men profeminist allies' engagement with challenging MVDAW. By critically understanding and strengthening their relationships with women and feminism, and with themselves and other men from a profeminist standpoint, men allies can contribute to challenging patriarchy and ending MVDAW.

Allyship is messy and demands vulnerability. It can be productive and rewarding, creating opportunities for personal growth, interpersonal support and structural change towards equality. All allies are works-in-progress regardless of their years or level of engagement with anti-oppressive work. Social workers need not wait until they have 'figured it all out' before beginning their allyship journeys. A place of curiosity to learn about oppression (and unlearn oppressive attitudes and behaviours), openness to making mistakes and willingness to apologise and make amends to oppressed groups, and accountability to oppressed group members and following their leadership is a good place to begin.

Further readings

Bishop, A. (2002). *Becoming an Ally: Breaking the Cycle of Oppression*. Crows Nest: Allen & Unwin.
Messner, M.A., Greenberg, M.A. and Peretz, T. (2015). *Some Men: Feminist Allies and the Movement to End Violence against Women*. New York: Oxford University Press.
Pease, B. (2014). Reconstructing masculinity or ending manhood?: The potential and limitations of transforming masculine subjectivities for gender equality. In À. Carabí and J.M. Armengol (Eds.), *Alternative Masculinities for a Changing World* (pp. 17–34). New York: Palgrave Macmillan.

References

Adams, M. and Zúñiga, X. (2016). Getting started: Core concepts for social justice education. In M. Adams, L.A. Bell, D.J. Goodman and K. Joshi (Eds.), *Teaching for Diversity and Social Justice*, 3rd Edition (pp. 95–130). New York: Routledge.
Ayvazian, A. (2010). Interrupting the cycle of oppression: The role of allies as agents of change. In M. Adams, W.J. Blumenfeld, C. Castañeda, H.W. Hackman, M.L. Peters and X. Zúñiga (Eds.), *Readings for Diversity and Social Justice*, 2nd Edition (pp. 625–628). New York: Routledge.
Bailey, J. (2015). Contemporary British feminism: Opening the door to men?. *Social Movement Studies*, 14(4), 443–458.
Baines, D. (2011). Bridging the practice-activism divide in mainstream social work: Advocacy, organizing, and social movements. In D. Baines (Ed.), *Doing Anti-Oppressive Practice: Social Justice Social Work*, 2nd Edition (pp. 79–94). Black Point, NS: Fernwood Publishing.
Bhattacharyya, S., Ashby, K.M. and Goodman, L.A. (2014). Social justice beyond the classroom: Responding to the marathon bombing's Islamophobic aftermath. *The Counseling Psychologist*, 42(8), 1136–1158.
Bishop, A. (2002). *Becoming an Ally: Breaking the Cycle of Oppression*. Crows Nest: Allen & Unwin.
Boutte, G.S. and Jackson, T.O. (2014). Advice to white allies: Insights from faculty of color. *Race Ethnicity and Education*, 17(5), 623–642.
Bridges, T.S. (2010). Men just weren't made to do this: Performances of drag at 'Walk a mile in her shoes' marches. *Gender & Society*, 24(1), 5–30.
Brod, H. (1998). To be a man, or not be a man – That is the feminist question. In T. Digby (Ed.), *Men Doing Feminism* (pp. 197–212). New York: Routledge.
Broido, E.M. (2000a). The development of social justice allies during college: A phenomenological investigation. *Journal of College Student Development*, 41(1), 3–18.

Broido, E.M. (2000b). Ways of being an ally to lesbian, gay, and bisexual students. In V.A. Wall and N.J. Evans (Eds.), *Toward Acceptance: Sexual Orientation Issues on Campus* (pp. 345–369). Lanham, MD: University Press of America.

Case, K.A. (2012). Discovering the privilege of whiteness: White women's reflections on anti-racist identity and ally behaviour. *Journal of Social Issues*, 68(1), 78–96.

Casey, E. (2010). Strategies for engaging men as anti-violence allies: Implications for ally movements. *Advances in Social Work*, 11(2), 267–282.

Collins, P.H. (2015). Intersectionality's definitional dilemmas. *Annual Review of Sociology*, 41, 1–20.

Connell, R.W. (1997). Gender politics for men. *International Journal of Sociology and Social Policy*, 17(1/2), 62–77.

Connell, R.W. (2005). *Masculinities*, 2nd Edition. Berkeley: University of California Press.

Duhigg, J.M., Rostosky, S.S., Gray, B.E. and Wimsatt, M.K. (2010). Development of heterosexuals into sexual-minority allies: A qualitative exploration. *Sexuality Research and Social Policy*, 7(1), 2–14.

Edwards, K.E. (2006). Aspiring social justice ally identity development: A conceptual model. *NASPA Journal*, 43(4), 39–60.

Evans, N.J., Assadi, J.L. and Herriott, T.K. (2005). Encouraging the development of disability allies. *New Directions for Student Services*, 110, 67–79.

Fabiano, P.M., Perkins, H.W., Berkowitz, A., Linkenbach, J. and Stark, C. (2003). Engaging men as social justice allies in ending violence against women: Evidence for a social norms approach. *Journal of American College Health*, 52(3), 105–112.

Flood, M. (2003). Men's collective struggles for gender justice: The case of anti-violence activism. In M. Kimmel, J. Hearn and R.W. Connell (Eds.), *The Handbook of Studies on Men and Masculinities* (pp. 458–466). Thousand Oaks, CA: Sage Publishing.

Flood, M. (2007). Involving men in gender policy and practice. *Critical Half*, 5(1), 9–13.

Flood, M. (2011a). Involving men in efforts to end violence against women. *Men and Masculinities*, 14(3), 358–377.

Flood, M. (2011b). *Men Speak Up: A Toolkit for Action in Men's Daily Lives (Research Series No. 4)*. Sydney: White Ribbon Australia.

Flood, M. (2014). Men's antiviolence activism and the construction of gender-equitable masculinities. In À. Carabí and J.M. Armengol (Eds.), *Alternative Masculinities for a Changing World* (pp. 35–50). New York: Palgrave Macmillan.

Getz, C. and Kirkley, E.A. (2003). Identity development models: One size fits all? Heterosexual identity development and the search for 'allies' in higher education. Paper presented at the 84th Annual Meeting of the American Educational Research Association, Chicago, IL, 2–5 April.

Gibson, P.A. (2014). Extending the ally model of social justice to social work pedagogy. *Journal of Teaching in Social Work*, 34, 199–214.

Goodman, D.J. (2011). *Promoting Diversity and Social Justice: Educating People from Privileged Groups*, 2nd Edition. New York: Routledge.

hooks, b. (2000). *Feminist Theory: From Margin to Center*, 2nd Edition. Cambridge, MA: South End Press.

International Federation of Social Workers. (2014). *Global Definition of Social Work*. http://ifsw.org/get-involved/global-definition-of-social-work/

Kahane, D.J. (1998). Male feminism as oxymoron. In T. Digby (Ed.), *Men Doing Feminism* (pp. 213–235). New York: Routledge.

Kaufman, M. (1994). Men, feminism, and men's contradictory experiences of power. In H. Brod and M. Kaufman (Eds.), *Theorizing Masculinities* (pp. 142–163). Thousand Oaks, CA: Sage Publishing.

Linder, C. and Johnson, R.C. (2015). Exploring the complexities of men as allies in feminist movements. *Journal of Critical Thought and Praxis*, 4(1). http://lib.dr.iastate.edu/jctp/vol4/iss1/.

Lorde, A. (1983). The master's tools will never dismantle the master's house. In C. Moraga and G. Anzaldúa (Eds.), *This Bridge Called My Back: Writings by Radical Women of Color* (pp. 94–101). New York: Kitchen Table Press.

Macomber, K. (2018). 'I'm sure as hell not putting any man on a pedestal': Male privilege and accountability in domestic and sexual violence work. *Journal of Interpersonal Violence*, 33(9), 1491–1518, https://doi.org/10.1177/0886260515618944.

Messner, M.A., Greenberg, M.A. and Peretz, T. (2015). *Some Men: Feminist Allies and the Movement to End Violence against Women*. New York: Oxford University Press.

Patton, L.D. and Bondi, S. (2015). Nice white men or social justice allies?: Using critical race theory to examine how white male faculty and administrators engage in ally work. *Race Ethnicity and Education*, 18(4), 488–514.

Pease, B. (2001). Developing profeminist practice with men in social work. *Critical Social Work*, 2(1). http://www1.uwindsor.ca/criticalsocialwork/developing-profeminist-practice-with-men-in-social-work

Pease, B. (2008). Engaging men in men's violence prevention: Exploring the tensions, dilemmas, and possibilities. Issues Paper No. 17. Sydney: Australian Domestic & Family Violence Clearinghouse.

Pease, B. (2017). *Men as Allies in Preventing Violence against Women: Principles and Practices for Promoting Accountability*. Sydney: White Ribbon Australia.

Pinto, S.A. (2014). ASEXUally: On being an ally to the asexual community. *Journal of LGBT Issues in Counseling*, 8(4), 331–343.

Precopio, R.F. and Ramsey, L.R. (2017). Dude looks like a feminist!: Moral concerns and feminism among men. *Psychology of Men & Masculinity*, 18(1), 78–86.

Reason, R.D., Roosa Miller, E.A. and Scales, T.C. (2005). Toward a model of racial justice ally development. *Journal of College Student Development*, 46(5), 530–546.

Sabat, I.E., Martinez, L.R. and Wessel, J.L. (2013). Neo-activism: Engaging allies in modern workplace discrimination reduction. *Industrial and Organizational Psychology*, 6(4), 480–485.

Scott-Samuel, A. and Crawshaw, P. (2015). 'Men behaving badly': Patriarchy, public policy and health inequalities. *International Journal of Men's Health*, 14(3), 250–258.

Sharma, A. (2015). Hegemonic masculinity as a conceptual lens to understand the experiences of men and boys who are survivors of child sexual abuse. In C. Hällgren, E. Dunkels and G. Frånberg (Eds.), *Invisible Boy: The Making of Contemporary Masculinities* (pp. 125–136). Umeå: Umeå University.

Spanierman, L.B. and Smith, L. (2017). Roles and responsibilities of white allies: Implications for research, teaching, and practice. *The Counseling Psychologist*, 45(5), 606–607.

Waters, R. (2010). Understanding allyhood as a developmental process. *About Campus*, 15(5), 2–8.

Williams, L. (1990). Men in feminism. *Women: A Cultural Review*, 1(1), 63–65.

9
Women and Older Age: Exploring the Intersections of Privilege and Oppression Across Lifetimes

Tina Kostecki and Selma Macfarlane

We acknowledge that our chapter was written on the lands of the Gadigal people of the Eora nation, and the Wathaurong people of the Kulin nation, who are the Traditional Owners and continuing Custodians of their lands, winds and waters. We acknowledge that we are on this land as beneficiaries of an uncompensated and unreconciled dispossession, which continues today. We also pay respect to their Elders past, present and emerging. Given the themes of social justice in this collection, and our personal commitments, we believe such an acknowledgement to be a fitting preface.

Introduction

In neoliberal social and policy contexts there are many areas of concern for critical social workers and others promoting social justice. Our focus on the intersections of privilege and oppression across women's lifetimes arises from growing evidence of disturbing inequalities based on class, gender, race and other structural factors that accumulate for women in older age (see, for example, Asquith, 2009; Carr et al., 2015; Hooyman et al., 2002; Lui et al., 2011). Inequalities and disadvantage encompass a range of factors which, over a lifetime, can alter significantly to shape life experiences such as in the areas of income, economic (in)security, caring responsibilities, access to health care, as well as the impacts of racism, sexism and heterosexism. In neoliberal societies such as Australia alongside the social impacts of ageism for both women and men (Hastings and Rogowski, 2015; Maidment and Macfarlane, 2011), older women are increasingly experiencing concerning levels of poverty, housing insecurity and marginalisation as indicated by recent research (see Australian Human Rights Commission, 2009; Hetherington and Smith, 2017; Committee for Economic Development of Australia, 2015; and the Australian Council of Social Service, 2015 submission to the Australian government's Retirement Incomes Inquiry).

We take the view that while comparable social forces and structures configure individual life experiences for older women, and while many women may share commonalities in relation to ageing and older age, there is also significant diversity in women's experiences, not only in older age but across the lifespan. Consequently we are interested in how adopting an intersectional lens might highlight diverse experiences amongst women that shift and merge over a lifetime to produce complex amalgams of economic advantage/disadvantage, social and cultural inclusion/exclusion and agency or disempowerment (Hankivsky, 2014). We argue that this is particularly important considering neoliberal contexts that have dominated Western societies such as Australia, with discourses of self-responsibilisation and market-driven meritocracies.

Social work, as a social justice and rights-based profession, has an important role to play in developing research that enables us to hear and explore the narratives of older women's lived experience in relation to the diverse structural and contextual factors that have characterised their lives, which might inform the development of enhanced and meaningful responses to redress growing inequality for older women. In tandem with research approaches that privilege the perspectives of those most affected by unjust practices, we contend that understandings which include the nuanced and particular circumstances of older women are crucial in addressing inequitable policy or service responses. Our aim is to join with the voices of those advocating for social justice, social change, recognition of diversity and the end to inequalities, by providing an opportunity for older women to consider and speak about the ways in which their lives have been shaped by interlocking contexts of privilege and oppression.

Theoretical orientations for intersectional research

Our theoretical orientation includes critical theory (including critical gerontology) and postmodern feminism which, in combination, draw attention to nuances of power, diversity and inequality. Critical theory is founded on three core assumptions. First, that Western democracies are highly unequal; second, this political context is maintained through the self-regulating systems of dominant ideology; and third, attempts to understand this state of affairs are necessary in order to make changes and advance equality (Brookfield, 2005, p. viii). Critical theory with respect to age provides possibilities for politicising and foregrounding ageism (Twigg and Martin, 2015), bringing attention to the connections between personal experiences of later life and social or structural inequalities (Biggs, 2008, p. 115).

Additionally, critical gerontology provides a focus on exploring the limitations of individualising biomedical models, towards more comprehensive understandings of identity and experience that include consideration of gender, sexual identity, race, class, geographical location and health status (see Figure 9.1 for further examples). Anderson (2011, p. 49) defines critical gerontology as a 'paradigm shift away from the dominant understanding of age, as represented in the positivism of the biomedical model, to the alternative view, a critical stance which exposes the underlying power structures and socially constructed "age conceptualizations" on both micro and macro levels'.

Feminist perspectives make another specific contribution to developing critical perspectives on women and ageing, by prioritising a gender lens to highlight the nature of inequality in later life for women. Key insights to the development of feminist thought and the nature of later life for women is the work of Black feminist scholars and activists who demonstrate how intersections of race, class and gender shape women's lives. For instance, Patricia Hill Collins refers to axes of oppression that together characterise the lives of Black women within a 'more generalized matrix of oppression' (Collins, 1990, p. 224).

Postmodern feminism further contributes to the construction of our framework by acknowledging diversity and fluidity within the category of 'women' and the lives of individuals. Moreover, feminist intersectional scholarship conceptualises social inequalities as power relationships constructed in specific historical and geographical contexts, creating 'fluid, shifting group relations that ... persist through time and space' (Weber, 2006, p. 24), which are shaped differently in different contexts and communities. This approach extends our thinking beyond fixed structural categories to consider the complexity of human identity, accepting and working with 'both the points of cohesion and fracture within groups' (Zambrana and Dill, 2006, p. 194).

Problematising women's later life experiences

Walker (2006) argues that it is false to think of agency and identity on the one hand and structural determination on the other as mutually exclusive; there are constant tensions over the life course between structure and agency in everyday life. This 'both–and' positioning (Sands and

Nuccio, 1992) enables, for example, group consciousness-raising in terms of a sense of collective identity, but also possibilities for exploring notions of agency and self-subjugation experienced by diverse individuals in specific contexts (Wood and Tully, 2006, p. 18). So, for example, normative discourses, popular within neoliberal regimes, on 'active' or 'successful ageing', may be empowering for some older women, but oppressive for others for whom ill health, lack of access to resources and/or poverty add complex layers of experience in growing old (Asquith, 2009; Biggs, 2001; Gattuso, 2003; Ranzijn, 2010).

According to Polivka and Longino (2006, p. 188), this discourse 'is expressly designed to divide the elderly into those who can fully provide for themselves and those who cannot and to dramatically reduce public support for the latter'. Thus economic hardship, poor health and/or inadequate access to resources in older age indicate that the individual has failed to look after themselves properly (Polivka and Longino, 2006). These ideas are socially powerful because they constitute 'radical acts of decision and institution, which involve the drawing of political frontiers via the creation of multiple lines of inclusion and exclusion' (Howarth, 2010, p. 309).

Neoliberal policy discourse and its practices also quite remarkably 'tend to omit gender, race, ethnicity and sexuality as categories of analysis, ignoring feminist analysis, and rendering women, race, class and gender invisible or insignificant' (Hawkesworth, 2010, p. 269). Dominant discourses and policies regarding 'successful ageing' largely ignore the notion of cumulative inequality, although superannuation policies are, ironically, intrinsically built on ideas of cumulative wealth and privilege. Cumulative inequality (or cumulative advantage/disadvantage) has been defined as 'the systematic tendency for interindividual divergence in a given characteristic (e.g., money, health, status) with the passage of time' (Dannefer as cited in Ferraro and Shippee, 2009, p. 333). For women in older age this has several implications. Throughout their lives, women in paid work have often occupied lower paid positions compared to men; this more likely for some groups of women, for example women with disabilities, non-English-speaking women, women from minority cultural or racial backgrounds (Zink et al., 2003).

The lower financial position and income of women throughout their lifespan is often compounded by caregiving responsibilities, which may mean significant portions of time out of the paid workforce altogether, or in part-time and casual jobs (AHRC, 2009; Calasanti, 2010). While accumulated financial strain has been clearly documented as negatively correlated with women's health in older age (see, for example, Shippee et al., 2012), the cumulative effect of other experiences, such as abuse and re-victimisation over many years, may be less widely acknowledged but equally significant given the pervasiveness of violence against women globally (Hightower et al., 2006). Older women are more likely than older men to experience poverty, widowhood or living alone (Chambers, 2004), make greater use of health and social services, experience institutionalisation in later old age (Sharma, 2016) and live longer than men with chronic morbidity or disability (Kalache et al., 2005). The growth in homelessness among older women in Australia is also significant. Travia and Webb (2015, p. 52) describe older women as one of the fastest growing groups of people experiencing homelessness and housing insecurity 'in the aftermath of a lifetime of income inequality and taking "time out" for caring responsibility'. This vulnerability is exacerbated, they argue, if women encounter illness, divorce or unemployment in mid to older age. Accordingly, approximately 70% of those seeking housing support services in Sydney are women, which is hardly surprising given that, for example in some Sydney suburbs, weekly rent alone is 38% more than the existing aged pension (Osborne-Crowley, 2015).

While gerontologists 'obviously consider later life as a period of profound change and adaptation ... the seeds of many of these changes may have been planted decades earlier' (Ferraro and Shippee, 2009, p. 338). Inequalities in retirement income is a case in point, with the gender gap in retirement savings, accumulated across a lifespan, and retirement incomes posing a threat to women's economic security in older age (Australian Government Workplace Gender Equality Agency, 2015). The Australian Human Rights Commission report (2009) into women's experiences of inequality over the lifecycle provides a sobering review: retired men between the ages of 55 and 64 years have around 1.7 times the disposable weekly income of retired women of the same age (p. 8); women are less likely to have sufficient income to make voluntary contributions to their superannuation without significantly undermining their ability to meet current financial responsibilities (p. 12); the onset of caring responsibilities after the birth of children has a significant impact on lifetime earnings and level of paid workforce participation of women; and, in 2003, men who separated experienced an average drop in their household disposable income by $4,100 per year, while women who separated experienced a decrease of $21,400 (p. 21). Therefore the 'most serious consequence of the gender gap in retirement savings is the likelihood of poverty for women in retirement' (Australian Human Rights Commission, 2009, p. 22). Thus, we argue, it is crucial, in redressing these disparities to explore how lifetimes of privilege and oppression accumulate to shape the lives of older women.

An intersectional approach to research on women and ageing

Like many critical social workers and qualitative researchers, we believe that stories of the lived experience can contribute to a nuanced representation and understanding of older age, without essentialising experience. Alongside narrative therapy approaches, programs, research projects and one-to-one work, reminiscing and remembering practices have been constructed as empowering for older persons. Research based on this approach is not only informative in terms of the structural factors which construct life experience across the lifespan, but the process of talking about their lives can be empowering and affirming for participants. For example, in their study of older women in the community-based Concerned Older Women's (COW) group in inner-city Sydney, Rawsthorne and colleagues (2017) found that women coming together to share their stories found this process not only empowering but also enabling in terms of challenging ageism through social action. As influential black feminist Patricia Hill Collins observed several decades ago, narratives of lived experience politicise women's stories and position their stories 'as agents of knowledge' (Collins, 1990, p. 221). Collins (1990) observes that:

> Placing black women's experiences at the center of analysis offers fresh insights on the prevailing concepts, paradigms and epistemologies that characterise Eurocentric masculinist worldviews. The telling and sharing of women's stories, which are embedded in overlapping social and cultural contexts, then, is more than therapeutic or individually empowering, it is a mechanism by which both individual women's consciousness can change as well as contributing to political and institutional change. (p. 221)

We believe that combining an individually focused narrative approach with one that brings structural and contextual factors to bear on women's life stories is, politically, highly instructive and is a significant contribution to critical social justice research practice that recognises and politicises the diverse social, historical and economic contexts of women's lives. So via the exploration of 'guiding narratives', alongside an intersectional lens, the way that discourses such as 'active ageing' and neoliberal self-responsibilisation agendas become part of the personal identities and inner self-governing worlds of older women (see, for example, Biggs, 2001; Rudman, 2015) can be revealed and act in resistance to neoliberal discourse or policy. Intersectional research approaches augment the processes and nature of the ways in which some personal identities are legitimated, for example those which conform to dominant discourse expectations (Biggs, 2001).

Neoliberal discourse and the policies and practices it engenders not only shape material realities for individuals but invade people's hearts and minds, potentially holding subjects fast through the 'fantasies' they spin about the way things are, and securing consent by controlling thoughts and desires (Howarth, 2010, p. 310). Social workers are not immune from this; social work professional identities and practices can sustain dominant ideology through their own 'fantasies' that serve to conceal the political implications of social work practice, for example when empowerment serves as a cloak for self-responsibilisation (Vitus, 2017, p. 472).

Intersectional research can assist to identify internalised discourse, as in Rudman's (2015, p. 10) exploration of older women's embodiment of 'positive aging and neoliberal rationality' in retirement. Drawing on Foucauldian-informed governmentality scholarship, Rudman (2015) was interested in how older women talked about their physical selves. As a result of her findings, she describes how the older Canadian women in her research had internalised messages about working on their ageing bodies as a means of resisting or denying ageing, despite discrepancies and tensions between bodily changes and chronological age, and 'fight[ing] all signs of aging by remaining active, autonomous and in control' (Sandberg cited in Rudman, 2015, p. 12). The ageing bodies of the women in Rudman's analysis were perceived, by the women themselves, as '"at risk" and in need of continuous surveillance, self-care and self-enhancement' (2015, p. 18), producing anxiety associated with failure in the face of physical decline. She concludes that further research needs to examine the implications of positive ageing discourses, with their implicit demands for individual body management, that is 'differentially realizable and fails to create meaningful spaces for those who embody oldness' (Rudman, 2015, p. 20).

Messages regarding financial independence in older age also have impacts on older women's sense of themselves which lead to feelings of precariousness and disempowerment in terms of inadequate retirement incomes, with older women more likely to live in poverty than older men. This was felt quite profoundly by women in Craciun and Flick's (2016) study on gendered views of ageing. As Fanon (1978) observed, some decades ago, the oppressor without becomes the oppressor within and this is an important pillar of self-governance in a neoliberal agenda.

A research approach which explores and considers oppression and privilege as a dynamic and fluid expression of the complexity of our social and political experience is a befitting approach for feminist social justice research practice interested in understanding the nature of older women's lives holistically and inclusively. Hulko (2014) discusses the advantages of an intersectional approach to research with 'equity seeking groups' including 'that it makes visible the invisible, honours voice and subjectivity, links micro (subjective) experiences with macro (social structures) and embraces the complexity and messiness of life' (p. 73).

Adopting intersectionality in research provides a nuanced understanding of 'what is considered relevant to women as a group facing diversity within and significant political challenges without' (Hancock, 2007, p. 248), for example public health inequalities to inform policy which more accurately address health inequity (Bauer, 2014). Rather than a focus on 'master categories of difference' (Bauer, 2014), an intersectional approach allows multi-vocality and acknowledges causal complexities, which is vital for public policy such as in relation to welfare reform and women's experiences of the paid workforce (Hancock, 2007). This represents an acknowledgement of women's lives as existing at intersections of race, age, sexual orientation, relationship status and so on, and the connection between individuals and institutions (Hancock, 2007).

In another example, Ferrer and colleagues (2017) demonstrate the advantages in using an intersectional approach to research in order to understand the stories and experiences of older Filipino people living in Montreal and systems of racial domination, with particular emphasis on sites of resistance or agency. The usefulness of an intersectional approach (in this case, an intersectional life course perspective) 'presents an important analytical lens to focus on the heterogeneous experiences of aging, to offer a richer consideration of the complex biographies of communities, to consider a broader and more detailed analysis of the dynamics of power, and to account for the fluid nature of identity that is embedded within particular times, contexts and spaces/places' (Ferrer et al., 2017, p. 15).

Consideration of the historical context is also an important intersectional axis which affects individual women's experience, as some factors disadvantaging today's older women, such as lower levels of education, may change in the next decades. Herron and Rosenberg (2016), by exploring the nature of caregiving responsibilities for women, highlight the importance of diversity to understand the potential negative consequences so that 'Culture, gender, geography, life stage, and material resources affect both the opportunities of caregivers and the person for whom they cared during end-of-life care' (p. 204). The ongoing effects of historical and cultural contexts, such as that of colonisation for example, have profound impacts on all periods of the life course, culminating in older age. Writing in the Australian context, Ranzijn (2010) discusses a research project involving Australian Aboriginal Elders (presumably both male and female) in relation to conceptions of ageing. He concludes that genericised concepts of ageing serve to devalue the life experiences of diverse non-dominant cultural groups who have been excluded from a range of resources over a lifetime and whose worldviews may not 'fit' with dominant neoliberal individualised narratives of success. Writing specifically about their community-based research with Aboriginal women elders, Dune and colleagues (2017, p. 70) discuss how these strong and agentic Indigenous women 'consistently negotiate (cross-)cultural expectations as they aim to retain a strong sense of indigeneity and community while navigating an Anglo-dominated society'.

Given the multiplicity of structural factors shaping the lives of older women, and concern that these factors are inadequately understood and addressed, we turned our attention to how we might construct a research project that would recognise intersectionality in the lives of older women, and contribute to a body of research telling these stories and insisting they be heard.

Challenges in intersectional research practice

In constructing our own intersectional research project on oppression and privilege for women in later life, we planned to recruit a small number of older women (approximately 12 women, aged 60 and over) from advertisements placed in community organisations frequented by older women in inner-city Sydney and Geelong, Australia. We created a tool called an 'intersectionality wheel', to use as a visual prompt when inviting women to tell us their stories (see Figure 9.1) during individual interviews.

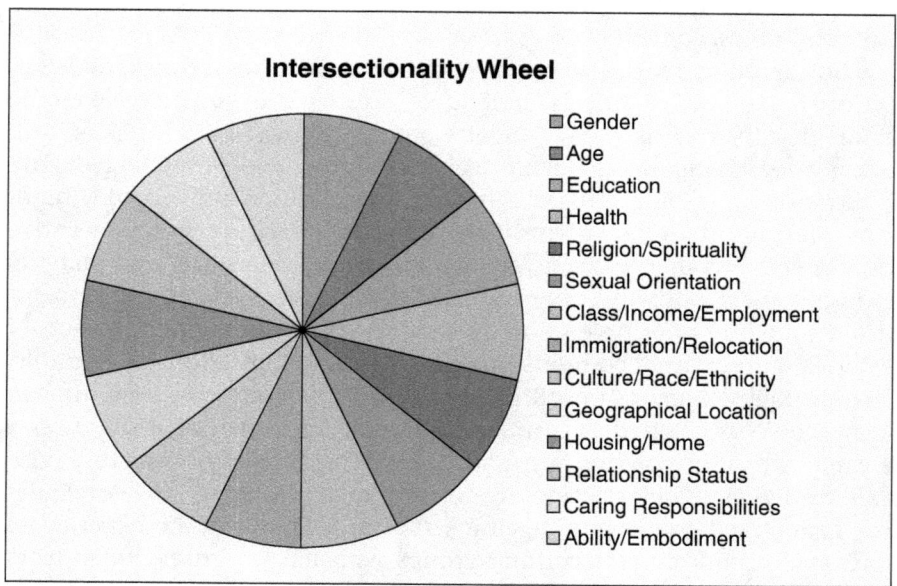

Figure 9.1 Intersectionality wheel

Each interview begins with an introduction to the 'wheel' and an explanation of how each section represents potentially important elements that have shaped the person's experience over their lifespan. At the start of the interview, we ask a general introductory question such as, *'In thinking about any of the areas represented on the wheel, are there any that stand out to you in terms of what has been important in your own life experience?'*

Our preparation for the research involved one of us conducting a test interview with a family member, after which we decided that responses to our guiding questions might arise organically in a conversation where we share our own significant social locations and how they have interacted to colour our own life experiences. This decision was based on a desire to practise as critical researchers and adhere to principles of feminist poststructural research practice and include critical reflexivity as part of the research process. It would also continue to be part of an ongoing process of critical reflection, as our interviews and responses from participants, as well as our own embodied experiences, further informed our project. By including, in various ways, the nature of our own privilege/ oppression as older women we sought to examine the extent to which our social location is necessarily embedded in the research (Strega, 2005, p. 229).

In conducting the interviews we sought to encourage exploration of the pertinent realms of life experience by using prompts like *'Can you tell me more about why you chose "x" (e.g. caring responsibilities) as a particularly important element in your life?'* Following identification of the initial area/s discussed by the participant, we asked whether other areas of the wheel might relate and intersect with those the interviewee had already identified. We anticipated using prompts such as *'I wonder if what you're saying about your experience of, for example, housing over the years has impacted on your experience of "y" (e.g. safety or vulnerability).'*

During the interview, if it seemed useful, we would potentially introduce the second wheel (see Figure 9.2), where an outer circle has been added to the intersectionality wheel, where the terms 'advantage/disadvantage', 'privilege/oppression', 'social policy', 'historical and social context' have been added.

The interviewee is invited to consider her experience in relation to these wider social contexts/concepts, using prompts such as *'You've told me about how your caring responsibilities have been a major factor in your life history even today as an older woman, so how might you see your caring responsibilities in light of the advantage or disadvantage they have created in your life?'* Or, *'We've talked about how gender has shaped your expectations for what you might achieve across your life history, how much do you think this was shaped by social messages such as social policies or the media, or other representation of what is considered "normal"?'* The interviews would be taped and

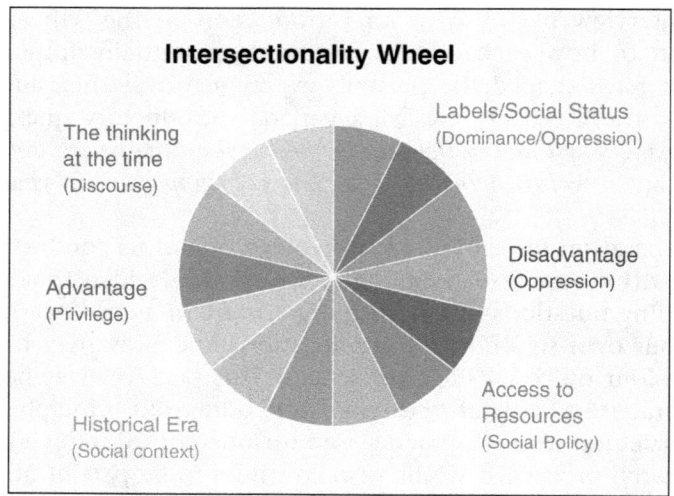

Figure 9.2 Second intersectionality wheel

transcribed by the researchers and a copy of the transcript sent to those participants who wish to review and/or amend it.

In the process of constructing and conducting our research, several questions and issues have become apparent, some of which resonate strikingly with the intersectionality research literature. Although, as we have suggested, intersectionality can potentially 'answer new questions as yet unanswered ... and generate strategies for policy change that incorporate all of us as political beings, not simply a subset of the population' (Hancock, 2007, p. 49), lack of conceptual clarity and specificity about its use can generate practical research design issues (Hulko, 2014).

One of these, as Hulko (2014) has identified, is how to sample for diversity. For example, as we considered our recruitment strategies, it became clear that, depending on where we advertised for participants, we might be more or less likely to speak with women with higher educational backgrounds or dominant racial identities. Given that we were only able to work with a small number of participants, targeting our recruitment for diversity raised some challenges. There is the potential risk of essentialising experience based on small numbers and, as well, issues regarding the nature and meaning of diversity. Warner (2008) identifies intersectionality research design issues as including constraints in the number of identities researchers are able to explore, questions about how researchers determine which identities to focus on, and questions of how much to include and focus on dominant privileged groups and identities.

The latter is a particularly interesting issue, as feminist intersectionality research is, arguably, aimed at addressing injustice and oppression. Hulko (2014) has provided some guidance here, suggesting that, in her research, rather than focusing on specific social locations, she attempted to select participants who lay at different points on axes of privilege and oppression ranging from multiply privileged to multiply oppressed, based on known information.

Another research design challenge was what, if any, visual prompt to use in our interviews. The 'wheel' we developed was something we thought would identify a range of structural aspects of women's lives that had shaped their individual experiences, and provide food for thought and a focal point for discussion. However, this representation may not be an ideal method of structuring our interviews. To some, the image may not be conducive to consideration of their own life and it has a necessarily limited number of identity categories/social locations. Apart from the use of the wheel and our underlying intersectionality orientation, our interviews were designed to be quite unstructured. However, while freedom for exploration is in keeping with an anti-oppressive, narrative approach, it also may mean that the data we seek remains elusive. 'Getting good data', or 'asking directly what you really want to know', is crucial to meaningful findings; this may mean starting with a vague self-exploratory question followed by something more specific about intersectionality (Hulko, 2014). In her intersectionality research with women, Hulko (2014) also used a visual prompt, a deck of image cards whereby participants were invited to pull out the image of a woman that is most similar to them, and another that is different. She found this elicited various responses to the same pictures, based on women's diversely intersecting social locations.

Finally, there are issues of how to locate and present ourselves, both in our research interviews and in this chapter. As feminists and researchers this has been a point of considerable discussion alongside helpful feedback from our colleagues. While we have not reached a final conclusion, we too have grappled with the intersectionality of our own lives and experiences and which elements of our social locations to share explicitly. For example, in a society where power and privilege is white, how do we adequately represent our race privilege and, importantly, how has this affected our opportunities and experience? Further, if we say that we have had our own experiences of relative poverty and discrimination, what assumptions and beliefs have underpinned this choice of disclosure? If we say that, as ageing women, we hold fears for our financial well-being in later life, does this mask that at least we have some superannuation accumulated as a result of our privileged position in academia? We are still pondering these questions.

Conclusion

We like to think we are critical social workers, and therefore we want to work in ways so that our research endeavours and our writing reflects that foundation. By 'critical social work', particularly in relation to the area of women and ageing, we mean a number of things (see our article, Macfarlane and Kostecki, 2016, for a comprehensive exploration). We view our research practice as social justice work that questions taken-for-granted assumptions and is open to diverse sources of knowledge. Our research reflects an effort to 'speak up' to imposed versions of genericised 'successful' ageing and neoliberal responsibilisation mantras by acknowledging the social contexts of privilege and oppression in which women's lives are lived. Research approaches that privilege the voices of older women can influence, as part of a larger and growing body of knowledge, policy directions providing alternatives to destructive and disenabling neoliberal agendas.

Second, critical social work seeks to contribute to social change and be attentive to the political nature of our everyday actions. Critically informed research on ageing, in the words and experiences of diverse older Australians, can chronicle the direct impact of social and economic policies, and, more subtly, reveal the effect on material and psychological experiences of daily life, well-being, dignity and empowerment in older age. As a policy rights and justice practice, individual workers and service users can join with other advocacy groups to lobby for more equitable retirement, taxation, housing and income support for older Australians, where particular factors relating to the intersection of gender with other structural elements are acknowledged (Macfarlane and Kostecki, 2016).

Third, critical social work research involves making connections between personal experience and broad social structures and inequalities. While we have argued that diversity is a crucial factor in experiences across the lifespan, culminating in older age, there are a range of common experiences that result from structural inequalities that produce particular forms of advantage and disadvantage in later life.

Finally, in documenting the complexities of older women's lives, research from a critical intersectional perspective aims to contribute to progressive social change and give voice to those who are marginalised and invisibilised and this involves reflexivity in order to examine assumptions implicit in all forms of practice. This is important in uncovering how our own – often invisibilised – assumptions, and that of our profession, as well as those of the organisations in which we work, guide understandings, practices and actions. This can enable the generation of emancipatory alternatives. Turning the spotlight on ourselves – whether as researchers, policy advocates or practitioners – is an attempt to uncover our own uncritical acceptance of ageist and other stereotypes. We are all embedded in powerful dominant narratives of ageing that contain assumptions about what constitutes 'right choices', 'responsibility', 'entitlement', 'active ageing' and so on, and less explicit narratives of moral failure, irresponsibility and dependence, which can unwittingly be reflected in our work (Macfarlane and Kostecki, 2016). Critical reflection is a process that may help us to be more emancipatory in our work; at whatever level or method of practice we are engaged.

While we are still in the early stages of this research project, we have attempted to locate our research, its aims, processes and purposes within a critical social work framework and to argue the relevance and importance of selecting an intersectional approach to this type of research. We are mindful that this not just be an intellectual exercise because inequalities that coalesce in older age have real consequences for real people. As critical social workers, and as ageing women, we believe that all members of society, in all their diversity – and here we are thinking particularly of older women – deserve to be valued, heard and respected, and to live well in a socially just society.

Further readings

Feldman, S. and Radermacher, H. (2016). *The Time of Our Lives? Building Opportunity and Capacity for the Economic and Social Participation of Older Australian Women*. https://www.lmcf.org.au/LMCF/media/05-Knowledge/PDFs/2016-03-07-LMCF-Time-of-Our-Lives-Report.pdf.

Freixas, A., Luque, B. and Reina, A. (2012). Critical feminist gerontology: In the back room of research. *Journal of Women & Aging*, 24(1), 44–58.

Hulko, W. (2014). Operationalizing intersectionality in feminist social work research: Reflections and techniques from research with equity-seeking groups. In S. Wahab, B. Anderson-Nathe and C. Gringeri (Eds.), *Feminisms in Social Work Research: Promise and Possibilities for Justice-Based Knowledge* (pp. 69–89). New York: Taylor & Francis.

References

Anderson, A. (2011). How critical gerontology challenges anti-aging ideology and leads the individual to a self-defined later life. Master's thesis, Marylhurst University, USA. http://digital.collection.marylhurst.edu/cdm/ref/collection/p15184coll1/id/7189.

Asquith, N. (2009). Positive ageing, neoliberalism and Australian sociology. *Journal of Sociology*, 45(3), 255–269.

Australian Council of Social Service (ACOSS) (2015). *Inquiry into Economic Security for Women in Retirement*. Sydney: ACOSS.

Australian Government Workplace Gender Equality Agency (2015). Women's economic security in retirement. Perspective paper. https://www.wgea.gov.au/sites/default/files/PP_womens_economic_security_in_retirement.pdf.

Australian Human Rights Commission (2009). *Accumulating Poverty? Women's Experiences of Inequality over the Lifecycle*. Sydney: Australian Human Rights Commission.

Bauer, G. (2014). Incorporating intersectionality theory into population health research methodology: Challenges and the potential to advance health equity. *Social Science & Medicine*, 110, 10–17.

Biggs, S. (2001). Toward a critical narrativity: Stories of aging in contemporary social policy. *Journal of Aging Studies*, 15, 303–316.

Biggs, S. (2008). Aging in a critical world: The search for generational intelligence. *Journal of Aging Studies*, 22(2), 115–119.

Brookfield, S. (2005). *The Power of Critical Theory for Adult Learning and Teaching*. Berkshire: Open University Press.

Calasanti, T. (2010). Gender relations and applied research on aging. *The Gerontologist*, 50(6), 720–734.

Carr, A., Biggs, S. and Kimberley, H. (2015). Ageing, diversity and the meaning(s) of later life. *Contemporary Readings in Law and Social Justice*, 7(1), 7–60.

Chambers, P. (2004). The case for critical social gerontology in social work education and older women. *Social Work Education: The International Journal*, 23(6), 745–758. https://doi.org/10.1080/0261547042000294518a.

Collins, P.H. (1990). Black feminist thought in the matrix of domination. In P. Collins (Ed.), *Black Feminist Thought: Knowledge, Consciousness, and the Politics of Empowerment* (pp. 221–238). Boston, MA: Unwin Hyman.

Committee for Economic Development of Australia (CEDA) (2015). *The Super Challenge of Retirement Income Policy*. Melbourne: CEDA.

Craciun, C. and Flick, U. (2016). Aging in precarious times: Exploring the role of gender in shaping views on aging. *Journal of Women & Aging*, 28(6), 530–539.

Dune, T., Firdaus, R., Mapedzahama, V., Lee, V., Stewart, J., Tronc, W. and Mekonnen, T. (2017). 'Say to yourself: Do I want to be a doormat?' Ageing Indigenous Australian women's reflections on gender roles and agency. *Australian Aboriginal Studies*, 1, 69–85.

Fanon, F. (1978). *The Wretched of the Earth*. Middlesex: Penguin.

Ferraro, K. and Shippee, T. (2009). Aging and cumulative inequality: How does inequality get under the skin? *The Gerontologist*, 49(3), 333–343.

Ferrer, I., Grenier, A., Brotman, S. and Koehn, S. (2017). Understanding the experiences of racialized older people through an intersectionality life course perspective. *Journal of Aging Studies*, 41, 10–17.

Gattuso, S. (2003). Becoming a wise old woman: Resilience and wellbeing in later life. *Health Sociology Review*, 12(2), 171–177.

Hancock, A. (2007). When multiplication doesn't equal quick addition. *Perspectives on Politics*, 5(1), 63–79.

Hankivsky, O. (2014). Rethinking care ethics: On the promise and potential of an intersectional analysis. *American Political Science Review*, 108(2), 252–264.

Hastings, S. and Rogowski, S. (2015). Critical social work with older people in neo-liberal times: Challenges and critical possibilities. *Practice: Social Work in Action*, 27(1), 21–33.

Hawkesworth, M. (2010). Policy discourse as sanctioned ignorance: Theorizing the erasure of feminist knowledge. *Critical Policy Studies*, 3(3–4), 268–289.

Herron, R. and Rosenberg, M. (2016). Aging, gender and 'triple jeopardy' through the life course. In M. Geisbrecht and V. Crooks (Eds.), *Place, Health, and Diversity: Learning from the Canadian Experience* (pp. 200–219). New York: Routledge.

Hetherington, C. and Smith, W. (2017). *Not so Super, for Women: Superannuation and Women's Retirement Outcomes*. Sydney: Per Capita.

Hightower, J., Smith, M.J. and Hightower, H.C. (2006). Hearing the voices of abused older women. *Journal of Gerontological Social Work*, 46(3/4), 205–227.

Hooyman, N., Browne, C., Ray, R. and Richardson, V. (2002). Feminist gerontology and the life course. *Gerontology & Geriatrics Education*, 22(4), 3–26.

Howarth, D. (2010). Power, discourse, and policy: Articulating a hegemony approach to critical policy studies. *Critical Policy Studies*, 3(3–4), 309–335.

Hulko, W. (2014). Operationalizing intersectionality in feminist social work research: Reflections and techniques from research with equity-seeking groups. In S. Wahab, B. Anderson-Nathe and C. Gringeri (Eds.), *Feminisms in Social Work Research: Promise and Possibilities for Justice-Based Knowledge* (pp. 69–89). New York: Taylor & Francis.

Kalache, A., Barreto, S.M. and Keller, I. (2005). Global ageing: The demographic revolution in all cultures and societies. In M.L. Johnson (Ed.), *The Cambridge Handbook on Age and Ageing* (pp. 30–46). New York: Cambridge University Press.

Lui, C., Warburton, J., Winterton, R. and Bartlett, H. (2011). Critical reflections on a social inclusion approach for an ageing Australia. *Australian Social Work*, 64(3), 266–282.

Macfarlane, S. and Kostecki, T. (2016). Growing old in the lucky country. *Social Alternatives*, 35(4), 54–58.

Maidment, J. and Macfarlane, S. (2011). Crafting communities: Promoting inclusion, empowerment and learning between older women. *Australian Social Work*, 64(3), 283–298.

Osborne-Crowley, L. (2015). Homelessness and older women: The accumulation of a lifetime of inequality. *Women's Agenda*. https://womensagenda.com.au/latest/homelessness-older-women-the-accumulation-of-a-lifetime-of-inequality/.

Polivka, L. and Longino, C. (2006). The emerging postmodern culture of aging and retirement security. In J. Baars, D. Dannefer, C. Phillipson and A. Walker (Eds.), *Ageing, Globalization and Inequality: The New Critical Gerontology* (pp. 183–204). Amityville, NY: Baywood.

Ranzijn, R. (2010). Active ageing – Another way to oppress marginalized and disadvantaged elders?: Aboriginal elders as a case study. *Journal of Health Psychology*, 15(5), 716–723.

Rawsthorne, M., Ellis, K. and de Pree, A. (2017). 'Working with COW': Social work supporting older women living in the community. *Journal of Gerontological Social Work*, 60(1), 32–47.

Rudman, D. (2015). Embodying positive aging and neoliberal rationality: Talking about the aging body within narratives of retirement. *Journal of Aging Studies*, 34, 10–20.

Sands, R. and Nuccio, K. (1992). Postmodern feminist theory and social work. *Social Work*, 37(6), 489–494.

Sharma, A. (2016). Assessing risk of institutional entry: A semi-nonparametric framework using a population-based sample of older women. *Women's Health Issues*, 26(5), 564–557.

Shippee, T., Wilkinson, L. and Ferraro, K. (2012). Accumulated financial strain and women's health over three decades. *The Journals of Gerontology Series B: Psychological Sciences and Social Sciences*, 67(5), 585–594.

Strega, S. (2005). The view from the poststructural margins: Epistemology and methodology reconsidered. In L. Brown and S. Strega (Eds.), *Research as Resistance: Critical, Indigenous, and Anti-Oppressive Approaches* (pp. 199–236). Toronto: Canadian Scholars' Press.

Travia, B. and Webb, E. (2015). Can real property law play a role in addressing housing vulnerability? The case of older women experiencing housing stress and homelessness. *Law in Context*, 33(2), 52–86.

Twigg, J. and Martin, W. (2015). The challenge of cultural gerontology. *The Gerontologist*, 55(3), 353–359.

Vitus, K. (2017). Policy and identity change in youth social work: From social-interventionist to neoliberal policy paradigms. *Journal of Social Work*, 17(4), 470–490.

Walker, A. (2006). Re-examining the political economy of aging: Understanding the structure/agency tension. In J. Baars, D. Dannefer, C. Phillipson and A. Walker (Eds.), *Aging, Globalisation and Inequality: The New Critical Gerontology* (pp. 59–80). Amityville, NY: Baywood Publishing.

Warner, L.R. (2008). A best practices guide to intersectional approaches in psychological research. *Sex Roles*, 59(5–6), 454–463.

Weber, L. (2006). Reconstructing the landscape of health disparities research: Promoting dialogue and collaboration between feminist intersectional and biomedical paradigms. In L. Mullings and A. Schulz (Eds.), *Gender, Race, Class and Health: Intersectional Approaches* (pp. 21–59). San Francisco: Jossey-Bass.

Wood, G. and Tully, C. (2006). *The Structural Approach to Direct Practice in Social Work: A Social Constructionist Perspective*, 3rd Edition. New York: Columbia University Press.

Zambrana, R. and Dill, B. (2006). Disparities in Latina health: An intersectional analysis. In L. Mullings and A. Schulz (Eds.), *Gender, Race, Class and Health: Intersectional Approaches* (pp. 192–227). San Francisco: Jossey-Bass.

Zink, T., Regan, S., Jacobson, C.J. and Pabst, S. (2003). Cohort, period, and aging effects: A qualitative study of older women's reasons for remaining in abusive relationships. *Violence Against Women*, 9(12), 1429–1441.

10
Uncovering Games of Truth: A Collaborative Exploration of the Ways Transgender and Non-Binary Young People Access Health Care and Support

Rebecca Howe, Amy Harper and Sekneh Hammoud-Beckett

> *Cis people are going in the wrong direction. It's not 'imagine your gender was something other than the one that was assigned', it's about imagining 'what would it be like if I was this gender and nobody saw me as this gender?'*

> *We have to try and live our lives with the cards that we've got, but sometimes when there's a card that we need, we have to use what cards we've got to get that extra card.*

Descriptions of 'games of truth', in the words of young people.

> *This collaborative project occurred on the land of the Gadigal people of the Eora nation, who continue their ongoing custodianship of the land and waters. We acknowledge that we are on this land as beneficiaries of an uncompensated and unreconciled dispossession, which continues today. We pay respect to Elders past, present and emerging. We pay respect to our LGBTI elders, particularly those of colour, who have created many of the paths we now travel. We pay respect to trailblazing Sistergirls, Brotherboys, as well as non-binary Aboriginal and Torres Strait people. Within acknowledgement, there should be action. So we remind ourselves to act in solidarity with First Nations peoples and resist racism, oppression and colonisation.*

The project is a collaboration with three workers, Amy Harper, Sekneh Hammoud-Beckett and Rebecca Howe, and a number of young people with lived trans and non-binary experience connected through a youth service. We made a group agreement that no identifying information would be used to protect the privacy of these young people. As workers, we all share an emphasis on honouring the knowledge of the young people we support. As with Pease (2013) who is conscious of writing about challenging heterosexism from within the dominant position of a straight man who benefits from heterosexual privilege, we are conscious of writing about trans and non-binary people as workers who benefit from our access to cis privilege. However, like Pease (2013), we also see the 'problems with silence' (p. 129) and agree that it should not only be people who designate their own gender who deconstruct cisgenderism. Collaborating has extended our practices and nourished us as workers.

In this chapter, we discuss therapeutic work with trans and non-binary young people. This discussion assumes that you, the reader, are familiar with the terms, 'trans', 'non-binary' and 'cis', which are used to describe gender expressions; and that the reader has a background understanding of core issues affecting trans and non-binary populations. For introductory reading in this area, see the National LGBTI Health Alliance's Knowledge Hub at: https://lgbtihealth.org.au/hub/.

We draw on Foucault's (1997) concept 'games of truth' to explore how 'truth' is formed and plays out for trans and non-binary young people, workers and the structures that connect them. Our collaboration explores 'being trans is a medical condition' as a powerful truth game that we are all recruited into. At the most fundamental level 'being trans is a medical condition' operates under the assumption that, currently, in Australia all trans and non-binary people need to engage in medical assessment to access gender affirming technologies. Thus, young people are being directed 'through the hoops of psychiatrists' (Kirby and Burstow, 2014, p. 165) to access treatment and support. Our critical analysis brings to light how many of the processes involved in accessing services and health care are oppressive to trans and non-binary people, and these are embedded within this 'game of truth'.

Throughout this chapter we use the term 'worker' in the broadest sense possible, so that it encapsulates not only those engaged in roles such as social workers, counsellors, psychologists, researchers and policy writers but also those engaged in unpaid and emotional labour, peer work, activism and other forms of advocacy. We invite you to shine a light on your work with trans and non-binary people. As workers, we typically believe that we are practising to support clients. Reynolds (2010) points out that, despite this, 'many of us, whether we intend to or not, benefit from the oppression of others' (p. 14). We also invite you to shine a light on work within health and welfare sectors that are increasingly shaped by conditions of neoliberalism, where autonomy and capacity for creativity are restricted by funding requirements and predetermined outcome measurements.

We discuss how Foucault's 'games of truth' can support engagement in critical analyses of power at interpersonal, structural and societal levels. Foucault (1997) suggests that 'one escaped from a domination of truth not by playing a game that was totally different from the game of truth but by playing the same game differently, or playing another game, another hand, with other trump cards' (p. 295). Drawing on this, we consider ways that workers can use 'games of truth' to reflect on their practice and use practical strategies of listening and openness to form a therapeutic stance in support of trans and non-binary people.

Our collaborative process

This writing is a collaboration between workers and a group of trans and non-binary young people aged 17–27, who shared their original work, joined group discussions and helped co-edit this chapter. We drew on Sekneh's original concept of 'inviting in' (Hammoud-Beckett, 2007), where connections between young people and workers become opportunities to 'give voice to' the alternative ways people 'define their existence' (p. 31). This approach honours the experience and knowledge of young people, and 'opens up the sort of communicative spaces wherein an alternative politics of mental health might be realised' (McKeown et al., 2014, p. 145).

We present this process in consideration of McRuer's (2006) critical perspective that 'neoliberalism and the condition of postmodernity, in fact, increasingly need able-bodied, heterosexual subjects who are visible and spectacularly tolerant of queer/disabled existences' (p. 2). In the context of working alongside people whose gender is self-designated (Ansara and Hegarty, 2012), our collaboration stands in resistance to that particularly subtle form of oppression this 'tolerance' perpetuates. The lessons and legacies of our elders have taught us 'that there are structures that support problems of injustice' (Reynolds, 2008, p. 5). We must take up a stance of 'collective accountability' to 'address problems together, both in the individual lives of the people we work with and also in the wider society' (Reynolds, 2008, p. 5). We agree with the assertion by McKeown and colleagues (2014) that alliances formed from collaboration are 'ever more urgent in the context of neoliberal threats to the provision of welfare', and these hold 'great potential for personal and wider social change, as well as reciprocal benefit' (p. 146).

What sort of 'games' are we talking about?

The term Intersectionality is increasingly being used as a frame of analysis (Cho et al., 2013) to guide ways of undoing privilege (Pease, 2013) and working anti-oppressively. Within this chapter, we offer 'games of truth' as a tool to further reflect/explore the relations and operations of power, and in doing so aim to deepen that work. This critical analysis of the game of truth 'being trans is a medical condition', stands on the shoulders of other writers and advocates exploring how power relationships operate at interpersonal and structural levels. These power relationships intersect with other systems of power inherent in settler-colonial societies and the global medical-industrial complex.

Ambrose Kirby, an activist and psychotherapist, involved in organising resistance to psychiatry in Canada, speaks from his experience as a trans man, saying 'our strategies for surviving are being taken out of context and individualized as "mental illnesses"' (Kirby and Burstow, 2014, p. 163). Kirby goes on to say:

> People who are setting themselves up as gatekeepers or insisting that people who are gender-different or gender-independent need to go to clinics to get support, are missing a huge part of the puzzle, which is the social, the societal – a political issue that prevents adults and children from being who they are. (p. 171)

Gender non-conforming performance artist, writer, and educator Alok Vaid-Menon (2016b) highlights the obsession Western settler-colonial states have with categorising everything about a person and the assumptions based on the assigned categories. Vaid-Menon exposes the limitations of Western discourses of medical transition, saying:

> When I started to experience dysphoria ... I started to really read and, talk to people and learn, and what I found was that for thousands of years there were ways of understanding gender that was not about our bodies, and not about the medicalisation of our bodies. And then I began to recognise that the medical industrial complex is profiting from trans people's trauma ... it actually has to do with the ways in which we're still reproducing this pathology that trans people are the problem that need to be fixed by a medical institution versus society's the problem for actually producing dysphoria. I actually think that all the dysphoria I experience comes from the oppression I experience ... I often say 'I was not born in the wrong body, I was born in the wrong world'. Like, this is on you. (Nur et al., 2016)

The work of these activists, grounded in their lived experiences as a trans man and as a non-binary feminine person of colour, shaped the conversations within this collaboration.

The game of truth, 'being trans is a medical condition', is deeply embedded in the consciousness and structures of Australian settler-colonial society. In the social consciousness, gender identity is constricted to biological sex and is expected to operate neatly within binary categories of male and female. These social constrictions are replicated in Australian laws. In New South Wales, there are three gender marker options on birth certificates, M, F and 'non-specific'. At the time of writing, to change the gender marker on a birth certificate there must be proof that 'a surgical procedure involving the alteration of a person's reproductive organs' (ICLC, 2015, para. 3) has been undertaken. Surgery on reproductive organs is also required for a non-binary person 'to be considered to be a member of the opposite sex; or to correct or eliminate ambiguities relating to the sex of the person' (ICLC, 2015, para. 3). Thus, 'only some people ... are legally regarded as being the gender they identify with, rather than their (assigned) birth gender' (Anti-Discrimination Board of NSW, n.d., para. 14). The requirement that trans and non-binary people receive a psychiatric diagnosis in order to access gender affirming medical technologies (i.e. access to hormone blockers, hormone replacement therapy and/or surgeries), and that medical transition is needed for protection under anti-discrimination laws, is an example of why we are interested in creating a dialogue with workers. This 'evidence' is inaccessible and/or unwanted for many and poses a significant cost both financially and in terms of emotional labour.

When Foucault said 'game' he did not mean it in the way of soccer or a game of Dungeons and Dragons. Rather, the game operates as a set of rules within society. When people play by these rules they are led to a certain truth (Foucault et al., 1997). The rules and the ways of playing are caught up in power dynamics that play out across multiple levels of society. In academic literature 'games of truth' have been used as a means to analyse power relationships between service users and workers (Nelson, 2017; Ning, 2005). However, it is Sekneh's analysis that is the inspiration for our use of 'games of truth' to explore the complex power dynamics affecting trans and non-binary young people.

Through her work, Sekneh found the discourse associated with 'coming out' (i.e. a person disclosing to others their sexuality identity) to be fraught with many complexities and contradictions. Sekneh highlighted the importance of 'coming out' in terms of giving voice to ongoing struggles, rendering visible human rights issues and creating a sense of community (Hammoud-Beckett, 2007). However, she also recognised that 'coming out' operates within white, Western, settler-colonial discourse, and it is a binary that carries with it an inherent pressure to name and visibilise identity or risk being shut in or, worse, dishonest (Hammoud-Beckett, 2007).

Sekneh's original exploration of the 'coming out' game of truth, focused on the significant distress it caused for Muslim young people in the context of their sexuality. Instead of coming out, Sekneh created a way young people could play the game of truth on their terms, through the process of giving 'invitations in to their life' (Hammoud-Beckett, 2007). Foucault and colleagues (1997) suggest that, since power is not a thing but a relation, it is not only repressive but can also be productive. Nelson (2017) extends this by stating: 'power relations are not fixed in a power/powerless binary but in perpetual flux, made and re-made recursively through power-laden processes and relationships' (p. 183). A game of 'inviting in' inverts the game of 'coming out'. Through adopting this practice, workers gain the opportunity to unpack relations of power in clients' lives. This can support service users to recognise their choices regarding who they give the opportunity to understand certain parts of their identity.

Foucault suggests that relations of power are rarely evident to the uncritical eye and are 'perhaps among the best hidden things in the social body' (Foucault, 1988, p. 118). Because there is productive power to be found in critique and adjustment, the game of truth 'being trans is a medical condition' can both limit and open up opportunities. Playing the game differently by playing another hand, with other trump cards (Foucault et al., 1997), creates ways that trans and non-binary young people come to experience themselves. Cultivating critique and analysis of how we all play games of truth also opens up opportunities for us as workers to expand our practice to respond to the needs of the people we support.

Being trans is a medical condition

'Being trans is a medical condition' operates in a way that privileges the worker's knowledge often as an expert or specialist. In our roles as workers, and through this collaboration collectively, we have heard countless examples of practices that have served to invalidate a person's own knowledge and identity. A 17-year-old collaborator shared her experience of trying to gain the support and understanding of her family around her gender identity. After many months of raising it with her parents, they would not accept her knowledge of herself and believed only a psychiatrist could verify it. The young woman was sent to her father's psychiatrist saying he feared that a practitioner with any understanding of gender diversity would be inherently biased and set her on a journey of transition. Her father spoke with the psychiatrist before seeing her and again after the appointment. She believes this set the agenda of siding with his anxieties. Little opportunity was given for her to speak for herself. The psychiatrist instead talked of her apprehensions, as her only experience was prescribing hormones for menopause. The psychiatrist informed the young woman she is too young to know if medical transition is what she really wants. This experience with a biased and powerful practitioner invalidated this young woman and undid her attempts to get her family members onside.

We have come across many stories from young people about workers, and spoken to many workers ourselves, who've refused to, or believe that they can't, support their client who is trans or non-binary. In our collaboration, young people reflected on how it felt to be referred elsewhere. For a young person who has already established a relationship with their practitioner enough to share issues surrounding their gender; who has used most of the allocated sessions on their mental health care plan; or who has to travel great distances to see someone who is 'specialised', being 'passed on' tells them that they are 'too complex to work with'. For non-binary people, this compounds gender essentialist views that their gender identity is 'too complicated' to understand (Vaid-Menon, 2017).

While there are elements of power in the game of truth 'being trans is a medical condition' that are prevalent in society, Foucault (1997) draws us to the ways power present in worker–client relationships can become harmful to the individual in the form of domination. He defines these as cases in which 'power relations are fixed in such a way that they are perpetually asymmetrical and allow an extremely limited margin of freedom' (Foucault, 1997, p. 292). When a worker positions trans and non-binary service users as 'too complicated', they are acting to oppress – protecting their own power and unearned privilege, while perpetuating difficult conditions for others (Baines, 2017). These beliefs and actions sit inside the game of truth 'being trans is a medical condition' and perpetuate the idea that trans and non-binary people can only get the care they need in the hands of a 'specialist'. When elements of power operate in this way, they have the capacity to exacerbate distress and harm.

In the National Transgender Discrimination Survey of more than 6,000 trans and non-binary respondents in the USA, 70% reported experiences of health care discrimination, with a majority also stating they *expect* to experience discrimination when accessing health care (Grant et al., 2010). Half of the respondents also cited lack of provider knowledge as one of the major hurdles in accessing care (Grant et al., 2010). In the Trans Pathways study (Strauss et al., 2017), an Australian study of the mental health and care pathways of trans and gender diverse young people aged 14–25, more than half of participants reported they 'experienced feeling isolated from medical and mental health services' (p. 97). The above-mentioned young person's experience with the psychiatrist, the experiences of others in this collaboration and our experience as workers call into question the belief that only a 'specialist' has the knowledge to support these young people. Moreover, this disparity between 'specialist' knowledge and the experiential knowledge of young people demonstrates there are powerful games at play.

In querying how knowledge around gender comes to be specialised and privileged, one health care student who is part of this collaboration said references to gender diversity were 'limited to invisible' within her training. She felt that 'even if people are interested in helping us they don't get the opportunity to learn ... if you think of all the practitioners that exist in Sydney, the fraction of them that have any understanding of gender stuff is tiny'. Another recounted how the absence of adequate training or information on gender for health care providers means that there is almost no post-surgical care to support people who have had gender affirming surgery. She expressed frustration seeking information for her own health care needs: 'the reality is we end up having to research ourselves more than doctors ever do'. Others shared how they and others have trawled through websites and 'compared hundreds of anecdotal experiences to find any answers'. Thus, it is useful to consider how in the absence of formal training and recognition in these fields, what qualifies practitioners to take up a role of a 'specialist'?

For many young people, the game 'being trans is a medical condition' involves a succession of decisions that come under scrutiny by workers, amid expensive legal, medical and bureaucratic hoops to jump through. One young person talked about the year-long waiting list to see the specialist in her state, to then be referred to the next specialist to oversee hormones. Another expressed her anger at the energy it took to get support: 'I spent three years trying to get all the specialist letters and eventually gave up. Do they know how stressful this is for all their patients?'

For many young people, what is wrapped up in this game of truth is a promise that prescribed pathways of treatment become the answer or end to the difficulties they may experience. Yet, as one young person pointed out:

> No one within the medical institution tells you or prepares you for this not necessarily being the case ... it took me so long to accept that there are people who are trans or gender diverse without really being dysphoric and I was so angry that I had to go through all this stuff to feel good about myself ... this game we are playing is a product of society just as much as it is a product of ourselves and our place in society.

With limited options and with everything that is at stake, many collaborators felt they could not take chances speaking about the complexities of their personal experiences with workers: 'you feel like you've got to play the game ... say their words ... surely they know that people lie?' One person said she hates being asked and wants to be able to ask the questions. This young person described the palatable story she had repeated so many times to different practitioners that the line between truth and reality blurred. Others talked about downplaying to workers their other mental or physical health issues for fear they would not get support, saying: 'We omit the fact that life is not fine and dandy – and who talks about this? ... and then when things don't go to plan you wonder why you're not happy yet and why it hasn't solved all your problems.' For these young people, the game becomes: 'how do I say the right thing to get what I need, whilst not omitting my own medical needs?' Without this game, which has been termed by many trans women of colour as the 'tragic trans narrative' (Sarkisova, 2014, p. 292), many felt that access to wanted forms of treatment seemed untenable.

The oppressive realities of these configurations of power in the lives of trans and non-binary young people mean that resistance becomes a valuable card in the game. Collaborators often spoke about how they and their peers had learnt to play, both in and outside of the game 'being trans is a medical condition'. Collaborators talked about queer- and trans-friendly spaces and organisations, activism and the internet *especially* as key spaces they could just be themselves. One non-binary person said that for them 'the internet is everything, especially because medical stuff may not be the first thing you seek out'. Personal writing, social media, articles, gaming, music and much more have become communicative spaces constructed by networks of trans and non-binary people to connect and share their truths. Through their searching, young people had found communities who staunchly support one another, share advice and ways to access the things that they need – legitimately or otherwise. They described how, through these spaces, they had learnt strategies to protect themselves when accessing services – such as finding a trans-informed practitioner who won't pathologise them and/or how to represent themselves to get the support they need. In situations where 'most of us can't control and self-determine our genders without considering the very real threat of intimate, familial, interpersonal, and state violence' (Vaid-Menon, 2016a, para. 1), these spaces bring recognition and validity to ways trans and non-binary people play their hand across intersectional games of truth.

The reality of violence is particularly concerning. Research from both Australia and Canada reveals trans and non-binary young people experience high rates of self-injury and thoughts and actions of suicide in response to external factors such as abuse, harassment or discrimination (Kirby and Burstow, 2014; Smith et al., 2014; Strauss et al., 2017). Reynolds (2016) emphasises how society's reliance on psychiatric labels such as depression, anxiety and gender dysphoria operate to obscure the violence and oppression trans and non-binary people experience, and place 'the responsibility for a hateful society' (p. 183) onto the person. Under neoliberalism, the game operates so that narratives are individualised, depoliticised and decontextualised; where structures appear fixed in privileging knowledge that maintains the status quo. Yet the ways trans and non-binary young people still come to play this game speak to the fact that there is something more precious about their genders, which they are able to hold on to despite what they are up against (Hammoud-Beckett, 2007).

Listening for truths and openness

In her paper on health access for trans women, one collaborator argued that rather than locating physical and mental health outcomes as part of the trans experience, workers must examine the structures they work within and how they perpetuate barriers for trans and non-binary people. That it is only through this exploration that we can work to expose and dismantle them. In our contact with young people, family members, other workers and structural bodies, we must recognise that 'we are always participating simultaneously in domains of power and knowledge', and critique how our practices have been formed in these domains (White and Epston, 1990, p. 29). This includes the assumptions that are made about people's bodies and identities, and who has the power to name bodies and identities.

In her therapeutic work, Sekneh invites us to consider how we can 'free ourselves from prescribed ideas about "identity acceptance" and open ourselves to learn something new, something different?' (Hammoud-Beckett, 2007, p. 31). The critical practice of interrogating the construction of truths creates opportunities for workers to cultivate a deeper understanding of issues affecting their various client groups. In this section, we use the phrases 'listening for truths' and 'openness' to discuss how these kinds of critical analyses can manifest as practical strategies to expose them.

Listening for truth in our practice involves considering how our work has been situated historically, culturally and institutionally. We must also consider how this has influenced the way we occupy our privileged positions as workers, and who this serves to benefit. Conditions of neoliberalism often lead to services that are underfunded and workers that are overstretched. Despite increasing LGBTI visibility within services, it is not uncommon that this visibility is not extended to inclusion within policies, processes or training of staff. Thus, the needs of these service users become swept up among many competing demands (McNair et al., 2017).

Many collaborators shared how past invalidation from workers and services have impacted their willingness to make new connections. They unanimously want workers who 'instead of ticking boxes listen to understand why they need what they need'. When young people first access a service, they are usually faced with a request for their personal information. Within our practice this is an opportunity to open conversations about why we ask for this information, how it will be recorded, how it could be used (for example, to advocate for systemic change), their right to opt out of questions, and how they can access information held about them. Service users are then better equipped to make decisions about what information they share with the service. Extensions of this practice include workers and young people collectively writing summary points at the end of a meeting or counselling session; and, taking up a practice of transparency and accountability by providing clients with copies of their case notes. We demonstrate our use of critical analysis within our practice by talking openly about how we position ourselves in our roles, the position of our service, and the structures we live and work among. We believe this cultivates a safe-enough space for service users to name and critique their own experiences. This practice, as in the case of this collaboration, contributes to a richer shared knowledge.

Trans and non-binary young people often rely on family and carers for their physical well-being. Thus, their rejection is likely to place the young person at significant risk. Families and carers are often in urgent need of information, guidance and support (Strauss et al., 2017). When first engaging, we show recognition of the efforts they have made to adapt to the young person's gender, as well as acknowledging their struggles and concerns. It is important, however, that we recognise that our roles as workers are political, and are concerned with relationships of power even when we think we're taking a 'neutral' stance (Reynolds, 2010). In these discussions, we support the young person by using their preferred pronoun rather than the one that family members or carers use. Using the pronoun preferred by a parent or carer sides with their rejection of the young person's identity and ultimately perpetuates cisgenderism (Ansara and Hegarty, 2012). Taking an active stance by using affirming language and sharing practical, supportive resources and strategies to talk about gender can be crucial in addressing concerns, as well as beliefs and practices that position them at odds to the child or young person.

Within our practice, we have taken a number of steps to address the scarcity of referral pathways for trans and non-binary young people. We have compiled resources aimed at clients, workers and families. With others, we have also formed an expanding network of workers who support and learn from each other online and in monthly supervision. When workers contact us wanting to refer a client who is trans or non-binary, we take this as an opportunity to address misinformation and support worker confidence. We discuss how attitudes such as 'not knowing enough' work to limit the supports available to trans and non-binary people, and encourage an openness to reflect on the relationship they have developed with the client. We share elements of our experiences of learning alongside clients, and offer resources to support the worker to continue their journey.

We utilise our position and experience as 'professionals', alongside other fierce advocates at our service, at a structural level. An example is our ongoing advocacy for changes to the database our funders require us to use, which only has male or female as options for recording a client's gender. Trans and non-binary young people are over-represented in Australian homelessness services (Mission Australia, 2015), yet the lack of representation within data collection has effectively erased experiences specific to this client group, limiting service ability to track and respond to LGBTI needs (McNair et al., 2017). After seven years of regularly tabling these issues with funding bodies, an LGBTI working group was created. The recommendations for more representative options for gender within the database, alongside the development of training packages for workers to develop skills needed to ask clients respectfully about their gender identity, were supported by homelessness services across the board. This is an example of inviting openness to include those whose genders are self-determined in data collection. It highlights the importance of taking up a stance of 'collective accountability' (Reynolds, 2008) not just with service users, but within and between service providers and those who fund them.

To work across our differences we as workers must take active steps to acknowledge and recast power with clients. Without collective accountability, the work falls back onto people who designate their own gender to self-advocate and challenge their oppression.

Conclusion

This collaboration provided an opportunity for workers and trans and non-binary young people to recast power relationships, in recognition of the role service users play in the development of practice knowledge. Using Foucault's 'games of truth' analogy, we sought to expose how 'being trans is a medical condition' plays out for trans and non-binary young people and the people who work with them. In a neoliberal context, which operates to downplay systematic problems, these collaborations assist us to expose them. Through doing so, we can take a position of collective accountability in seeking not just social but transformative justice for trans and non-binary people.

Our practices are imperfect. They are a work in progress informed and adjusted through our engagement with young people. Precisely by not being a 'specialised expert', being open to discomfort and uncertainty, means all of us as workers can create space to be able to listen out for, and hear, the ways trans and non-binary people play games of truth. Cultivating a practice of open curiosity, reflecting on our discomfort and extending our critical analysis in order to 'embrace our power and be accountable to it' (Reynolds, 2016, p. 184) are steps we can all take in support of our clients. Every person should be able to walk into a service and receive respectful and just care. In solidarity with your clients, we invite you to consider these critical self-reflections:

➣ Are you able to identify the games of truth you are recruited into?

➣ When identified, how do you negotiate and respond to the games of truth?

➣ Do you know the histories of these games of truths?

➣ What sorts of conversations are required to expose the different types of power in advocacy work, for example institutional, legal, medical, media, societal, political, etc.?

➣ Are there times you play within these games of truth? Who benefits from the ways you play?

➣ What are the practices you take up to centre the individual seeking your support?

➣ How do you safeguard against 'linguistic sleepwalking' (i.e. using labels without critiquing their application/why you are using them)?

➣ How do you name and take responsibility for your uncertainty?

➣ How do you show that the service you deliver is accessible and affordable?

➣ If you are seen to hold 'specialised' knowledge, how and under what conditions do you share it?

➣ How do you embody and model respectful practices for other workers?

➣ And how do you actively address clients' experiences of mistreatment within your own or another service?

Further readings

Kirby, A. and Burstow, B. (2014). Trans jeopardy/trans resistance: Shaindl Diamond (SD) Interviews Ambrose Kirby (AK). In B. Burstow, B.A. LeFrançois and S. Diamond (Eds.), *Psychiatry Disrupted: Theorizing Resistance and Crafting the (R)evolution* (pp. 163–176). Ontario: McGill-Queen's University Press.

Hammoud-Beckett, S. (2007). Azima ila hayati – An invitation into my life: Narrative conversations about sexual identity. *International Journal of Narrative Therapy & Community Work*, 1, 29–39.

Sharman, Z. (2016). *The Remedy: Queer and Trans Voices on Health and Health Care*. Vancouver, BC: Arsenal Pulp Press.

Acknowledgements

We would like to thank Twenty10 Inc. GLCS NSW for providing resources and support to the workers and young people connected through this project. We acknowledge the ongoing commitment of our colleagues and volunteers at Twenty10 in supporting LGBTQIA+ communities in NSW.

References

Ansara, Y.G. and Hegarty, P. (2012). Cisgenderism in psychology: Pathologising and misgendering children from 1999 to 2008. *Psychology & Sexuality*, 3(2), 137–160. https://doi.org/10.1080/19419899.2011.576696

Anti-Discrimination Board of NSW (n.d.). Transgender discrimination. http://www.antidiscrimination.justice.nsw.gov.au/Pages/adb1_antidiscriminationlaw/adb1_types/adb1_transgender.aspx#Whoiscountedastransgenderunderanti-discriminationlaw

Baines, D. (2017). Anti-oppressive practice: Roots, theory, tensions. In D. Baines (Ed.), *Doing Anti-Oppressive Practice: Social Justice Social Work*, 3rd Edition (pp. 2–22). Black Point, NS: Fernwood Publishing.

Cho, S., Crenshaw, K.W. and McCall, L. (2013). Toward a field of intersectionality studies: Theory, applications, and praxis. *Signs Journal of Women in Culture and Society*, 38(4), 785–810.

Foucault, M. (1988). Power and sex. In L.D. Kritzman (Ed.), *Politics, Philosophy, Culture: Interviews and Other Writings 1977–1984*, trans. A. Sheridan (pp. 110–124). New York: Routledge.

Foucault, M. (1997). The ethics of the concern of the self as a practice of freedom. In P. Rabinow (Ed.), *Ethics: Subjectivity and Truth*, trans. R. Hurley (pp. 281–301). New York: The New Press.

Foucault, M., Rabinow, P. and Faubion, J.D. (1997). *The Essential Works of Foucault 1954–1984*. New York: New Press.

Grant, J.M., Mottet, L.A,. Tanis, J., Herman, J.L., Harrison, J. and Keisling, M. (2010). *National Transgender Discrimination Survey Report on Health and Health Care.* Washington, DC: National Center for Transgender Equality and the National Gay and Lesbian Task Force.

Hammoud-Beckett, S. (2007). Azima ila hayati – An invitation in to my life: Narrative conversations about sexual identity. *International Journal of Narrative Therapy & Community Work*, 1, 29–39.

ICLC (Inner City Legal Centre) (2015). *Changing Sex Listed on Identification Documents.* Inner City Legal Centre Fact Sheet, 12 June. http://www.iclc.org.au/factsheets/changing-sex-listed-on-identification-documents/

Kirby, A. and Burstow, B. (2014).Trans jeopardy/trans resistance: Shaindl Diamond (SD) Interviews Ambrose Kirby (AK). In B. Burstow., B.A. LeFrançois. and S. Diamond (Eds.), *Psychiatry Disrupted: Theorizing Resistance and Crafting the (R)evolution* (pp. 163–176). Ontario: McGill-Queen's University Press.

McKeown, M., Cresswell, M. and Spandler, H. (2014). Deeply engaged relationships: Alliances between mental health workers and psychiatric survivors in the UK. In B. Burstow, B.A. LeFrançois and S. Diamond (Eds.), *Psychiatry Disrupted: Theorizing Resistance and Crafting the (R)evolution* (pp. 145–162). Montreal: McGill-Queen's University Press.

McNair, R., Andrews, C., Parkinson, S. and Dempsey, D. (2017). *Stage 1 Report LGBTI Homelessness: Preliminary findings on risks, service needs and use.* GALFA LGBTI Homelessness Research Project. https://www.launchhousing.org.au/wp-content/uploads/2017/03/LGBTI-Homelessness-project-LMCF-and-ACF-report_Final-31-Jan-2017.pdf

McRuer, R. (2006). *Crip Theory: Cultural Signs of Queerness and Disability.* New York: University Press.

Mission Australia (2015). *Mission Australia's Review of Homelessness 2015.* https://www.missionaustralia.com.au/documents/position-statements/homelessness-1/469-mission-australia-s-review-of-homelessness-2015

Nelson, E. (2017). Re-thinking power in student voice as games of truth: Dealing/playing your hand. *Pedagogy, Culture & Society*, 25(2), 181–114.

Ning, A.M. (2005). Games of truth: Rethinking conformity and resistance in narratives of heroin recovery. *Medical Anthropology*, 24(4), 349–382.

Nur, A., Hart, E., Cooke, A., Hanna, J. and Pham, T.H. (Producers). (2016). In conversation with Alok Vaid-Menon. *Women on the Line*, Radio 3CR [Audio podcast], 10 October. http://www.3cr.org.au/womenontheline/episode-201610100830/conversation-alok-vaid-menon

Pease, B. (2013). *Undoing Privilege: Unearned Advantage in a Divided World.* London: Zed Books.

Reynolds, V. (2008). An ethic of resistance: Frontline worker as activist. *Women Making Waves*, 19(1), 5.

Reynolds, V. (2010). Fluid and imperfect ally positioning: Some gifts of queer theory. *Context, Association for Family and Systemic Therapy*, 111, 13–17.

Reynolds, V. (2016). Hate kills: A social justice response to suicide. In J. White, I. Marsh, M.J. Kral and J. Morris (Eds.), *Critical Suicidology: Transforming Suicide Research for the 21st Century* (pp. 169–187). Toronto: UBC Press.

Sarkisova, X. (2014). (Beyond) Suffering as a measuring tool. In L. Erickson-Schroth (Ed.), *Trans Bodies, Trans Selves: A Resource for the Transgender Community* (p. 292). New York: Oxford University Press.

Smith, E., Jones, T., Ward, R., Dixon, J., Mitchell, A. and Hillier, L. (2014). *From Blues to Rainbows: Mental Health and Well-being of Gender Diverse and Transgender Young People in Australia.* Melbourne: The Australian Research Centre in Sex, Health, and Society. https://www.beyondblue.org.au/docs/default-source/research-project-files/bw0268-from-blues-to-rainbows-report-final-report.pdf?sfvrsn=2

Strauss, P., Cook, A., Winter, S., Watson, V., Wright Toussaint, D. and Lin, A. (2017). *Trans pathways: The mental health experiences and care pathways of trans young people. Summary of results.* Telethon Kids Institute, Perth, Australia. https://www.telethonkids.org.au/globalassets/media/documents/brain–behaviour/trans-pathways-summary.pdf

Vaid-Menon, A. (2016a). There is no one way to be trans, *ALOK* (blog), 22 November. https://www.alokvmenon.com/blog/2016/11/22/there-is-no-one-way-to-be-trans

Vaid-Menon, A. (2016b). Transphobia doesn't capture the violence of gender binarism, *ALOK* (blog), 10 December. https://www.alokvmenon.com/blog/2016/12/10/transphobia-doesnt-capture-the-violence-of-gender-binarism

Vaid-Menon, A. (2017). Shift your paradigm: Non-binary people aren't too complicated, *ALOK* (blog), 11 January. https://www.alokvmenon.com/blog/2017/1/11/shift-your-paradigm-nonbinary-people-arent-too-complicated

White, M. and Epston, D. (1990). *Narrative Means to Therapeutic Ends.* New York: WW Norton & Co.

PART FOUR
CRITICAL PERSPECTIVES ON NORMALITY AND DIFFERENCE

11
Accepting My Illness? Problematising the Claims of Mental Health Anti-Stigma Efforts

Emma Tseris

The author commences this chapter by acknowledging the Traditional Owners of the land across Australia on which she works and lives, paying respect to Elders past, present, and emerging, and recognising the invaluable contributions of Aboriginal and Torres Strait Islander world views relating to social and emotional well-being.

Introduction

Historically, to be deemed mentally ill has carried the consequence of a highly marginalised social positioning; mental illness has been a marker of social difference often coupled with a range of negative circumstances, including social isolation and unemployment, alongside despair and hopelessness about probable life outcomes (Hansson, 2006). In an attempt to reduce the stigma attached to mental illness, and to address the marginalisation of people labelled as mentally ill, contemporary mental health community education campaigns have focused their attention on a major reframing of mental illness – not as an experience to be hidden or ashamed of but as a common occurrence, which can affect people of all backgrounds and across all contexts. Examples of such education efforts include Australia's *beyondblue* Ambassador program, in which famous sporting and entertainment personalities share their stories of mental illness in order to 'raise awareness and reduce stigma' and 'provide messages of hope and encouragement to others' (Beyond Blue, 2016); and the United Kingdom's *Time to Talk* campaign, aimed at generating 'thousands of conversations about mental illness' within schools, workplaces and communities, in order to 'end discrimination and change attitudes and behaviour' (Time to Change, 2017). These shifts in the public conversation about mental illness are often seen as deeply embedded in social justice principles – for example, the hopelessness and fear of societal rejection that has traditionally surrounded mental illness is replaced with a reassurance that compassionate help and effective treatments are available, combined with a message that recovery from mental illness is possible. As anti-stigma education efforts are becoming increasingly commonplace and influential in shaping both community and professional understandings of difference, it is necessary for human service professionals to understand both their strengths and their limitations in transforming the social positioning of people diagnosed with mental illness. Within this chapter, critical mental health theory, the ideas of Mad activists and the voices of people with lived experience of mental illness diagnosis are drawn on to explore the key assumptions contained within education campaigns designed to 'de-stigmatise' mental illness, in order to address the complexities of working across difference within mental health policy and practice contexts.

The attention and influence that mental health awareness-raising campaigns have achieved have led to more recent notions that to 'speak out' about one's mental distress can be an 'empowering' experience, with some people going so far as to 'celebrate' their identity as a person with mental illness. For example, autism rights activists coined the term 'neurodiversity' to reposition autistic traits as differences rather than deficiencies, which, given enough support, can actually become advantageous – a view that has since been applied more generally to a range of mental illness diagnoses (Runswick-Cole, 2014). Other less radical claims have critiqued the assumption that a person's future prospects are determined by a mental illness diagnosis, arguing instead that a mental illness should not be viewed as the defining characteristic of a person, and emphasising the capacity for mental health recovery, given adequate support and treatment (BpHope, 2017). Such identity claims stand in stark contrast to the notion that people with mental illness should be pitied, or that they will experience lifelong dysfunctions, thereby challenging previously dominant narratives about the need to maintain secrecy surrounding the experience of mental illness, and that people diagnosed with mental illnesses are dangerous or should be feared. Nevertheless, concerns have been raised by some mental health activists that anti-stigma campaigns do not go far enough in their critique of dominant understandings and practices relating to mental health, and that they often strengthen and perpetuate an individualised and biomedical discourse of mental illness, at the expense of other understandings. For example, McWade and colleagues (2015) claim that while anti-stigma efforts offer a less dire outlook on the life course of people diagnosed as mentally unwell, they do not sufficiently problematise the role and social legitimacy afforded to professional mental health workers in the treatment of mental disorders; furthermore, anti-stigma campaigns are often limited in their transformative capacities due to their connections to pharmaceutical interests and their uncritical acceptance of the validity of the psychiatric knowledge base that underpins the practice of separating people into categories of mental health and mental illness (Cohen, 2016).

Examining key messages

Common threads that can be frequently seen within mental health anti-stigma efforts include:

- *Mental illness is a common experience* – for example, 'No one should feel alone in his or her mental health journey. Everyone should have a place to realise, "me too"' (NoStigmas, 2017).
- *Mental illness can affect anyone* – for example, 'Anyone can develop a mental illness. There is no immunity to mental illness. Not everyone develops a mental illness during their lives, but anyone could' (Sane Australia, 2017).
- *Mental illness does not define you (we should separate the illness from the person)* – for example, 'Mental illness is a flaw in chemistry, not character' (Imagine Thriving, 2017).
- *The general public needs education in order to reduce stigma* – for example, 'A key part of ending the stigma is education … [through] regular workshops for consumers, families, carers and the general public' (One Door Mental Health, 2017).
- *Effective help is available* – for example, 'It can often take a while to realise that you need help but once you do, it's important to know where help is available … It is usually appropriate to see a mental health professional for a more thorough assessment. They are qualified to prescribe medication and/or therapy recommendations' (WayAhead, 2016).
- *Recovery is possible* – for example, 'Most people with mental health problems can get better. Treatment and recovery are ongoing processes that happen over time. The first step is getting help' (US Department of Health and Human Services, 2017).
- *Talking about one's own experience of mental illness is empowering* – for example, 'batyr [sic] provides programs that train young people to speak about their personal experience with mental ill health … the

programs engage, educate and empower the audience to learn from the experiences of others and to reach out to the great services around them' (Batyr, 2017).

On first glance, stigma reduction and mental health awareness-raising campaigns appear in many ways to be strongly aligned with social justice principles of inclusion, participation and full citizenship. To an extent, the positive effects of these campaigns are undeniable, and it is difficult to not contrast their optimistic attempts to move towards social inclusion with the long history of inhumane and violent treatments perpetuated towards people labelled as mentally deviant (Scull, 2015). Nevertheless, although critical theories of mental health are certainly interested in exploring ways to reduce the social exclusion of people labelled with mental illness diagnoses, they also examine a range of other concerns relating to psychiatric labelling processes and professional power. For example, contributions within LeFrancois, Menzies and Reaume's (2013) collection on Mad Studies challenge the commonplace assumption that help-seeking in relation to mental distress is always useful, by discussing experiences in which unsatisfactory – or, worse still, harmful – responses have been received by service users when attempting to access psychiatric or therapeutic services, highlighting the ongoing unacceptable use of coercion within mental health treatment. More far-reaching than a psychosocial analysis of mental illness, critical perspectives are interested in how notions of mental illness invisibilise social justice issues, by shrinking them to the level of individual minds, whereby a clinical response is offered that situates individuals as the site of the problem (Ecclestone and Brunila, 2015). Key to this analysis is an exploration of the sociopolitical work that is accomplished through psychiatric labelling practices, for example the ways in which mental health diagnoses both reflect and perpetuate patriarchal, racist, heterosexist and classist biases (Cohen, 2016). Furthermore, Summerfield's (2012) analysis of the attempt to create a 'global mental health' agenda questions the assertion that mental health professionals are the only people who are capable of providing useful support at times of mental distress, discussing this assumption as a form of cultural imperialism that has invisibilised non-Western knowledges relating to diverse experiences and perceptions. Consequently, conventional attempts to de-stigmatise mental health diagnoses, focused predominantly on encouraging people to speak out about their experiences of 'illness' and to seek professional assistance, often fall short of fully capturing the principles embedded within critical mental health theory and practice. To explore these potential limitations in more depth, it is useful to revisit the dominant themes contained within mental health education campaigns while utilising the lenses offered by critical theory.

Mental illness as a common experience

While it is true that mental illness diagnoses are becoming increasingly prevalent in contemporary times, leading to discussions about mental illness 'epidemics', alternative arguments have suggested that these trends are reflective not of an objective rise in mental illness but of a decreasing tolerance for difference, whereby the parameters for what is considered 'normal' or 'acceptable' behaviour have become increasingly narrow; for example, within the American Psychiatric Association's ever-expanding *Diagnostic and Statistical Manual*, shyness can now be labelled as Social Anxiety Disorder, grief as Major Depressive Disorder and childhood temper tantrums as Disruptive Mood Dysregulation Disorder. While it may be comforting to feel less alone when diagnosed with a mental illness, critical scholars have raised concerns that the proliferation of mental illness diagnoses can be linked to both pharmaceutical and professional interests, coupled with a neoliberal political agenda in which forms of personhood that are not useful to marketplace productivity are deemed to be 'abnormal' and requiring 'treatment' (see, for example, Moncrieff, 2008).

Mental illness can affect anyone

This claim, although potentially reassuring, ignores the unequal distribution of mental illness diagnosis within society, whereby heightened social marginalisation carries with it an increased possibility of being labelled as mentally unwell (prominent examples being asylum seekers, women who have experienced violence, queer people and so on). Assertions about mental illness as a ubiquitous experience therefore sidestep the role played by psychiatric diagnoses in misnaming and reinterpreting experiences such as poverty, patriarchy, heterosexism and racism as individual dysfunction and illness, rendering individuals as the site for treatment and intervention (see, for example, Ussher, 2011). As a result, Mad activism is most effective when connected to other liberation struggles, including feminism, anti-racism and anti-classism (LeFrancois et al., 2013).

Mental illness does not define you

This claim, based on the humanistic idea that it is important to separate a person from their illness, emphasises the importance of language usage whereby a mental illness is viewed as merely one aspect of a person's identity, rather than as the defining characteristic of a person (for example, 'a person experiencing depression' is preferred over 'a depressed person'). Such changes in language, though subtle, can have significant effects of a person's self-identity as well as how others relate to them (Mental Health Coordinating Council, 2013). Nevertheless, the limitations of political efforts such as these are often limited due to their uncritical acceptance of the binary categories of mental health and mental illness. In other words, within such constructions, mental illness is constructed as a tolerable, and yet unwanted, deviation from the 'norm' – which may in fact perpetuate, rather than transform, social divisions, contributing to an 'us' and 'them' politics that is inherent to neoliberal ideology (Runswick-Cole, 2014). Furthermore, it is important that the potential benefits of attempting to reframe public attitudes about mental illness, as well as service user's self-perceptions, are not overstated. An attempt to shift societal *attitudes* about mental illness, in and of itself, is unlikely to achieve a goal of transforming mental health service users' position in society in terms of their vastly unequal opportunities and access to material resources, including housing and employment, nor can it alleviate the unfavourable treatment that they often receive, within both community and professional treatment contexts (Sayce, 1998). In contrast to the attempts of anti-stigma campaigns to intervene at the level of beliefs and attitudes towards mental illness, wider political efforts in relation to mental health aim to connect psychiatric practices – including the very use of diagnostic labels – to the continuation of broader societal inequalities. From this perspective, psychiatric labelling practices are called into question and mental health knowledge is viewed not as neutral and unchallengeable but as deeply embedded in sociopolitical contexts and power relations. A practical implication might be workers recognising their own privilege if they have not been labelled with a mental illness diagnosis, and choosing not to use mental health language to describe the lives of others.

The general public needs educating

Anti-stigma efforts nearly always take the position that the stigma experienced by people diagnosed with mental illness arises from ignorant community understandings of mental illness, with the resulting assumption being that the general public is in need of education by mental health professionals in order to address stereotypes and myths about mental illness. The assumption that professional workers are immune from stigmatising beliefs about mental illness has created a significant reflexive blind spot to the sometimes violent practices that occur within contemporary mental health services, as well as the symbolic violence contained within mental health labelling practices themselves (Liegghio, 2013). For example, critical scholars have noted that psychiatric practices of labelling people as 'dysfunctional' and 'disordered' are at least as equally stigmatising as a layperson's use of the term 'crazy'. In a fascinating study conducted in the United Kingdom (MindFreedom, 2012), which explored the origins of messages of hopelessness received by mental health service users, participants most frequently responded that they received this message from a mental health professional, pointing clearly towards the need for mental health professionals to revisit dominant ideas about the origins of the stigma of mental illness.

Effective help is available

Although the claim that effective treatments are available in response to mental illness does act to counter historical notions of hopelessness and lifelong difficulties, it also provides undue legitimacy to biomedical and individualised therapy pathways, strengthening the social power of mental health professionals and ignoring alternative knowledges. As well, it brushes over ongoing human rights concerns relating to the use of force and coercion within mental health settings, which can take the form of seclusion and restraint, as well as less overt forms of harm, for example the practice within cognitive behavioural therapy of situating distress as arising from 'thought distortions' rather than from any hostile and unfair aspects of a person's external environment (Hagan and Donnison, 1999). Furthermore, although the de-institutionalisation of mental health services has resulted in an increased availability of treatment options outside of involuntary and hospital interventions, people with the fewest resources are least likely to be able to access support within privately operated (and potentially less coercive) therapeutic services (Martin, 2013). Consequently, effective and responsive service provision is not evenly distributed within society, but exists along a social gradient, meaning that an intersectional analysis of the varying social locations of people accessing mental health support is needed. Finally, it is important to recognise the experiences of some people who attempt to seek mental health support, who are subjected to risk assessment tools that deem them to be 'too well' to receive a service (Sawyer, 2008).

Recovery is possible

To explore in detail the critical literature pertaining to recovery discourses within contemporary understandings of mental well-being is beyond the scope of this chapter, however limitations include the focus on neoliberal personhood and individual responsibility at the expense of considering the social and material resources that might be required to 'recover' from mental distress, and the narrow possibilities encompassed within medical definitions of recovery, as opposed to social or personal definitions (Harper and Speed, 2012); along with a concern that recovery from mental illness has shifted from being seen as 'impossible' to being 'compulsory', without any attention being paid to the need to shift the effects of 'intolerable social and economic conditions' on the lives of people classed as mentally unwell (Recovery in the Bin, 2017).

Talking about one's own experience of mental illness is empowering

In contrast to a long history of silencing people with a psychiatric diagnosis, and assuming that their voices are less legitimate or reliable due to the belief that they lack competency or coherence, the stories of people who have been labelled as mentally ill are now readily available within a broad range of settings, and an effort to incorporate the voices of service users is often pivotal to mental health awareness-raising campaigns. Nevertheless, apprehensions have been raised among some mental health activists that while it is a welcome change that the perspectives of people with a lived experience of the psychiatric system are no longer being invisibilised and ignored, service user narratives are being increasingly appropriated and co-opted by mental health organisations in order to bolster conventional biomedical interests (Costa et al., 2012). For example, rather than being drawn on to contribute towards a critique of dominant professional practices as well as broader societal change, service user narratives are at times used to support conventional biomedical approaches, such as the importance of medication compliance or being willing to receive a mental illness diagnosis. Our Consumer Place (2016) notes that service users who participate in community education about mental illness can be subjected to 'coaching' processes, whereby they are encouraged to frame their experiences in ways that support, rather than challenge, dominant understandings of mental illness – for example, they are directed to affirm the importance of professional help, or the validity of a particular psychiatric label, which may not genuinely reflect their own understandings. In this way, the transformative potential of service user narratives is significantly undermined.

In summary, while anti-stigma and mental health awareness-raising efforts offer an affirmative view of people labelled as mentally ill, in contrast to a message of hopelessness and social exclusion, the silences within many of these campaigns relating to the professional and social power relations that underpin psychiatric labelling practices are of concern for human service professionals who are interested in exploring ethical ways of working across difference. While they offer simplistic ideas for advocacy, they do not recognise the privileged position held by people whose lives are not described using the language of mental illness. Drawing on the principles of critical mental health theory, it is possible to construct an alternative 'awareness-raising' campaign:

> *Peta was recently diagnosed with depression. As a result of this diagnosis, her family and friends grew more distant, and she commenced medication that made her feel drowsy. Many of us have been given mental health labels, which do not always offer the deep explanations of our experiences that we need. The most helpful thing for Peta was making space to consider the root causes of her distress – which largely originated within her life context, not her biochemistry. While some people find medication and therapy useful, often the most helpful responses are found elsewhere – it is important that people are supported to find what works best for them, rather than imposing a one-size-fits-all solution.*

This reconstruction differs from conventional anti-stigma messages in several ways, not least being that the diagnosis of mental illness is problematised as resulting in potentially devastating consequences, rather than as a straightforward pathway to effective support. Importantly, there is still space provided for people who have found medical and therapeutic support helpful, thus reflecting a commitment to multiplicity rather than the creation of an alternative, yet no less rigid, counter-narrative of mental health. In a subtle way, the reconstruction also highlights the political work that is performed by diagnostic practices, in invisibilising social contexts and emphasising individual dysfunction. Although the reframed campaign could be criticised for being significantly wordier and less straightforward than most existing efforts, arguably its less simplistic and more nuanced description of mental illness is entirely justified, as a strategy to counteract the dehumanising effects of a narrow biomedical narrative.

Reflexivity and lived experience

In developing a critique of conventional awareness-raising narratives and constructing this reimagined vignette, it is necessary that I acknowledge the position of privilege from which I write, as an academic who is currently unmarked by a mental illness diagnosis and consequently not subject to mental health intervention, either involuntary or otherwise. For this reason, it is useful for my critical analysis to be complicated by the voices of people who have been labelled as mentally ill and directly affected by a psychiatric framing of their experiences. To achieve this, I draw on a qualitative research study that explored women's experiences of being given one or more mental health diagnoses during the time of their adolescence (Tseris, 2014). Eighteen women participated in the study, each of whom had an experience of mental health service system intervention; as well, each participant had experienced child abuse perpetrated within a family context. The study utilised a semi-structured interview approach that aimed to provide an in-depth exploration of their perceptions and understandings. The study found that a majority of the participants did not have their experiences of abuse understood and validated within the mental health intervention that they received. For the most part, they reported that there were weak connections drawn between their life contexts and their emotional distress. Despite these adverse system experiences, however, most participants did not entirely reject the usefulness of psychiatric knowledges. Rather, participants had multiple responses to psychiatric discourses, and the medicalisation of their experiences through the use of diagnostic categories had both affirming and harmful effects on them. Accordingly, participants simultaneously adopted and problematised psychiatric understandings of their experiences, resulting in rich narratives about their engagement with mental health services. Two key themes within the participants' narratives will now be briefly outlined.

Order and legitimacy

Receiving a mental health diagnosis was linked by many participants to being 'not crazy', reflecting the ability of psychiatric discourses to legitimate distress by rendering it as distinct from the stigmatised identity of a person in inexplicable emotional turmoil (Walter and Rosen, 1997). The highly legitimate paradigm of psychiatry allowed participants' experience of distress to gain credibility as 'reasonable' and 'acceptable':

Interviewer: What do you think of those labels [of PTSD and Dissociative Identity Disorder] that you've been given now?

Participant: It just makes me feel like I'm not crazy.

The weight given to psychiatric labels also meant that participants experienced their distress as being 'taken seriously' as a medical condition that required attention (Kvaale et al., 2013). For example, although the following participant was sceptical about the soundness of psychiatric labels as accurate descriptors of the effects of abuse, she recognised the affirming effects that come about as a result of being given a diagnosis:

Interviewer: So what is your opinion about the different labels [panic attacks, agoraphobia, psychogenic non-epileptic seizures] that were given to you?

Participant: At the time, look I have to say there is a strand that, for me, any attention was good attention. And that it felt like people ... were concerned about me and had my best interests at heart.

All participants in the study believed that the distress that they had experienced in their lives was linked to their abuse histories, and they claimed that they would not be experiencing emotional distress to the same extent, or at all, if they had not experienced abuse. However, for the majority of participants, a medical narrative of their distress, rather than a social analysis, was the considerably more salient explanatory narrative:

Interviewer: Could you describe the relationship between feeling suicidal and the things that have happened in your life?

Participant: Yep. If I didn't go through the horrific things that I've gone through, I don't think I ever would have thought about suicide.

[Later in the interview]

Interviewer: Could I ask, in terms of the DID (Dissociative Identity Disorder) diagnosis, what does that mean for you?

Participant: It's a relief. It's a relief knowing that I'm not actually going nuts.

Within these excerpts, the perceived benefits of a diagnosis, in terms of providing validation and relief, occurred even though the social model offered significant explanatory value to the participant. Despite her statement about the social causation of her distress, a social explanation did not offer the same level of authoritative weight as a medical explanation, as medical language was the means through which the participant developed a socially acceptable narrative of her struggles. Psychiatry thus operated as a dominant discourse with the capacity to make distress 'thinkable' (Fullagar, 2009). However, participants also discussed the limited nature of psychiatric classification as adequately describing the effects of violence, and their desire for a less restrictive discursive space to articulate the complexities of their experiences.

Rigidity and meaning-making

In engaging with the psychiatric classification system, participants were faced with the rigidity of psychiatric labels. The 'price' of engaging with the legitimising discourse of diagnostic classification was a lack of autonomy offered by labels, which they viewed as highly prescriptive. For example, a participant discussed diagnostic classification as being linked to authoritative or 'expert' knowledge and the sense of security that comes from this. However, she had grave reservations about the constraints placed by diagnoses on her capacity to fully and uniquely understand and express herself:

> I think at certain time when I had labels put on, it sort of did make me feel better, that there was a name for it. But then, as well it kind of puts you in a box … A couple of years ago, I decided that I was going to disregard any label that was put on me, and just call it 'Ruth's disease'. And that way then, that box, fits me because it's my box … Sort of like, you want [a diagnosis] because then they know what they're doing, but at the same time, it sticks you in this little box.

In summary, each of the participants in the study was compelled to form a relationship to the psychiatric classification system, as a result of being involved in mental health or therapeutic services, in which the language and paradigm of psychiatry constrained the ways in which their experiences were able to be understood. At the same time, they also engaged with psychiatric discourses for the more subtle reason of attaching legitimacy to their distress, which was useful even when they were aware of the social causation of their difficulties. The costs of allowing oneself to be understood within the psychiatric paradigm, however, were often immense. Participants were left to negotiate a discourse that was rigid, deficit-based and biomedically oriented in its analysis of the origins of their distress. Therefore, the participants' engagement with psychiatry was unavoidable and yet complicated. Diagnostic classifications offered both hope and harm to participants, who positioned themselves as both accepting of and resistant to their effects.

Conclusion

A linear narrative of progress within mental health systems, whereby horrific and violent practices are said to have been replaced by 'evidence-based' and empowering responses to mental distress and difference, is an appealing and yet overly simplistic view of a more mixed picture of change over time. Critical mental health theory contests the legitimacy of a singular biomedical lens for understanding emotional distress and differences, instead highlighting the need for multiple cultural perspectives and a sociopolitical analysis of psychiatric practices. Within this chapter, critical theory has been used to problematise the notion that anti-stigma campaigns offer a straightforward pathway towards the empowerment of people who have been labelled with a mental illness. At the same time, the words of women directly affected by psychiatric labels have been used to complicate this critical analysis, by demonstrating the ways in which aligning oneself to a mental illness diagnosis can be at times an act of resistance to societal invalidation and – for the participants quoted – a subversion of the trivialisation of women's despair, particularly in relation to gender inequality and violence. In this way, claiming a mental illness identity may provide the possibility of a refuge from the unrelenting demands of neoliberal personhood and the requirement to constantly engage in rational, productive forms of citizenship – expectations that leave no room for women to express their distress and dissent towards the injustices produced by patriarchal power relations. Critical social work practice in mental health, then, requires balancing an awareness of the capacity for psychiatric labels to do harm (through invisibilising inequalities, supporting professional and corporate interests, perpetuating neoliberal ideals and so on), while at the same time advocating strongly for people labelled as mentally unwell to be able to voice their concerns, whether or not they draw on psychiatric language to do this. The tensions raised in this chapter pose particular challenges for human service workers, then, to consider how it might be possible to both engage in improving the social well-being of psychiatrised people in the short term (which could include drawing on the imperfect claims of anti-stigma efforts, recognising the usefulness of mental illness categories for some people, or acknowledging the sometimes life-saving effects of medicalised interventions for distress) and, at the same time, work towards more ambitious changes to how distress and difference can be understood outside of biomedical hegemony.

Further readings

Cohen, B.M.Z (Ed.) (2018). *Routledge International Handbook of Critical Mental Health*. Abingdon and New York: Routledge.

LeFrancois, B.A., Menzies, R.J. and Reaume, G. (Eds.) (2013). *Mad Matters: A Critical Reader in Canadian Mad Studies*. Toronto: Canadian Scholars' Press.

Poole, J.M., Jivraj, T., Arslanian, A., Bellows, K., Chiasson, S., Hakimy, H., Pasini, J. and Reid, J. (2012). Sanism, mental health and social work/education: A review and call to action. *Intersectionalities*, 1, 20–36.

References

Batyr. (2017). Batyr: Giving a Voice to the Elephant in the Room (website). http://www.batyr.com.au/

Beyond Blue (2016). Ambassadors. Beyond Blue (website). https://www.beyondblue.org.au/connect-with-others/ambassadors

BpHope (2017). 19 Inspirational Quotes to Help Cope with Bipolar Disorder. BpHope (website). http://www.bphope.com/bipolar-buzz/20-inspirational-quotes-to-help-cope-with-bipolar-disorder/

Cohen, B. (2016). *Psychiatric Hegemony: A Marxist Theory of Mental Illness*. London: Palgrave Macmillan.

Costa, L., Voronka, J., Landry, D., Reid, J., McFarlane, B., Reville, D. and Church, K. (2012). Recovering our stories: A small act of resistance. *Studies in Social Justice*, 6(1), 85–101.

Ecclestone, K. and Brunila, K. (2015). Governing emotionally vulnerable subjects and 'therapisation' of social justice. *Pedagogy, Culture & Society*, 23(4), 485–506.

Fullagar, S. (2009). Negotiating the neurochemical self: Anti-depressant consumption in women's recovery from depression. *Health: An Interdisciplinary Journal for the Social Study of Health, Illness and Medicine*, 13(3), 389–406.

Hagan, T. and Donnison, J. (1999). Social power: Some implications for the theory and practice of cognitive behaviour therapy. *Journal of Community & Applied Social Psychology*, 9(2), 119–135.

Hansson, L. (2006). Determinants of quality of life in people with severe mental illness. *Acta Psychiatrica Scandinavica*, 113(s429), 46–50.

Harper, D. and Speed, E. (2012). Uncovering recovery: The resistible rise of recovery and resilience. *Studies in Social Justice*, 6(1), 9–25.

Imagine Thriving (2017). Common Mental Illnesses A–Z. Imagine Thriving (website). http://www.imaginethriving.org/mental-illnesses/

Kvaale, E.P., Gottdiener, W.H. and Haslam, N. (2013). Biogenetic explanations and stigma: A meta-analytic review of associations among laypeople. *Social Science and Medicine*, 96, 95–103.

LeFrancois, B.A., Menzies, R.J. and Reaume, G. (Eds.) (2013). *Mad Matters: A Critical Reader in Canadian Mad Studies*. Toronto: Canadian Scholars' Press.

Liegghio, M. (2013). A denial of being: Psychiatrization as epistemic violence. In B.A. LeFrancois, R. Menzies and G. Reaume (Eds.), *Mad Matters: A Critical Reader in Canadian Mad Studies* (pp. 122–139). Toronto: Canadian Scholars' Press.

Martin, J. (2013). Accredited mental health social work in Australia: A reality check. *Australian Social Work*, 66(2), 279–296.

McWade, B., Milton, D. and Beresford, P. (2015). Mad studies and neurodiversity: A dialogue. *Disability & Society*, 30(2), 305–309.

Mental Health Coordinating Council (2013). *Recovery Oriented Language Guide*. http://mob.mhcc.org.au/media/5902/mhcc-recovery-oriented-language-guide-final-web.pdf

MindFreedom (2012). *Hope in Recovery Health Care Survey Executive Summary*. http://igotbetter.org/campaign/i-got-better/learnings/igb-exc-sum

Moncrieff, J. (2008). Neoliberalism and biopsychiatry: A marriage of convenience. In C.I. Cohen and S. Timini (Eds.), *Liberatory Psychiatry: Philosophy, Politics and Mental Health* (pp. 235–256). New York: Cambridge University Press.

NoStigmas (2017). The NoStigmas Project. NoStigmas (website). https://nostigmas.org/nostigmas-project/

One Door Mental Health (2017). Advocacy. One Door Mental Health (website). http://www.onedoor.org.au/advocacy

Our Consumer Place (2016). *Pluck, Acceptance, Defiance and Fortitude: Telling Mental Illness Stories to Change the World*. Melbourne: Our Community Pty. http://www.ourcommunity.com.au/files/ocp-stories2016.pdf

Recovery in the Bin (2017). RITB – 20 Key Principles. Recovery in the Bin (website). https://recoveryinthebin.org/recovery-in-the-bin-19-principless/

Runswick-Cole, K. (2014). 'Us' and 'them': The limits and possibilities of a 'politics of neurodiversity' in neoliberal times. *Disability & Society*, 29(7), 1117–1129.

Sane Australia (2017). Fact vs myth: Mental illness basics. Fact Sheet. https://www.sane.org/mental-health-and-illness/facts-and-guides/fvm-mental-illness-basics

Sawyer, A. (2008). Risk and new exclusions in community mental health practice. *Australian Social Work*, 61(4), 327–341.

Sayce, L. (1998). Stigma, discrimination and social exclusion: What's in a word? *Journal of Mental Health*, 7(4), 331–343.

Scull, A. (2015). *Madness in Civilisation: A Cultural History of Insanity, from the Bible to Freud, from the Madhouse to Modern Medicine*. London: Thames & Hudson.

Summerfield, D. (2012). Afterword: Against 'global mental health'. *Transcultural Psychiatry*, 49(3–4), 519–530.

Time to Change (2017). Be in your mate's corner. Time to Change (website). https://www.time-to-change.org.uk/what-you-should-know/be-your-mates-corner

Tseris, E. (2014). *Diagnosing Distress? Psychiatric and Therapeutic Constructions of 'Traumatised' Young Women*. Sydney: University of Sydney.

US Department of Health and Human Services (2017). *Recovery Is Possible*. https://www.mentalhealth.gov/basics/recovery/index.html

Ussher, J.M. (2011). *The Madness of Women*. East Sussex: Routledge.

Walter, G. and Rosen, A. (1997). Psychiatric stigma and the role of the psychiatrist. *Australasian Psychiatry*, 5(2), 72–74.

WayAhead (2016). Help! It's out there. WayAhead (website). https://wayahead.org.au/download/help-its-out-there/?wpdmdl=4101

12
Supported Employment and Social Inclusion: An Analysis from the Perspective of People with Intellectual Disabilities

Barbara Soares e Madureira

I acknowledge the Gadigal people of the Eora nation as the Traditional Custodians of the land where this project was written; and I pay my respects to the Elders both past and present.

Introduction

A growing literature explores and problematises the social inclusion of people with disabilities. This chapter draws on data collected for a thesis of Master of Social Work in the University of Sydney. The data was collected in February 2017. The purpose of the research was to investigate supported employment for people with intellectual disability in order to explore whether this form of employment promoted social inclusion, particularly forming social relations and undertaking community participation.

The aim of this research was to demonstrate the importance of policies aimed at the social inclusion of people with intellectual disability in the labour force and in the community. The objective of the research was to gain insight into how people with intellectual disability perceive work and employment through their own experience and to provide a place in which their voices could be heard on this complex set of issues. The data showed that people with intellectual disabilities interviewed for this study placed particular attention on the number and kinds of meaningful relationships with work friends in the workplace and outside; the tasks performed at work; the means of transportation available to get them to and from work; relationships with carers; and training and opportunity for equal remuneration. These themes paint a complex picture of supported employment and suggest that, while it may provide employment opportunities for people with intellectual disabilities, it does so in a way that fails to address their segregation from mainstream society and does little to provide real inclusion. 'This is another manifestation of the conceptual limitations of the single-issue analyses that intersectionality challenges' (Rimmerman, 2012, p. 149). People with disabilities can experience many ways of discrimination, and addressing only one of them is not sufficient for a more inclusive society.

Work

This research project was concerned with the social aspects of work, particularly the social relationships built as a result of work and employment, and the ways that these relationships fold people into wider community or leave them in small enclaves outside of it. This study started with the assumption that work is central to most people's sense of social inclusion and value; therefore it is an important aspect of social inclusion for all people, including those with intellectual disabilities. Grint (1998, p. 1) argues that work 'has often been taken as a symbol of personal value'.

Work cannot be separated from the other important spaces of meaning in neoliberal society: 'The spheres of work, employment and home are all necessarily intertwined and to separate them as if they could exist independently is to misconceive the complex reality of work and misunderstand the significance of the relationships which it embodies' (Grint, 1998, p. 2).

Underscoring its centrality and importance in modern life, and particularly within neoliberalism, with its emphasis on individualism and labour market attachment, the right to work is encoded within bills of rights in many countries. Some of these bills are focused exclusively on labour market or employment relations, while others focus on issues of equity and inclusion. For example, employment is seen as a fundamental right accordingly with the Australian Human Rights Commission (AHRC, 2016).

Disability as difference

The National Disability Insurance Agency, the agency in Australia charged with the responsibility to implement the National Disability Insurance Scheme (NDIS), defines disability as it is described by the United Nations Convention on the Rights of Persons with Disabilities (CRPD) as: 'Persons with disabilities include those who have long-term physical, mental, intellectual or sensory impairments which in interaction with various barriers may hinder their full and effective participation in society on an equal basis with others.' These definitions fit with the medical model of disability. As Stanley notes: 'This model sees disability as being about impairment and focuses on addressing the impairment or the consequences of the impairment' (Stanley, 2005, p. 31). In contrast, disability researchers and advocates have developed a definition of disability that does not focus only on the impairment of a person; it takes into consideration the environmental factors. Known as the social model of disability, this approach places the emphasis on the ways that society marginalises people with disabilities and notes that their greatest disability may be society itself (Connell, 2014). In Australia, for legal reasons, the medical model of disability is the most widely used. This reflects the neoliberal drift of the state away from social and human rights and towards models that provide justification for marginalising those less able to compete vigorously in the labour market. 'The state is a key to the power of medical models: it has been the provider of services and has defined or denied rights' (Connell, 2014, p. 10).

In recent studies, the Australian Bureau of Statistics (ABS) reported that in Australia there were more than 4.3 million people with disabilities, representing 18.3% of the population (ABS, 2015). The labour force participation for people with disability in working age is only 53.4% (ABS, 2015), compared with the rate of 82.5% for those of working age without disabilities (ABS, 2015). In the past, people with disabilities were outside of the workforce. In recent days, policies around employment for people with disabilities have been implemented aimed at facilitating social inclusion. As the Human Right Commission notes: 'There are many factors which impact on how a person with disability is able to live, participate in society and realise their potential. Employment is one factor' (Australian Human Rights Commission, 2016, p. 38).

Supported employment

In Australia, one option for employment for people with disabilities is open employment in a workplace that does not provide supports of any kind. The other option is supported employment in Australian Disability Enterprises (ADE). These are not-for-profit organisations that provide supported employment for more than 20,000 people with disability across Australia (www.ade.org.au). Supported employment is available to those who meet criteria as 'disabled'. Employees, or people with disabilities, are hired and work with the assistance of a support worker. ADEs are funded by the Australian government, provide employment only to people with disabilities and are one of the major government disability employment initiatives (Australian Human Rights Commission, 2016, p. 204).

Supported employees are paid a pro rata wage rate (a percentage of the full rate). The rationale for this lower wage is because, as supported employees, people with disabilities are paid a proportion of a full, legal wage because their disability is assumed to restrict their productive capacity (www.ades.com.au). The largest portion of people with disabilities working in supported employment earn around AUD$3 per hour, in contrast to the minimum wage, which, in Australia in 2017, is $17.70 per hour, a difference of $14.70 per hour.

However, employment for people with disabilities is not only beneficial for economic purposes and economic participation. People with disabilities who are entirely outside the labour market are more prone to social isolation (Stanley, 2005). Combating isolation is seen as a major achievement of the ADEs: 'Having a vision for disabled people that includes recognition of the fact that creating greater opportunities for disabled people to work is a social justice issue and success here will impact on success in other areas' (Stanley, 2005, p. 37).

Social inclusion

Social inclusion is a broad concept that refers not only to economic participation. In order to be included a person must be able to access community and services, to have a job, to be an informed member of the public, to have friends and networks; and to be able to participate in the civic society (Chanan, 2000, p. 203). In contrast, social exclusion is a complex concept; Fawcett and colleagues (2010) argue that 'social exclusion captures the ways in which some groups and individuals are excluded from the ordinary living patterns, customs and activities of the broader community' (p. 160).

Social inclusion is a complex domain – difficult to be wholly achieved. It is very possible that some minority groups may achieve social inclusion in one sphere but will not in another, leaving full social justice unrealised. Employment has been seen as a central plank in full social inclusion for many groups, including people with intellectual disabilities as Riddel and Banks (2005) argue: 'Employment is an important factor that impacts the inclusion for people with disabilities in society' (p. 5; see also Australian Human Rights Commission, 2016, p. 38).

Though employment and work are not exclusively responsible for social inclusion, integrating people with intellectual disability in the labour force can increase their participation in other spheres as well, such as community participation and relationships. Other aspects of participation often overlap with employment. For example, Verdonschot and colleagues (2009) define community participation in terms of 'ability to engage in domestic life, interpersonal relationships, education, work and employment, and community, civic and social life'. Often, it is not only access to employment, education or other aspects of participation that prevent social inclusion, discrimination also plays an important role. 'Discrimination takes the form of continuing segregation and exclusion – community care policies notwithstanding. It has deep historical roots – and has still not, at root, been challenged' (Sayce, 1998, p. 334).

The purpose of this study was to obtain insights from people with intellectual disabilities working in ADEs regarding how this employment impacted their experience of social inclusion. It was hoped that the data from this study would be beneficial for the development of new policies around employment for people with intellectual disabilities, reduce discrimination and increase inclusion. It was also hoped that the findings might encourage disability services to review strategies for more inclusive employment experiences for people with disabilities.

Method

The purpose of this qualitative and emancipatory research was to understand how the participants experienced social participation in the context of paid, supported employment. This was done in order to more clearly understand possible links between paid employment in supportive environments and full social inclusion. As Alston and Bowles (2012) argue: 'Qualitative researchers are less interested in recognizing patterns of behavior, attitude or other phenomena than they are in understanding social reality' (p. 81). Alston and Bowles (2012) argue further that 'the job of the emancipatory researcher is to uncover the myths, beliefs and social constructions that contribute to the continuation of the status quo, in order to reveal how power relations are really operating to control the powerless' (p. 18).

The research participants in this study were people with intellectual disabilities who worked in ADEs for at least two years; and were in the age bracket of 18 to 65 years old. The qualitative semi-structured interviews adopted a very conversational style. This facilitated the participation of people with intellectual disabilities through the use of open-ended questions that could be reworded in order to provide greater clarity and participation. This interview strategy was consistent with Fortune's (2013) observation that, 'For researchers, one purpose of interviewing others it to understand someone else's life experiences from his/her point of view' (p. 213).

This flexibility fits well with semi-structured interviewing principles: 'Semi structured interviews allow the interviewer to explore additional information that the respondent has raised, to ask other questions, or to follow up issues that were not originally included in the interview schedule' (Alston and Bowles, 2012, p. 142).

All thirteen participants interviewed for this project could communicate verbally and most had a mild intellectual disability. The researcher interviewed only people with intellectual disabilities because other people such as family, support workers and other representatives usually represent this group and speak on their behalf. This research sought to give voice to people with disabilities to talk about their own experiences.

The interviews were audio recorded and transcribed verbatim; they were not edited to ensure that the data, voice of the participants and meanings were preserved. Aliases were provided by the researcher to protect confidentiality. The Ethics Committee of the University of Sydney approved this research. All participants were capable of signing the consent form for themselves. Data analysis identified five aspects of social inclusion which are discussed in the sections that follow: work, social relations with friends and family, personal and social changes, training at work and community participation.

The experience of work

Interestingly, all participants stated that they were satisfied that they are working. The data shows that before gaining employment some participants stayed at home with few outside activities, and noted that they preferred working. Jesse notes: 'I felt more happier now that I am coming to work, I am not home wasting electricity going on computer or on TV.' Similarly, Laura asserts: 'there is something to do, if you are at home for 4 or 8 hours a day you get bored. It is worth coming out and experience some life and doing something for yourself and not just for others as well.'

Relationships

When asked what they liked about being at work, participants emphasised the importance of having friends and having something to do outside the house. Nick noted that he liked 'Just being around my friends. My friends from work.' Laura added that work was important for her self-worth and to learn new skills: 'Basically I feel like I am doing something for myself as well and also meeting a lot of nice people and socialising and also doing the job, learning new skills on the workplace.' All the participants said that they socialised and made friends at work. For some of them, the workplace was the only place where socialising happened.

Most respondents explained that they only see these friends at work or at the social outings promoted by work; never outside of work. The data seems to show that, while research participants had built relationships that were important to them, by occurring exclusively within the workplace, they were conditional or sheltered friendships. Conditional social interaction exists when relationships are only formed on the condition that participants are physically at work or involved in some activity organised by the workplace (Haring, 1991). In conditional social interaction, there are no spontaneous or planned actions undertaken to see these friends in other places, such as at home or in the community. As Simon reported, regarding his friends at work, 'Here they are just people that I chat to at work. They are friends but I don't hang out with them.'

The ADE workplace promoted a kind of friendship based in the environment that occurred because people are working together, but there was no further development or meaning in these relationships beyond the workplace. Yet, disturbingly, these relationships were probably the most meaningful relationships that the participants have created outside their homes and their families, within their lifetime. Support workers and manager were never cited as friends in the data, signalling the market-basis to these relationships.

In other words, research participants were socially included because they had friends at work, namely within the ADEs, but they were still segregated from the outside world. On the other side of the coin, people without disabilities also continue to have little or no contact with people with disabilities, which perpetuates social exclusion and segregation. The inability to fully include people with disabilities promotes a society with little capacity to work across difference or to build relationships and understanding across or about differences such as intellectual disabilities.

A few participants had friends from other disability projects, programs or their church. For example, Simon told me: 'Most of my friends are from church and I just see them at the church.' Spencer noted that he had a number of friends and contacts from programs and organised activities: 'Basically over the years I have done a lot of community programs, community access, life skills.'

Personal and social changes as a result of employment

Work was felt to improve the social and interpersonal skills of supported employees. Personal skills and confidence are important qualities for further opportunities in employment and in other aspects of social life. Nicole, for example, who had worked at the same ADE for 15 years noted: 'When I first started here I had hardly any friends, like all shy, wouldn't talk. I used to be quiet, I never spoke. Now I am a lot more confident.'

Training and further opportunities for employment

Supported employment and ADEs fail to bridge unemployment and other kinds of employment, such as open employment. Though the ADEs provide training, the training mostly related to the tasks that employees performed at work, such as work health and safety. There was very limited training available for transferable skills, further education and other job opportunities.

When asked about what employees did in their job, the respondents almost always described the tasks that they perform. They noted that the activities they performed at work were not meaningful tasks, and had low levels of autonomy and responsibility. Justin said: 'I did a couple of courses. Cleaning and lifting boxes.' Similarly, when asked what participants learned at work most would say they have learned the tasks they do as part of the job. As Walter asserted: 'I just learned how to do my job.'

Working in an environment with people with different needs and types of learning often promotes inclusion, understanding and respect. Jesse confirmed that he learned some tasks at work but he also learned how to work with other people with disabilities: 'I've learned how to do a good job, I was learning how not ever say anything when I am cleaning because someone with a disability could pay a contribution to what they have done, I am learning not to ever be judging.'

Community participation

Salary

When asked about their salary, most participants said they know how much they earn. However, for all of them, unlike the non-disabled community, improving their economic situation was not the reason why they were working. The respondents understood that money was a crucial factor in life; yet most of them were not responsible for looking after their own money and had very little knowledge or interest in it. Some of them said the salary was not much, but they never said it was unfair pay though, ironically, the low pay is often seen by outside groups as deeply inequitable and unjust. Nicole noted, regarding her wages: 'It goes into my account. My mum pays the bills and I pay my own bills. I don't know, do you think it is enough?'

People with disabilities working in supported employment in Australia earn around $3 per hour. If the salary is higher than a certain amount per week, they are not entitled to a disability pension. This places people with disabilities in a difficult position. As they have very little choice and opportunities, a great number are not in the workforce and those who are generally accept the idea that they do not make much, in part, as a way to ensure that their pensions are not jeopardised.

Carers

Mothers were the main caregiver for most of the participants and employment was the main disability service and form of socially inclusion undertaken by most of the respondents. Spencer is typical of many of the research participants: 'I've got my mum, which is my full-time carer.'

Public transport

All the participants are able to use public transport. Transportation was not seen as an obstacle preventing supported employees from participating more actively in the community. Spencer, for example, responded: 'Yes, I catch public transport by myself.'

Open employment

Some of the participants had worked in open employment for a period. All of them declared that it was a difficult experience and they did not feel supported in open employment, and found it discouraging to face the difficulties of being different. Laura said that she felt stressed when working in open employment and she liked supported employment because she felt more accepted, saying she found open employment 'A bit more stressful. I found this employment because they accept the disability, it makes easier and less stressful, so they are totally dedicated to help.'

In short, it would seem that open employment without the right support can be segregating, exclusionary and not very attractive for people with disabilities.

Discussion and conclusion

The theme of this book is working across difference and inequity. The data analysed in this chapter suggests that ADEs are not a fully successful way to work across difference. Rather than reduce inequity and increase social inclusion, they cocoon people with intellectual disabilities in a sheltered, supported, segregated experience that meets some of their needs for friendship and social interaction. The analysis presented here suggests that within ADEs there is an increase in social inclusion for people with intellectual disabilities, even if this experience of social inclusion remains segregated.

Wistow and Schneider (2003) interviewed 30 people with disabilities in supported employment in the United Kingdom. Supported employment is a situation in which a person with disability works in open employment with a support worker. The researchers found that 'the picture of social inclusion was variable, lending further support to the view that physical integration does not necessarily mean social integration' (Wistow and Schneider, 2003, p. 173).

In this research, I discovered much the same situation. People with disabilities felt part of a group defined by the physical environment of their work, but at the same time they were excluded from larger society. As noted earlier: 'It is entirely possible to live a fully integrated lifestyle, and yet be maximally socially segregated' (Haring, 1991, p. 195). The participants in this research have an integrated lifestyle, they are mobile and use public transport, they have workplace and family relationships, they have a social life and go to work, but all these activities happen within their own segregated environment.

While ADEs are not entirely failing, other measures are necessary to enable more inclusive forms of social interaction. Relationships developed in the ADEs are, probably, the most important in the participants' lives outside of their home environment. However, the ADEs are the condition for these friendships; other interactions with other members of the community and in other settings are very limited. As Hall (2009) notes: 'Many people with disabilities have limited friendships that are constrained to the settings that initiate them' (p. 169).

The main reason for social exclusion seems to be that the labour market, community and society are not prepared and open to live in a fully integrated way with difference, in this case intellectual disability. Sadly, supported employment settings, or day programs and services especially designed for people with disabilities, segregate people with disabilities and reinforce their differences while purporting to fully integrate people.

One of the participants in my study identified the ongoing stigma around disability in larger society and said that non-disabled people should learn about people with disabilities. An inclusive society needs to learn and be educated about difference. It needs to encounter and embrace difference on an everyday basis, including in the workplace, which claims such a central place in social life in all countries. This suggests further that more decisive action is required for the removal of social and segregational barriers for people with disabilities, to discourage segregation in all its forms and to fully realise social inclusion for people with disabilities in the workforce and beyond.

The term 'segregated' social inclusion was chosen by the researcher to describe the form of inclusion found in ADEs. This term was chosen after some consideration about two other terms: 'sheltered' or 'conditional' social inclusion. 'Sheltered' social inclusion describes a social inclusion generated in a sheltered workplace and implies a level of safety and seclusion alongside an underlying theme of paternalism. 'Conditional' social inclusion describes a social inclusion where the condition is to be physically in the same place – therefore, is a social inclusion that only happens when that particular condition is met. It suggests a benign situation in which exclusion can be remedied by meeting particular, apolitical conditions rather than recognising that exclusion is a painful experience requiring social and political remedies. 'Segregated' was chosen because the place or the ADEs are not the cause for this incomplete social inclusion; they are the consequence of a society that segregates, excludes, marginalises and exploits when it could create conditions for a group to be fully included. It is important to note that the data collected for this project shows that, for the research participants, even the low level of inclusion they have in ADEs is still felt to be very valuable. ADEs can play an important role in increasing training opportunities, working as preparation for open employment, a service where people with disabilities learn new social, interpersonal and professional skills to find other employment in the future. However, as current policy and practice stands, ADEs are an inadequate response to working across difference and addressing inequities.

The social model of disability highlights that the way society is organised is discriminatory and creates disability and, therefore, far-reaching social policies are needed in order to produce much needed change. Of particular importance are social policies with the objective to change employment opportunities to a more inclusive approach. There are examples of new approaches to employment for people with disabilities in the United Kingdom and United States, namely supported employment in open employment, in which people with disabilities have a support person while working in open employment (Rimmerman, 2012, p. 93).

Other countries such as Japan and Germany use quota employment policies (Rimmerman, 2012). The goals of quotas or affirmative action are to eliminate systemic discrimination, achieve social justice and empower groups that are traditionally socially, politically and economically disadvantaged (Kwok and Tam, 2003, p. 58). The quota system implies that an employer needs to hire a certain percentage of employees with disabilities. Advocates in Australia call for a more open debate about quotas for people with disabilities in the public service (Byrne, 2017).

We need a change in social policies around employment for people with disabilities in order to have more social cohesion and equality. More research is required regarding how to make employment fully inclusive and it is essential that this research includes the voices of people with disabilities. Even in research people with disabilities are usually represented by other people such as guardians or representatives. The objective of this research was to value the perspective of this group who too frequently has little choice and few opportunities. It seems fitting that this project gives the final word to a person with disabilities who captures the feelings of many in the quote below:

> I just want to say that people need to learn about us. They are not all bad, there are really good ones too, but because of the stigma associated with it (disability), it maybe sounds bad, but we are not really that bad. (Laura)

Further readings

Hills, J., Legrand, J. and Piachaud, D. (Ed.) (2002). *Understanding Social Exclusion.* Oxford and New York: Oxford University Press.
Meekosha, H. and Soldatic, K. (Ed.) (2014). *The Global Politics of Impairment and Disability: Processes and Embodiments.* Abingdon: Routledge.
Roulstone, A. and Barnes, C. (Ed.) (2005). *Working Futures? Disabled People, Policy and Social Inclusion.* Bristol: Policy Press.

References

ABS (Australian Bureau of Statistics) (2015). *Disability, Ageing and Carers First Results (Cat. No. 4430.0.001).* Canberra, Australia: ABS.
Alston, M. and Bowles, W. (2012). *Research for Social Workers: An Introduction to Methods*, 3rd Edition. Australia: Allen & Unwin.

Australian Human Rights Commission (2016). *Willing to Work: National Inquiry into Employment Discrimination against Older Australians and Australians with Disability (AHRC)*. Sydney: Australian Human Rights Commission.

Byrne, B. (2017). Advocates call for quotas to hire people with disabilities in the workplace. *Herald Sun*, 9 February. http://www.heraldsun.com.au/leader/news/advocates-call-for-quota-to-hire-people-with-disabilities-in-the-workplace/news-story/0c20671c59146a222f0ffbd924f4ad4c

Chanan, C. (2000). Community responses to social exclusion. In J. Percy-Smith (Ed.), *Policy Responses to Social Exclusion Towards Inclusion?* (pp. 201–215). Philadelphia, PA: Open University Press.

Connell, R. (2014). Bodies and disability: Re-thinking concepts. In H. Meekosha and K. Soldatic (Eds.), *The Global Politics of Impairment and Disability. Processes and Embodiments* (pp. 1369–1382). Abingdon: Routledge.

Fawcett, B., Goodwin, S., Meagher, G. and Phillips, R. (2010). *Social Policy for Social Change*. South Yarra: Palgrave.

Fortune, A.E.R.W.J. (2013). *Qualitative Research in Social Work*. New York: Columbia University Press.

Grint, K. (1998). *The Sociology of Work: An Introduction*. Cambridge: Polity Press.

Hall, S.A. (2009). The social inclusion of people with disabilities: A qualitative meta-analysis. *Journal of Ethnographic & Qualitative Research*, 3, 162–173.

Haring, T.G. (1991). Social relationships. In L.H. Meyer, C. Perk and L. Brown (Eds.), *Critical Issues in the Lives of People with Severe Disabilities* (pp. 195–217). Baltimore: Paul H. Brookes Publishing.

Riddel, S. and Banks, P. (2005). Disabled people, employment and the work preparation programme. In A. Roulstone and C. Barnes (Eds.), *Working Futures? Disabled People, Policy and Social Inclusion* (pp. 59–73). Bristol: Policy Press.

Rimmerman, A. (2012). *Social Inclusion of People with Disabilities: National and International Perspectives*. Cambridge: Cambridge University Press.

Sayce, L. (1998). Stigma, discrimination and social exclusion: What's in a word? *Journal of Mental Health*, 7(4), 331–343.

Stanley, K. (2005). The missing million: The challenges of employing more disabled people. In A. Roulstone and C. Barnes (Eds.), *Working Futures? Disabled People, Policy and Social Inclusion* (pp. 29–41). Bristol: Policy Press.

Verdonschot, M.M.L., De Witte, L.P., Reichrath, E., Buntinx, W.H.E. and Curfs, L.M.G. (2009). Community participation of people with an intellectual disability: A review of empirical findings. *Journal of Intellectual Disability Research*, 53, 303–318, https://doi.org/10.1111/j.1365-2788.2008.01144.x

Wistow, R. and Schneider, J. (2003). Users' views on supported employment and social inclusion: A qualitative study of 30 people in work. *British Journal of Learning Disabilities*, 31, 166–173, https://doi.org/10.1111/j.1468-3156.2003.00253.x

PART FIVE
POLICY WORK ACROSS DIFFERENCE

13

Feminist Gains Lost: Public Policy and the 'Genericising' of Women Survivors of Domestic Violence

Susan Heward-Belle

I acknowledge the Traditional Owners and Custodians of this ancient land on which I write this chapter and pay my respects to Aboriginal and Torres Strait Islander elders, past, present and emerging. It is impossible to write about violence against women and children without acknowledging the devastating impact of colonisation and successive oppressive public policies that have created and compounded private and collective pain. I also pay my respects to the many dignified and strong women – Indigenous and non-Indigenous – who have engaged in the struggle to redress social injustice in all of its forms; many of their voices can be heard in this chapter.

Introduction

Feminist activists and policy advocates in Australia have been highly successful politicising the distinctive needs of women and have advocated for gendered policy analyses of a wide range of issues. This kind of work has led to the development of a raft of new policies and services for women – often referred to as women's policies and women's services. One of the areas where feminist policy development has been key to improving the lives of women has been in relation to gender-based violence, and Australian feminists, or 'femocrats' (Sawer, 2007), were pioneers in establishing policies that assured services and resources were made available to survivors of domestic violence.

This chapter demonstrates how feminist perspectives about the specificities of women's experiences can be expunged from key areas of public policy through policy reforms. It serves as a cautionary tale and illustrates the way the productive politicisation of difference – in this case the differential needs and experiences of women and children escaping domestic violence – can be depoliticised and 'genericised'. Using the New South Wales (NSW) government's recent homelessness policy package 'Going Home, Staying Home' (GHSH) as a case study, it is argued that this has occurred through a process of constructing women and children seeking refuge from violent men as 'homeless' or at risk of becoming 'homeless'. I suggest that by categorising survivors seeking refuge from domestic violence as among the ranks of the general homeless, their needs and experiences have effectively been 'genericised' – framed as the same as, or similar to – other members of the 'homeless' population. As a result, the needs of domestic violence survivors have become primarily reduced to considerations about residential and tenancy status. Further, by producing survivors as 'homeless' – or in need of housing – differences between people are institutionally rejected (Lorde, 2012) and the feminist analysis of domestic violence is de-gendered and effectively neutralised.

The Australian example discussed in this chapter reflects broader shifts away from gendered policy and program development. A range of authors have linked these changes to neoliberalism. For example, Rimmer and Sawer (2016) suggest that, in a departure from previous policy directions, contemporary Australian policy based on neoliberalism has avoided a systemic gender analysis. Teghtsoonian and Chappell (2008) show how contemporary neoliberal policy has emphasised mainstreaming, the privileging of individualism and marketised relationships that challenge constructions of women as a disadvantaged group. These kinds of changes have resulted in the development of non-specific policies and service provision. This turn is not in keeping with recommendations of the United Nations, which caution against developing mainstream violence prevention and intervention plans, programs and services because they fail to acknowledge intersectional differences and produce non-specific services (Australian Human Rights Commission, 2012). Of particular relevance to this study is the mainstreaming of housing and homelessness policies and the concern that mainstreaming in this area fails to frame women's and children's experience of homelessness as a symptom of the problem of male violence (Nunan, 2009). In this chapter, I argue that the recent GHSH policy is an example par excellence of policy makers being gender-blind and reflects the general silencing in policy about the continuation of inequality based primarily but not only on gender in Australia. This chapter will also demonstrate how gender inequality intersects with other systems of power and oppression linked with women's social locations, including but not limited to racism, classism and ableism (Almedia and Lockard, 2005).

Drawing on research that obtained the first-hand accounts of 15 women's refuge workers in the state of NSW, this chapter will explore their perceptions of the impact of the GHSH policy on their ability to deliver holistic, women-centred services to women and children experiencing domestic violence. Specifically, this chapter presents findings regarding the key problems that specialist women's domestic violence workers identify as resulting from the 'genericising' of domestic violence policy. It also explores workers' perceptions of the impact of this policy on their work practice and job satisfaction.

Domestic violence, homelessness and housing

One in four Australian women over the age of 15 have experienced physical or sexualised violence by an intimate partner since the age of 15 years, and 60% of women survivors reported that they had children in their care when they had experienced domestic violence (Australian Bureau of Statistics, 2012).

Despite the fact that numerous enquiries, Royal Commissions, governmental reports and studies have highlighted the centrality of securing safe and affordable housing in order to leave violent and controlling men (Bland and Shallcross, 2015; Chung et al., 2000; State of NSW, 2008; State of Victoria, 2016), there remains a significant undersupply of affordable and safe housing and specialist women's domestic violence refuges. In 2007, the NSW Wood Royal Commission into the child protection system highlighted the issue, stating that 'affordable, accessible and liveable housing is essential for families, particularly women and children escaping violence. Its provision is a necessary component of a universal response to supporting families and ensuring child safety' (State of NSW, 2008, p. 259). The limited availability of refuge accommodation and temporary housing for women escaping violent men continues to be identified as a key concern; for example, it is linked to domestic homicide in the most recent report of the NSW Domestic Death Review Team (2017).

Moreover, there is a large body of evidence that demonstrates that, in order to meet survivors' housing needs, responses need to attend to the specificities of women's lives and the perpetrator's pattern of violence and control. A differentiated response includes the provision of a range of crisis refuges, transitional and long-term housing options including 'safe at home' programs, which aim to enable survivors of domestic violence to reside safely in their homes through a range of security and support strategies.

Feminist activism and the women's refuge movement

Women's refuge workers and feminist activists have long argued that women and children 'journeying away' (State of Victoria, 2004) from domestic violence have specific needs that extend beyond residential concerns. Historically, women's refuges were established to provide a safe space for women and children to escape men's violence. They were staffed by women and based within a feminist politics that understood domestic violence through a gender-based analysis that attended to the institutionalised subordination of women. Women's refuges were initially established as feminist, community-based collectives.

Government-funded women's refuges and programs did not emerge until the 1980s (Sawer, 2007). In more recent times, women's refuges have continued to provide a place of safety for women and children but their remit has expanded and their work has become more specialised – including assisting women to navigate a complex legal and service system. Generalist homelessness services, on the other hand, have been more focused on the housing component of homelessness and particularly on addressing long-term homelessness.

The provision of women's refuges as an effective intervention is supported by evidence. For example, a meta-analysis of 17 international studies examined the effectiveness of women's refuges and concluded that they play a critical role in violence prevention and intervention efforts (Sullivan, 2012). Given that women are at increased risk of severe violence and homicide when they leave violent and controlling male partners (Campbell et al., 2003), specialist women's refuges effectively play a crucial role in homicide prevention. For example, specialist refuge workers establish safety plans with women and children; provide trauma-informed emotional support and counselling; facilitate women's access to legal remedies to redress domestic violence; raise community awareness of domestic violence; facilitate women's access to the labour market; assist women to become financially independent; and provide a safe place for women and children to join with others who have shared experiences (Sullivan, 2012). In short, women's refuges offer a broad spectrum of services over and above the provision of a bed. Refuge workers have specialist knowledge and skills that enable women and children to navigate a complex legal and service system in order to help them journey away from domestic violence. The support and services they provide are also vital to domestic homicide prevention and intervention efforts (NSW Domestic Violence Death Review Team, 2017).

The policy context

At the international level, both violence against women and children and homelessness related to gender-based violence are considered human rights violations. Australia has obligations as a signatory nation that has ratified a number of United Nations Conventions that pertain to state obligations in relation to ensuring that women and children live free from violence and have access to safe housing. Relevant conventions include United Nations Convention on the Rights of the Child (United Nations, 1989); the International Covenant on Civil and Political Rights and the International Covenant on Economic, Social and Cultural Rights. Despite the existence of international conventions, Chung and colleagues (2000) argue that women and children survivors of domestic violence are often unprotected despite the existence of a human rights framework that constructs them as full citizens with human rights.

A key moment in the positioning of survivors of domestic violence within a homelessness discourse can be found in the Australian Government white paper, *The Road Home: A National Approach to Homelessness* (Dept. of Families, 2008). This policy provided the framework for government policy and funding to address homelessness, proposed a plan to reorient service delivery and funding in order to prevent homelessness, and prioritised the development and expansion of programs that aimed to remove violent perpetrators from the home. Breckenridge and colleagues (2016) argue that the shortage of specialist domestic violence refuges combined with the fact that many women cannot access specialist domestic violence services led to an increased call for 'safe at home' programs. These programs have the potential to address the additional social and economic disadvantage that women and children face when they have to leave their home. Philosophically, they offer a more socially just response – shifting the burden from the survivor to the perpetrator to leave the home.

For example, 'Stay at home' programs such as 'Staying Home, Leaving Violence' in NSW have as their primary aim the goal of ensuring that women and/or children can remain in independent accommodation, in either their own or another home. 'Stay at home' programs are housing-focused but can also provide case management, including risk assessment, safety planning and support (Breckenridge et al., 2016). Tually and colleagues (2008) argue that there is not a single solution to domestic violence-related homelessness because of the diversity of women's and children's identities and experiences. 'Safe at home' programs thus do not preclude the need for specialist domestic violence homelessness services such as refuges.

In NSW, support for domestic violence survivors at risk of homelessness has been predominantly provided through the state government's homelessness service system (Murray, 2007). Since 1985, women's refuges for survivors of domestic violence have been government-funded through a federal/state partnership called the Supported Accommodation Assistance Program, which was Australia's major policy response to homelessness for more than two decades (Bullen, 2009). Over this period, notwithstanding political and policy response changes to domestic violence, there was overall support for the provision of specialist domestic violence support through women's refuges.

The Going Home, Staying Home (GHSH) 'reform'

Between 2012 and 2014, the NSW government embarked on an unprecedented and large-scale overhaul of the funding and service provision of specialist homelessness services known as the 'Going Home, Staying Home' (GHSH) reform. The stated goals of the reform were to 'simplify access to specialist housing; balance the provision of early intervention, crisis and post crisis support and to centralize the structure of service provision' (KPMG, 2015). New 'service packages' delivering homelessness services to men, women, children and families were developed and there was a stated objective to consolidate and rationalise services across the state according to need, as determined by a 'resource allocation model' developed by a private consulting company, Deloittes Access Economics. The entire homelessness budget was recommissioned and service packages were advertised, with services having to compete against each other through a competitive tendering process. Small organisations delivering specialised services – like most women's domestic violence refuges – were required to join with other agencies and had to demonstrate that they would provide generalist homelessness services in order to be competitive. In many cases, specialist women's domestic violence refuges, underpinned by feminist principles, had to join with large organisations, underpinned by charitable and faith-based approaches to 'welfare', in order to be competitive in tendering to provide services to the 'homeless'. This process saw the number of government contracts drop from 336 to 157.

The relative merits of the GHSH reform are widely contested and there is a wide gulf between official government and community accounts of the tender process, as well as the quantitative and qualitative impact of the reform. For example, official government documents indicate an increase in the number of women's refuges; in the funding allocated to supporting women in crisis; and in the number of women and children helped. Specifically a NSW Government (2017) publication indicates that there were 76 women's refuges pre-reform (63 government-owned and 13 non-government-owned) and 81 women's refuges post-reform (65 government-owned and 16 non-government-owned). However, unpublished research conducted by the Coalition for Women's Refuges (2017) found that only 13 out of 62 accommodation services that participated in the study that had been identified as 'women's refuges' by the NSW government exclusively accommodated women and children escaping domestic violence. Twenty-seven percent of the remaining services provided generic services to homeless men, women and children and another 52% provided generic homeless services to all homeless women and children, including non-specialist services to those who were escaping domestic violence. Notably, another nine services listed by the NSW government as women's refuges were uncontactable and another five declined to participate, hence they are not included in the survey.

The funding allocated to women's refuges pre-reform was $40 million dollars. The latest figures in the post-reform era indicate that $59 million dollars were allocated for 'domestic and family violence specific service packages, and homelessness service packages that assist all women, including women's refuges' (NSW Government, 2017). However, the definition of 'help' is widely constituted and does not necessarily mean that women's and children's homelessness and housing needs have been addressed.

The study

The study was broadly concerned with exploring participants' perceptions of the impact of the GHSH reform on the delivery of specialist domestic violence services to women and children. Qualitative data from semi-structured interviews with 15 specialist women's refuge workers was collected. The research was underpinned by feminist research principles, emphasising a commitment to promoting women's interests and rights, improving their lives and producing knowledge useful to these ends (Reinhartz, 1992). Information was specifically obtained on the following aspects of the reform: changes to the scope and scale of service delivery; impact on ability to provide a holistic, woman-centred, empowering service; changes to referral patterns and women's access services; changes to workers' ability to engage in advocacy, political activism and violence prevention activities; changes to accountability and monitoring measures; gaps in services; experience of providing services to a broad range of homeless clients; changes in the relationships with funders auspicing organisations; and changes in workers' satisfaction.

The participants were sourced through organisations that had provided specialist domestic violence services, including refuge accommodation prior to the reform. These services had joined with other agencies (often large faith-based charities) and had been successful in the competitive tendering process, receiving government funding to provide general homelessness services, including services to women and children escaping domestic violence. As the research was concerned with looking at the impact of the reform, a condition of participation in the study was that participants had worked in the system pre- and post-reform.

Owing to the sensitive nature of the research, which posed potential risks to participants' job security and agency funding, particular attention was paid to ensuring the anonymity of workers and their workplaces. As a result, the only demographic details reported in this chapter are length of time employed in the women's refuge sector and gender of participants. In total, 15 female workers and/or managers with extensive experience working with women and children journeying away from domestic violence were interviewed. The average length of time that participants had been employed within women's domestic violence refuges was 15 years.

The study was approved by, and complied with, all requirements of the Human Research Ethics Committee of the University of Sydney.

Overview of the reform experience

The exploratory study provides a mainly negative image of the GHSR reforms for the majority of women and children seeking specialist domestic violence services, from the perspective of experienced domestic violence service providers. Furthermore, the study paints a predominantly negative picture of the impact of the reform on workers' job satisfaction in the domestic violence field. In contrast to the government's assurances that the reform would not result in any losses to pre-existing women's and children's domestic violence refuges, participants overwhelmingly indicated that the number of specialist women's refuges in NSW had been significantly reduced as had their capacity to deliver holistic, woman-centred, trauma-informed services.

The predominant concern expressed by participants was that the reform had genericised homeless people, rendering invisible the specific needs that women escaping domestic violence have. This approach is in opposition to contemporary notions of best practice in the domestic violence field. For example, Laing and Humphreys (2013) argue that women and children escaping domestic violence have diverse, multiple and complex needs that require specialist knowledge and skills. For example, women and children who have experienced domestic violence have particular medical, legal, social, emotional and financial needs. Suffice to say, securing safe and affordable housing is an important need but it is not the only need. Most participants expressed the view that the reform had resulted in practices that reduced women's and children's needs to a narrow consideration of their housing security. Most participants shared the view of one manager who said that 'viewing women's experience of domestic violence through the lens of homelessness is just completely and utterly inappropriate'. She described how women's refuge workers now feel like 'housing agents' whose practice has been reduced to assessing a victim/survivor's prospects of attaining a tenancy agreement:

> on intake we have to follow a set of questions that takes nearly an hour to interview a woman. Only three of those questions relate to DV [domestic violence] – they start out with questions about your finances, your rental history. It's all around establishing a sustainability for a tenancy. And it completely ignores somebody's experience of DV and what would be most important to a woman, which would be her safety and fear of the perpetrator. The questions on that intake are just appalling. Questions like when is your next pay, do you have a credit card, how much do you owe on your credit card ... that kind of detail to a woman whose life is in danger ... standardized questions that they have to answer before they even get told if there is a vacancy in a service ... so they can go through the whole thing to be told there's no vacancy.

Gains lost for domestic violence service provision

The paradigm shift from framing women and children escaping domestic violence as people with a particular set of complex needs to viewing them as part of the general 'homeless' population was identified as contributing to dangerous practices that were not informed by knowledge about domestic violence. The overemphasis on housing considerations eclipsed other considerations such as assessing the safety and risk issues, including lethality assessments for women and their children. Many, like the worker quoted below, despaired that the reforms had resulted in poor service provision that no longer addressed the complex and individual needs of women and children:

> These words are bandied about ... trauma informed, wraparound service provision and holistic service provision ... it's a complete load of rubbish ... it's absolutely corporatised and its process-orientated ... (in the past) we treated every woman who came into the refuge like they had their own customized wounds that we would attend to. Now it's a one size fits all shove them through the system and move onto the next woman.

Many participants indicated that women and children suffered terribly as a result of changes to operating hours which mandated 'homelessness services' open between the hours of 9 am to 5 pm. One worker expressed frustration with her attempts to explain to the charity that had taken over management of the refuge that this approach does not work with women experiencing domestic violence:

> They don't seem to understand what it entails [domestic violence]. Secrecy, darkness, power. It's not an open shut case like a baker opening up at 6 or 7 o'clock. It's not like that.

Another worker was aware that women had been 'directed to stay overnight in hotels until morning when they can access a homelessness service that may not operate overnight'. Similarly, a worker described how women who had suffered trauma were taken to inappropriate generic homeless shelters which increased their trauma:

> a woman who literally came out of hospital – she had a broken jaw and a broken wrist from domestic violence. She was brought to me by a constable. She had rung Link2home (a government-funded centralized intake service) and they had organized emergency accommodation. She was taken to a rundown suburb, an area that is partly industrial where there were some shops above these shops there was a ramshackle structure that looked like a little office annex and then an area of the roof that had a shed ... this was crisis accommodation, there were five bedrooms. Everyone else there was a male and they had to share a bathroom and a kitchen.

Gains lost for children and young people

All participants indicated that the therapeutic services for children that were previously delivered by specialist children's workers in women's refuges had been overlooked in the 'service packages'. One worker indicated that she knew of very few refuges that now had specialist children's workers and described the irony of this situation saying that 'we have more information now about the impact of trauma on children's health and well-being than ever before but less workers'. Many participants expressed a deep-seated sense of frustration and sadness about this turn of events, well expressed in the following statements:

> So again we spent 30 years trying to get services to recognise that children were not appendages of their mothers ... if they really wanting to put their money where their mouth is about early intervention and prevention then why would you get rid of child support workers in women's refuges?

The question posed by the worker is particularly salient when one considers the emphasis placed on working with children and young people in order to prevent domestic violence, which is an essential aspect of Australia's National Plan to Reduce Violence against Women and Their Children (Council of Australian Governments, 2010).

Most participants indicated that they had worked with women who had decided to return to abusive partners because their experiences in 'generic homelessness shelters' compounded their trauma and placed their children at further risk of harm:

> this is what women are saying. You've got other homeless women who are drinking and drugging ... would you take your children to a place like that? There's no vacancies and when you get into a refuge they're crap.

Gains lost for domestic violence recovery and survival

All participants expressed a view that, as one worker put it, 'all homeless people deserve a place' but maintained that the particular needs of women and children who had experienced domestic violence means that a one-size-fits-all approach to addressing homeless does not work.

> in a place where women are hyper-vigilant, suffering from PTSD because of their DV issues – to have a woman coming in who is suffering from an active psychosis who may just be, not necessarily threatening but their behaviour is uncertain for these women and children who have been living in unpredictable situations.

A further observation was that women and children who had experienced domestic violence were now commonly placed alongside women suffering from significant mental health issues and/or substance misuse problems or who had just been released from prison:

> I had a client severely traumatized by domestic violence ... she had a lifetime of trauma ... they put her into the Haymarket homelessness services – one floor for men, one floor for women, and one for families. She was in the floor, which was women. They had a room in which there were five women. You don't have a room to yourself at all. You had to leave in the morning and you couldn't come back until the evening ... She needed support and money. She was in this room with four other women. One of them had very severe mental health issues and she was terrified of this woman. Two of the other women were long-term substance abusers. The other woman was also a victim of domestic violence who would wake up in the middle of the night screaming. It was very difficult to sleep and every morning she had to get up and wander around Sydney and wasn't allowed back until the night ... she was in this position for several months.

Many participants were of the opinion that the reforms had increased the safety concerns for many women and children. For example, one worker believed that opening refuges to all homeless people heightened the physical risks to women and children escaping domestic violence because people who had not experienced domestic violence did not understand the particular risks posed by men who use violence and coercive control. Participants described how women and children were placed at risk when other residents failed to lock security doors or adhere to curfews, or revealed the refuge location. This worker indicated that, by way of contrast, women who shared a lived experience of domestic violence inherently understood the importance of abiding by strict security measures.

The impacts of the reforms extended beyond crisis accommodation and refuges. Participants also described how many women in transitional housing were placed at increased risk as a result of the reforms. For example, one worker explained that transitional housing units previously used to house only women and children escaping domestic violence were now designated for use by homeless clients. She described how a woman who had suffered years of domestic violence was housed in a transitional unit with a shared laundry next to a man with significant mental health issues. The woman alleged that the man was stalking her and as a result she increasingly isolated herself within her unit, compounding the depression and anxiety that she was experiencing as a result of domestic violence.

Gains lost for Aboriginal and Torres Strait Islander and migrant women

The deleterious impact of the GHSH reforms have had particular impacts for Aboriginal and Torres Strait Islander women and migrant women who do not have residency in Australia. One worker described how women's refuges, pre-reform, had discretion to allow migrant women to stay without cost for long periods of time. She stated that, post-reform, this had changed:

> Women whose Visas have not been processed are unable to work, they don't have an income. They have nowhere to go. They get referred but we don't take them so they go back to the same situation, they get abused, their children get abused, they get killed, they sleep in cars. Intake question does she have an income – no – she's on a spouse visa or bridging visa then we can't afford to take her in from the funding body; it's not up to us anymore it's up to the

funding body; we have to provide medication, food, clothes, everything until they get residency. We used to have time to work with migrant women; we don't now.

The amalgamation of previously independent specialist women's refuges with large charitable, mainly faith-based, organisations was identified as particularly problematic for Aboriginal and Torres Strait Islander women. A worker described how transferring a local, community-based women's refuge to a large faith-based charity rendered invisible the oppressive impact of colonialism, which includes the historical and widespread institutional abuse of Aboriginal people by people associated with religious organisations:

> They (Aboriginal women) don't have a personal relationship with the local refuge anymore ... they've said to me that they don't trust some of the, for obvious historical reasons, the large church-run organizations.

Many participants described how the strong relationships that they had developed over years with women from Aboriginal and Torres Strait Islander backgrounds had been decimated by the reform in many areas of the state, compounding the vulnerability of many women and children.

Gains lost for the domestic violence workforce: Specialist knowledge and skills

Mandel (2017) argues that effective work with women and children who have experienced domestic violence requires effective safety planning, including understanding and mapping the perpetrator's pattern of coercive control as well as partnering with survivors. Workers within services that had historically provided specialist services to women and children escaping domestic violence expressed concerns about the domestic violence knowledge and skill base of new workers employed in general homelessness services. One participant indicated that she was aware that workers within a centralised intake service 'don't have specialist skills to deal with the complex issues' associated with domestic violence and are expected to manage each call within six minutes. On the other hand, many participants with domestic violence expertise indicated that they did not have the requisite skills and knowledge to adequately respond to women with significant mental health and/or substance use issues. Moreover they expressed concern about the increasing number of women seeking a 'homelessness service' because they did not have access to specialist care to manage these serious health issues.

Gains lost for workers

Overwhelmingly, participants expressed the view that the reforms had not only delivered negative outcomes for women and children but had a devastating impact on workers in the domestic violence field. Participants indicated that the field lost many experienced, knowledgeable workers who had resigned.

Gains lost for the feminist movement

Many participants were of the opinion that the GHSH reforms had resulted in the decimation of the women's refuge movement. Whether this was by design or circumstance was a matter of conjecture. However, there was an overwhelming sense that the hard-fought wins of feminists before had been lost:

> I think we've gone back to the reason why women's refuges started where they said okay the church-run services are not adequate, they don't meet the needs of women escaping violence. There's too much judgment and there's too many strings attached. That's why services were started. We've gone back 40 years. Going home staying home reforms to me equates *to go home and shut up.*
>
> I said it was a war against women and I still think so.
>
> You know we spent 40 years trying to break down the stigma attached to women's refuges. You know that perpetrators and uninformed people used to say that refuges are horrible places and full of drug addicts and mad people ... and unfortunately the reforms are actually backing some of that up now. I had a woman pack up her bags and say I knew who to be scared of when I was living with my partner. I'm going back home. (emphasis added)

Many despaired about how the collaborative, collegial and relationship-based feminist movement had been eradicated and replaced with a marketised, corporatised and economic rationalist informed approach. At a time when much government policy in the area of child protection and domestic violence promotes interagency collaboration as a prerequisite for good practice; this turn of events had a particular sting for many workers:

> The fact that I'm calling other refuges agencies irks me ... that language and we don't have a personal relationship with the other supposed DV services that we used to have. Prior to the reforms we were members of the women's refuge

movement. We knew the other 56 refuges in the state that took women specifically escaping DV. We met as a group. We don't even know where to refer.

There's such a sense of competition around funds that the whole network of services that used to be around to support women escaping domestic violence, it's a closed shop now. We don't want to tell you what we're doing or we don't want to let you know what's going on at our service because there's every chance that the next round of funding you might be our competition.

Competition ... that's the biggest thing that's happened since the reforms, created that competition because people used to work together before, united to support the clients. Now it's dog eat dog.

Participants described how this competitive tendering process pitted small services against each other. Moreover, all participants talked about how they have experienced increased surveillance of their work practices. One worker stated: 'there is an over emphasis on compliance, efficiency, counting numbers of clients/nights stayed – it has a direct impact on the ability of workers to provide one to one crisis & ongoing care and support to people.' Every participant indicated that in the post-reform regime they were required to spend large amounts of time interfacing with computers doing data entry for multiple systems that did not 'speak to each other' – leaving minimal time for client contact.

The level of despair and feelings of powerlessness that participants expressed in relation to their experiences during and after the reform were palpable. It was difficult to hear strong feminist women with a long and proud history of gaining ground for women and children describe their accounts of feeling so powerless and helpless:

I don't say this lightly but the government is responsible for raping the domestic violence sector, the community sector.

I experienced Going Home, Staying Home as the most disempowering thing that had happened to me as a worker in the sector. There was nowhere we could take our disapproval and rage.

Conclusion

On her recent visit to Australia, the United Nations Special Rapporteur on Violence against Women cautioned against the risks of 'mainstreaming' and advocated strongly to design policies, plans, programs and services in a way that recognised difference (Australian Human Rights Commission, 2012). Such an approach draws on extensive research evidence that highlights how women and children journeying away from domestic violence have myriad, complex and diverse needs. Using the GHSH homelessness policy package as a case study, this chapter has demonstrated the devastating impact of gender-blind policy development on women and children. The direction of this state-based policy package is inconsistent with national and international best practice trends in violence against women and children prevention and intervention. The findings presented in this chapter demonstrate how gender-blind and domestic violence destructive policy (Mandel, 2017) can undermine rather than promote the safety of women and their children.

Further readings

Chung, D., Kennedy, R., O'Brien, B. and Wendt, S. (2000). *Home Safe Home: The Link between Domestic and Family Violence and Women's Homelessness*. Adelaide: Social Policy Research Group, University of South Australia.

Rimmer, S. and Sawer, M. (2016). Neoliberalism and gender equality policy in Australia. *Australian Journal of Political Science*, 51(4), 742–758.

Teghtsoonian, K. and Chappell, L. (2008). The rise and decline of women's policy machinery in British Columbia and New South Wales: A cautionary tale. *International Political Science Review*, 29(1), 29–51.

Acknowledgements

I thank the many dedicated women who participated in this study, as well as Associate Professors Lesley Laing and Susan Goodwin who contributed valuable suggestions and edits to draft chapters. I am also grateful to Nina Melander, David Wilkinson and Amelia Boyers who graciously volunteered their time to assist with this research.

References

Almeida, R. and Lockard, J. (2005). The cultural context model: A new paradigm for accountability, empowerment, and the development of critical consciousness against domestic violence. In N. Sokoloff and C. Pratt (Eds.), *Domestic Violence at the Margins: Readings on Race, Class, Gender and Culture* (pp. 319–332). London: Rutgers University Press.

Australian Bureau of Statistics (2012). *The Personal Safety Survey*. Canberra: Australian Bureau of Statistics.

Australian Human Rights Commission (2012). *Australian Study Tour Report: Visit of the UN Special Rapporteur on Violence against Women*. Sydney: Australian Human Rights Commission.

Bland, D. and Shallcross, L. (2015). *Children Who are Homeless with Their Family: A Literature Review for the Queensland Commissioner for Children and Young People*. Brisbane: Queensland University of Technology.

Breckenridge, J., Chung, D., Spinney, A. and Zufferey, C. (2016). *National Mapping and Meta-Evaluation Outlining Key Features of Effective 'Safe at Home' Programs that Enhance Safety and Prevent Homelessness for Women and Their Children Who Have Experienced Domestic and Family Violence: Research Report Horizons*. Sydney: ANROWS.

Bullen, J. (2009). Domestic violence and homelessness: Notes on the policy road so far. *Parity*, 22(10), 10–11.

Campbell, J., Webster, D., Koziol-McLain, J., Block, C., Campbell, D., Curry, M. and Laughton, K. (2003). Risk factors for femicide in abusive relationships: Results from multi-site case control study. *American Journal of Public Health*, 93(7), 1089–1097.

Chung, D., Kennedy, R., O'Brien, B. and Wendt, S. (2000). *Home Safe Home: The Link between Domestic and Family Violence and Women's Homelessness*. Adelaide: Social Policy Research Group, University of South Australia.

Coalition for Women's Refuges (2017). *Survey of Homelessness Agencies*. Sydney: Coalition for Women's Refuges.

Council of Australian Governments (2010). *The National Plan to Reduce Violence against Women and Their Children 2010–2022*. Canberra: Council of Australian Governments.

Dept. of Families (2008). *The Road Home: A National Approach to Reducing Homelessness*. Canberra: Dept. of Families, Housing, Community Services and Indigenous Affairs.

KPMG (2015). *Going Home Staying Home Post-Implementation Review 2015 Final Report*. Sydney: KPMG Health, Ageing & Human Services.

Laing, L. and Humphreys, C. (2013). *Social Work and Domestic Violence: Developing Critical and Reflective Practice*. Sydney: Sage Publishing.

Lorde, A. (2012). *Sister Outsider: Essays and Speeches*. New York: Crossing Press.

Mandel, D. (2017). *Why Is the Safe and Together Model Relevant for Welfare Workers*. Safe & Together Institute. https://safeandtogetherinstitute.com/safe-together/faq/why-is-the-safe-and-together-model-relevant-for-child-welfare-workers/.

Murray, S. (2007). Homelessness and domestic violence social policy in Australia. *Parity*, 20(10), 17–18.

NSW Domestic Violence Death Review Team (2017). *Domestic Violence Death Review Team Report 2015–2017*. Sydney: NSW Domestic Violence Death Review Team.

NSW Government (2017). *Help for Homeless Women and Children*. Sydney: NSW Government.

Nunan, C. (2009). Women, domestic violence and homelessness. *Parity*, 22(10), 7–9.

Reinhartz, S. (1992). *Feminist Methods in Social Research*. New York: Oxford University Press.

Rimmer, S. and Sawer, M. (2016). Neoliberalism and gender equality policy in Australia. *Australian Journal of Political Science*, 51(4), 742–758.

Sawer, M. (2007). Australia: The fall of the Femocrat. In J. Outshoorn and J. Kantola (Eds.), *Changing State Feminism* (pp. 20–40). London: Palgrave Macmillan.

State of NSW (2008). *Report of the Special Commission of Inquiry into Child Protection Services in NSW*. Sydney: State of NSW.

State of Victoria (2004). *Women's Journeys Away from Family Violence*. Melbourne: Department of Human Services.

State of Victoria (2016). Royal Commission into Family Violence: Summary and recommendations, Parl Paper No 132 (2014–16). Melbourne: State of Victoria.

Sullivan, C.M. (2012). *Domestic Violence Shelter Services: A Review of the Empirical Evidence*. Harrisburg, PA: National Resource Center on Domestic Violence.

Teghtsoonian, K. and Chappell, L. (2008). The rise and decline of women's policy machinery in British Columbia and New South Wales: A cautionary tale. *International Political Science Review*, 29(1), 29–51.

Tually, D., Faulkner, D., Cutler, C. and Slatter, M. (2008). *Women, Domestic and Family Violence and Homelessness*. Canberra: Commonwealth of Australia.

14

Who Can Argue with Blue Sky? The Questionable Alliance between Difference and the Market in Disability Policy

Amanda Howard

I acknowledge the Awabakal people, the Traditional Owners of the land where I live and where most of my research takes place, and pay my respects to Elders past, present and emerging.

A central debate in social policy in the twenty-first century is managing the tensions between collective and equity-based approaches and responses which attend to individual needs, recognising differences between people and the contexts impacting on life. One-size-fits-all approaches in providing economic and social support and sustenance can appear equitable but hide an uneven distribution of resources and create support systems driven by their own imperatives rather than those they are supporting. In relation to disability, this trend has been particularly marked with dramatic changes in a number of countries regarding the way in which support is funded and controlled (Glasby et al., 2009; Green and Mears, 2014; Hutchison et al., 2006; Laragy et al., 2015). The development of consumer-directed and consumer-controlled care in disability policy represents a significant paradigm shift, from services receiving funding and monitored to meet targets and outcomes to (in principle at least) funding and decision making about who provides support and how now resting with the person living with disability. This shift appears to represent a greater level of attention to difference and diversity as policy and funding is reshaped to place individual needs and preferences at the centre of decision making (this idea underpins person-centredness).

In Australia, this trend is embodied in the National Disability Insurance Scheme (NDIS), heralded as the most comprehensive policy reform since Medicare (Cortis et al., 2017; Warr et al., 2017), and set to provide individualised funding packages to eligible people living with disability where support is designed and directed by the person with the package. This reorganisation of funding arrangements has revolutionary implications for service design and delivery, resource distribution and regulatory governance. Most importantly, the change signals a revolution for the decision making power of people living with disability in Australia. After a long and complicated battle by disability advocates, organisations, individuals and families, person-centred approaches have now been established as the foundation for disability policy in Australia (APC, 2011).

The NDIS was launched in 2013 and from 2017 is being rolled out in all states of Australia. By 2019, the Scheme will have replaced all state-based disability departments – except in Western Australia where a bilateral agreement has been developed between Commonwealth and State governments (APC, 2017) – and services will operate completely within a fee-for-service insurance model via individualised funding packages.

The scale and complexity of this change, the diversity of needs and contexts experienced by potential participants in the NDIS, as well as the radical realignment of regulatory and access arrangements, mean that the Scheme is an important site for research, critical analysis and review. Bilateral political support, as well as widespread praise for the Scheme by people living with disability and their advocates, created an environment for rollout of both high expectations and unprecedented welcome. The risk in such universal and enthusiastic support as the Scheme is implemented is that the voices of those who identify oversights or areas for improvement, including people with disability highlighting their own experiences, may be seen as undermining the leap forward and jeopardising the potential of the NDIS. Some commentary has framed challenges experienced to date as 'teething problems', arguing that time and full Scheme rollout will address all concerns (Ireland, 2014).

In this chapter, I argue that key structural tensions that underpin the Scheme, and that are largely tacit in much of the debate, must be considered to ensure 'teething problems' are not converted to problems of exclusion and invisibility for some. Specifically, at the heart of the NDIS are two sets of divergent ideas, which have become intertwined, and which need to be disentangled if disability policy in Australia is to deliver properly on the promise of person-centredness.

These intentionally linked idea sets are:

1. The juxtaposition of individual decision making and person-centredness as the central tenet of NDIS – symbolised in the notions of *choice and control* – with a discourse of centralised policy decision making enacted through the imperative that only supports deemed *reasonable and necessary* can be provided through the Scheme.

2. The intertwining of human rights principles and discourse with the neoliberal notion that markets are the best way to organise and distribute resources.

From these two idea sets several key assumptions follow, which have shaped NDIS rollout to date, and which, if not addressed, could undermine Scheme aspirations. I argue that these assumptions need to be critically examined in the context of the driving idea sets of the Scheme if bespoke support recognising different needs is to be achieved.

Choice and control, reasonable and necessary

Two sets of foundational ideas govern and operationalise person-centred approaches in the NDIS. These are *choice and control* and *reasonable and necessary*. Both are enshrined in the National Disability Insurance Scheme Act 2013 ('the Act'), and their coexistence illustrates a central tension in Scheme implementation to date. In the Objects of the Act, *choice and control* are outlined as to:

> enable people with disability to exercise choice and control in the pursuit of their goals and the planning and delivery of their supports. (Part 2.3)

The Object sets clear parameters, but leaves room to move with regard to particular goals, the range of supports and the ways in which these will be organised. This principle fundamentally changes power relations between a person participating in the NDIS and the state, shifting decision making to the individual who now controls resources and their distribution in line with their own goals. The broader parameters of this principle were outlined by the NDIS Independent Advisory Committee, which argued that *choice and control* should be implemented in a way consistent with the United Nations Convention on the Rights of Persons with Disabilities and available research, so people living with disability can lead a 'good life' (NDIS IAC, 2013) through exercising the right to make the same range of choices as any other person in Australia.

This additional commentary on parameters of *choice and control* reflects a more generalised notion of this principle than is in the Act, but is consistent with a policy position, which values diversity in needs and circumstances. Symbolically, this principle has taken centre stage in much of the discussion of the NDIS by most interested people. The inclusion of *choice and control* principles in the Act represents a major step forward in framing person-centredness as a central policy idea in Australia.

The second set of principles, also in the Objects of the Act, equally influential in shaping NDIS policy and implementation, is that supports in the NDIS must be *reasonable and necessary*. According to its Object the Act aims to:

> provide reasonable and necessary supports, including early intervention supports, for participants in the National Disability Insurance Scheme launch. (Part 2(d))

The Act goes on to provide detail about how the principle of *reasonable and necessary* is to be understood and enacted. Section 34 details that in addition to supports being shaped by participant goals and aspirations, consideration must also be given to value for money, how the support facilitates social and economic participation, whether support is consistent with 'good practice' (34(d)) and whether support might be provided by an alternative means (including both informally through family and community or formally through other service sectors).

The *reasonable and necessary* principle places very specific parameters around the exercise of *choice and control*, providing a disciplining aspect to individual decision making. While choice of supports is in the hands of people accessing the NDIS, whether those supports make it onto the eligible list to be chosen remains in the control of the State. Different needs, contexts and goals are only able to shape *choice and control* within the centralised boundaries established within supports deemed *reasonable and necessary* according to the state. While in any legislation governments set parameters for funding provision, the National Disability Insurance Scheme Act 2013 appears to give power to people living with disability through the framing of *choice and control*, while simultaneously taking overarching decision making power back by setting a range of specific and limiting restrictions on individual decision making through the parameters for what is considered *reasonable and necessary*.

The juxtaposition of these two sets of principles symbolises a broader tension in the NDIS between the ambition to provide bespoke, person-led decision making and resource allocation and the imperatives of centralised policy and budget implementation to set close limits on the extent of resources available and the processes for access and allocation. The tension in relation to how power relations are shaped will have implications for the implementation of the Scheme and amplifies several assumptions evident as the NDIS is rolled out. Later in the chapter, the implications of this tension will be discussed as it plays out in the operation of the Scheme. The connection between the two ideas in the Act sets up a very particular relationship between principles of individual decision making and that of the State. Even within the Act constraints on the exercise of *choice and control* are at the forefront. It is the State that decides the parameters for available support, with choice ultimately controlled in a number of ways. This tension becomes more important in the context of the second idea set at the centre of the NDIS.

Human rights and the market

A second closely intertwined idea set, central to the narrative of the NDIS, is important to understand in examining the implementation of the Scheme to date, as well as how it might address challenges in the future. The two ideas are human rights – embodied in person-centred approaches and decision making – and the market – operationalised in (1) the organisation of resources as individualised funding packages, and (2) management of services/supports as competitive individuals and organisations vying for the opportunity to be the provider of choice for individuals with a funding package in a particular market. The marriage of these ideas and the discourse that has been built around them (rendering them virtually inseparable) should be understood if bespoke support responding to diverse needs is really to be achieved.

Discourses driven by human rights imperatives have been the key driver of disability advocacy in Australia and internationally (APC, 2011; Barnes, 2007). The United Nations (2006) Convention on the Rights of Persons with a Disability represents the pinnacle of this discourse, but, equally, human rights in the form of access and equity have been operationalised in national, state and local government legislation in Australia through the Disability Discrimination Act, 1992 Australian Building codes, and state-planning legislation. Disability support services, however, were slow to respond to increasing pressure from disability advocacy organisations that argued for people living with disability receiving support to be the central decision makers in who, how and how much support was provided, rather than state governments or service providers. In 2011, the Productivity Commission summarised what people living with disabilities had been experiencing for decades – a disjointed, piecemeal, underfunded and inadequate system (APC, 2011). For disability advocates, the question of who *has* the power to shape resource allocation and support system design and who *should* have that power was a fundamental human rights issue. The framework and method for enacting the imperative of person-centredness would be critical and it is here that broader trends in policy and funding would play a key role.

The rise of neoliberalism, with its mantra of market-driven solutions to social as well as economic challenges, has played a significant role in recalibrating the welfare state in Australia, as it has done overseas (Arthurson and Jacobs, 2009). Employment services, housing, aged care and out-of-home care all experienced radical changes in funding and service design at the behest of market-driven solutions from the 1990s onwards. Neoliberal policy makers viewed established policy and funding arrangements as inflexible, unresponsive and dictatorial. Higher quality and cheaper service provision, it was argued, could only be provided where services were in competition with each other and where the consumer could choose between providers rather than being compelled to use one, where funding was allocated under established policy.

In relation to disability support, the introduction of an insurance model of care, similar to health insurance, was seen as a way to address the uneven and one-size-fits-all approach used by state governments, where organisations were funded to provide a set of services with only tokenistic or no input from those needing support.

If people living with disability were able to control their own funding and choose which supports they preferred, and who they preferred to provide them, the power shift driving human rights arguments could be addressed, while the market orientation advocated by neoliberal policy makers as the most efficient arrangement for service provision seemed ideally suited and deftly positioned to deliver this human rights promise.

Bringing together human rights and the market framed the central principles of the NDIS: *choice and control*. This seemed like a perfect match that would address criticisms of market-oriented policy in employment services about false choice and punitive individualised blame allocation (Howard et al., 2016), and simultaneously address issues of human rights and power in relation to disability policy. Unlike those who were unemployed, where service 'choice' was framed as a policy mechanism to ensure compliance with State economic participation goals, the operation of the market in reshaping disability policy was framed in terms of human rights, of liberation from a funding regime that was clearly broken and exclusionary (APC, 2011).

The result was that the market and human rights were now inseparably linked in disability policy. The danger here is that any critiques of market aspects of the NDIS were now linked to and potentially seen as critiques of the human rights of people living with disability. The marriage of these two very different ideas has gone a considerable way to critique-proof the NDIS. As the title of this chapter references – *Who Can Argue with Blue Sky?* – who doesn't want a policy that champions human rights? Linking human rights with the market effectively creates a frame and discourse which render the two ideas as interchangeable – human rights delivery in disability policy equals the establishment of a market where individualised funding packages create demand for support providers, who must compete on a fee-for-service basis to win the business of the consumer.

These two ideas urgently need to be uncoupled and examined closely if the evolving NDIS landscape is to be responsive in addressing unintended consequences which now, or potentially, exclude people who may access and will benefit from accessing the NDIS.

Operationalising tensions

The two idea sets – (1) *choice and control, reasonable and necessary*; and (2) human rights and marketisation – have, to date, shaped the NDIS parameters and processes through operationalising central tensions focused on power. Questions about who gets to decide what and within which parameters, as well as how resources will follow whose decisions have taken a very particular turn in the NDIS rollout, and not one which may have been envisaged. In theory, the central decision makers are people living with disability accessing the NDIS, and central players are providers operating in a competitive market. The reality is much more complicated. Human rights, enacted through *choice and control*, have been directly and indirectly shaped through both the imperatives of the State via *reasonable and necessary* provisions and those of the market via individualised funding and realignment of service providers as competitors. An examination of the influence of state and market to date is critical in assessing the prospects for delivery of *choice and control* via these structures.

Rise of the National Disability Insurance Agency (NDIA): the state and the market

While the market is the mechanism of choice for the delivery of human rights through *choice and control*, the NDIS rollout has been largely orchestrated through the architecture of a proactive Commonwealth government, creating, scaling and managing the market. The launch of the NDIS triggered a shift from individual state to federal government arrangements for funding and regulatory coordination of disability support. This precipitated the creation of a new Commonwealth government department, the National Disability Insurance Agency (NDIA). This department (or Agency) has been built quickly from initial establishment in 2013, and controls all regulatory and monitoring aspects of the NDIS, as well as the distribution of funds. Price setting, plan development and sign-off, provider monitoring and policy shaping are all within the purview of the NDIA. The tension between principles of *choice and control* and *reasonable and necessary* is no more evident than in the rapidly expanding bureaucratic architecture of the NDIA. The expansive role of the NDIA in overseeing NDIS rollout includes regulating the market, monitoring and vetting service providers, and shaping inclusions in individual plans and packages. Key questions about both the integrity and the practicality of implementing disability policy, founded on recognition of individual difference, via a rigid and growing bureaucracy, remain a central concern for the success of the NDIS. The increasing size and breadth of the NDIA footprint calls into question the choice of market creation as the delivery mechanism for the NDIS. While all markets require some level of regulation, protections from abuse or exploitation, and monitoring, in its current and evolving form evidence suggests that the NDIA traverses boundaries between regulator, market shaper and ultimately sole buyer (or perhaps enabler) of supports. The NDIA tightly and increasingly regulates the parameters of the market using centralised price fixing, restrictive practices with regard to conditions of entry and operation for support providers, and itemised support and service menus from which people living with disability are compelled to choose.

Rather than a managed market (Cortis et al., 2017), there is increasing evidence that the NDIS resembles a reluctant market or at best an overmanaged one. Very particular duty of care, safety and human rights considerations are central to disability support provision. In practice, these considerations have rightly taken an increasing role. Alongside concerns for increasing costs of the Scheme based on launch site participation and plans, processes for addressing duty of care issues have been increasingly dealt with through NDIA structures and processes. Some of this work is also still being done by state government departments, which will no longer exist when the full Scheme is rolled out. In a market, prices and services are usually allowed to fluctuate and then settle in response to supply and demand. In the NDIS market, the stakes are too high to trust service provision to supply and demand, given the vulnerability of many accessing the Scheme, the ethical and duty of care costs of market failure, and the potential for exploitation that accompanies a free market.

The very managed market in implementation

So, the market as a mechanism for human rights delivery via *choice and control* in the NDIS may not in fact be a market after all. It turns out, so far, that without proactive intervention by the state (in the form of the NDIA) the conditions that will encourage competitive provision of *reasonable and necessary* supports either cannot or have not been allowed to emerge. Given that conditions in this very managed market have been expressly created to facilitate *choice and control* of supports for NDIS participants, it is worth briefly examining how recognition of difference is faring so far.

From these tensions, NDIS implementation to date has revealed several assumptions, which potentially threaten the capacity of the Scheme to deliver on different needs and provide *choice and control* in disability support. The ambitious nature of the NDIS, with its aim of providing funding for bespoke support systems for each individual eligible to access it, is dependent on a flexible, responsive and well-coordinated structure and processes for the development and delivery of funding packages as well as subsequent support systems. In the very managed and reluctant market of the NDIS – a market created through the intersection of idea sets outlined earlier in the chapter – four assumptions follow that cast doubt on the capacity of this market to practically deliver *choice and control* of supports:

- Available skilled workforce
- There is a market everywhere
- Fast, accurate and accessible planning process that attends to diverse needs
- Seamless whole-of-life support.

Available skilled workforce

Workforce development has been a centrepiece of ongoing debate regarding NDIS implementation. The 2017 Productivity Commission report highlights persistent challenges in this area and the need for urgent attention to ensure the aims of the NDIS can be achieved (APC, 2017).

Cortis and colleagues (2017) highlight significant challenges in the pricing structure of the NDIS, which is resulting, they argue, in a devaluing of disability support work through downwards wage pressure as organisations realign their service offer and workforce characteristics within the boundaries of the new fee-for-service model. The risk here is that a disincentive is created for organisations to employ more qualified workers (who cost more) and the result is a poorer quality of support provided to people living with disability.

The increasing casualisation of the workforce is also discussed as a potential threat to NDIS implementation, as cashflow issues and employment implications for organisations pose a challenge when people shift between providers, taking their funding with them.

In the area of Mental Health, where a number of complexities remain in relation to the NDIS, workforce make-up is a significant concern. In a submission to the Productivity Commission, Mental Health Australia reported that support pricing effectively excluded psychosocial support work for NDIS participants with a persistent and severe mental illness due to the cost of this support (McGrath, 2017). They argued that qualified and skilled workers required to support this group of people are being excluded from employment, with a resulting risk to effective support for people with a mental illness under the NDIS. Findings from the Productivity Commission regarding costs and pricing in the NDIS are pending, but submissions to the review highlight two fundamental structural factors impacting on the cost and availability of support. First, centralised price fixing and competition are driving down wages for disability workers, already a low-paid group, who have significant ethical and care responsibilities in relation to people with often complex needs. There is a very real danger that the managed NDIS market is creating exploitative conditions for workers and excluding more experienced and skilled workers (Cortis et al., 2017). Second, in addition to negative workforce impacts, duty of care to people with NDIS funding is also a potential consequence on both market forces driving down prices and the centralised price ceiling set by the NDIA. An increasingly casualised workforce is a consequence of flexible and responsive markets, and potential exploitation of workers on low wages set by the NDIA for packages requires close monitoring as the Scheme is fully rolled out, to ensure that human rights for people with a package do not come at the cost of those providing support. From the other side, the risk of low-quality support availability (or none at all) as a result of reliance on a poorly trained and low-paid workforce potentially jeopardises the capacity of the NDIS to fulfil its promise of *choice and control*, and raises duty of care concerns in relation to vulnerable and high-need groups accessing the Scheme.

There is a market everywhere

Feedback from disability organisations, advocates and NDIS participants draws attention to the very different circumstances experienced by people in rural and remote areas of Australia in terms of access and availability of support. The assumption that a viable market exists in all jurisdictions in Australia, where enough services and supports will be available to offer choice to the consumer, has been highlighted as an issue since the launch of the Scheme (Barton et al., 2015; Laragy et al., 2015). More recent policy discussion regarding NDIS implementation uses the strangely euphemistic term 'thin markets' (APC, 2017) to describe contexts where few if any supports are locally available for people accessing the NDIS. The existence of 'thin markets' and NDIS price limitations on transport pose a very real threat to people living with disability in rural and remote Australia in terms of access and equity. Although some additional allowance is made in packages to account for distance, reports from service providers indicate this is inadequate (Cortis et al., 2017; Warr et al., 2017). Given the cashflow challenges faced by all support providers in the NDIS, but felt keenly by small and medium-sized organisations (APC, 2017), a likely scenario is that rural and remote support will be provided by large organisations based in major cities, as these organisations are the only ones which have the economies of scale to cover costs. The flexibility and responsiveness of large organisations to provide specific and diverse support to people in rural and remote areas is a question needing further consideration. This is problematic, but a more negative outcome is likely if pricing structure means providing support to rural and remote participants is not viable at all, or will be shifted to other sectors such as health where market structures are not as evident. The assumption of a competitive market for services in rural and remote Australia is one that has not been borne out in tendering processes for other sectors, and there is no evidence that this will be different in relation to disability support. Implications here include not only availability of any suitable supports locally for rural and remote Australians accessing the NDIS but access to the Scheme at all.

Fast, accurate and accessible planning process that attends to diverse needs

A critical process for successful NDIS implementation is quick, effective access to funding via the planning process. It is here where the recognition and operationalising of choice and control are mapped out. The planning process involves the potential NDIS participant contacting a planner at the NDIA, providing documentation to the planner, undergoing an assessment of need and working with the planner to set goals, required supports and preferences about who will provide these and how.

The combination of the logistics involved in mobilising a large and skilled workforce of planners able to work with people with a range of diverse needs, communication and cognitive capacities poses a significant challenge. The need to transition people from previous support arrangements to the NDIS within the time frame set for the cessation of block funding, and the differing times and complexities involved in developing individualised plans, has created a number of tensions in the system. Key assumptions in the planning process related to these factors illustrate areas needing attention from the NDIA.

Time pressures have more recently led to a truncated planning process being implemented, known as the First Plan (NDIA). In this process, initial NDIS plans and funding packages are developed over the phone, with the intention of providing quick access to the Scheme for more people. The First Plan is then reviewed and any changes made at a later date, where planners meet people face to face and spend more time on goal setting and support design. Problems with the First Plan process include the need for short-term review, as plans are not well developed to account for diverse and changing needs and uncertainty, and poor processes for people with communication and cognitive challenges. It is difficult to argue that the First Plan process adequately attends to difference or to person-centredness, given its reliance on a one-size-fits-all phone process. The tension between *choice and control* and *reasonable and necessary* supports is enacted daily in the planning process where set menus of priced supports can be chosen rather than bespoke support designed due to time and budgetary constraints. With increasing pressure for planners to get more people enrolled in the Scheme before all block funding ceases, the time, detailed assessment and dialogue required to develop a plan where a person living with disability has real *choice and control* are an ideal rather than a practicality of NDIS implementation. This is compounded for particular groups, including those with intellectual disabilities, communication challenges and families with children under five.

Seamless whole-of-life support

The fourth assumption in NDIS rollout needing consideration is the Scheme's capacity to deliver seamless whole-of-life support for people living with disability. From the outset the NDIS, in the *reasonable and necessary* provisions, was clear that it would not provide supports that could be provided by other sectors, government departments or informal community and family networks (NDIS Act 2013). A significant gap remains, however, in developing the range of interfaces required between the NDIS market and other service sectors, including health, education, transport, housing, community services and aged care. This was highlighted in the Productivity Commission Position Paper (APC, 2017) and, if unaddressed, potentially increases the need for people living with disability to navigate complex bureaucracies rather than establishing seamless support. If the NDIA becomes an additional agency in a disjointed bureaucratic landscape, rather than a facilitator of connections between agencies, it is difficult to imagine that there will not be a return to the piecemeal and complicated experiences described by people living with disability to the Productivity Commission in 2011 prior to the commencement of the Scheme. The exclusion of specific areas, including health and education, potentially compounds the already limited consideration of intersectional factors impacting on people's access to the NDIS. In addition, this raises questions regarding the effectiveness of planning which does not engage with gender, race, culture, sexuality or structural disadvantage as key factors shaping the experience of people living with disability in Australia (Hancock, 2016).

Where to go from here?

There is a growing body of evidence that analysis of the very managed market established to deliver the NDIS must be separated from the human rights principles of *choice and control* embedded in the policy if key assumptions in the Scheme are to be addressed. I have touched on a number of the serious and legitimate questions already emerging from NDIS implementation regarding whether the market, very managed or otherwise, can deliver the promise of *choice and control* on which the Scheme is founded. The detailed actuarial forward planning for the NDIS, which the Productivity Commission has found is on track (APC, 2017), needs to be matched by equally detailed strategic planning for practical implementation in terms of access, assessment, support planning and provision; intersections with health, housing, education, transport and other sectors; and workforce development. Several of these issues may not be adequately addressed using a fee-for-service model. While all contingencies cannot be predicted in complex policy and practice change such as the NDIS, the disadvantages of letting the Scheme evolve, and addressing high-impact questions as they arise, mean the experience of people living with disability eligible for participation in the Scheme is potentially uneven rather than bespoke. The capacity of the NDIS to fulfil key principles of *choice and control* – principles that prioritise respect for difference – is undermined through processes that can seem chaotic rather than responsive. It is the practical details of implementation that are the stumbling blocks, but these are based on a marriage of ideas, which entangles human rights with imperatives of the state and the market. They must be separated in policy planning and discussion if the NDIS is to be viable over time.

Questions need to be asked about whether a fee-for-service market, based on individualised packages, is the only, or even most appropriate, mechanism for delivering *choice and control*. In this context, the question of what kind of workforce is available to deliver *choice and control* meaningfully must be examined across the spectrum of needs, locations and life circumstances of potential and existing NDIS participants. The process for a person living in a rural or remote community must reflect that context and the differences of experience compared with urban Australia.

Loyalty to market imperatives, albeit controlled by the state, as the deliverer of human rights for people living with disability belies the origins of the NDIS where *choice and control* took precedence as the driver of policy structure and process rather than the other way around. Additionally, building a person-centred and person-driven disability policy, which aims to change shape and size in response to individual needs and preferences, using a centralised and totalising bureaucratic architecture and fixed building materials is a paradox and one which must be resolved if the principles of difference are to be enacted in a meaningful way for those utilising the Scheme.

Further readings

Foster, M., Henman, P., Tilse, C., Fleming, J., Allen, S. and Harrington, R. (2016). 'Reasonable and necessary' care: The challenge of operationalising the NDIS policy principle in allocating disability care in Australia. *Australian Journal of Social Issues*, 51(1), 27–46.

Simpson, S. (2013). Choice means privatisation under NDIS. *Education*, 94(12), 15.

Townsend, C., White, P., Cullen, J., Wright, C. and Zeeman, H. (2018). Making every Australian count: Challenges for the National Disability Insurance Scheme (NDIS) and the equal inclusion of homeless Aboriginal and Torres Strait Islander peoples with neurocognitive disability. *Australian Health Review*, 42(2), 227–229.

References

Arthurson, K. and Jacobs, K. (2009). Discourses about Australian social housing, social exclusion and employment: Indications of the post welfare state?. *Housing, Theory and Society*, 26, 179–192.

APC (Australian Productivity Commission) (2011). *Disability Care and Support*. Canberra: APC.

APC (Australian Productivity Commission) (2017). *National Disability Insurance Scheme Costs Issues Paper February 2017*. Canberra: APC.

Barnes, C. (2007). Disability activism and the struggle for change: Disability, policy and politics in the UK. *Education, Citizenship and Social Justice*, 2(203), https://doi.org/10.1177/1746197907081259

Barton, R., Robinson, T., Llewellyn, G., Thorncraft, K. and Smidt, A. (2015). Rural and remote perspectives on disability and mental health research in Australia: 2000–2013. *Advances in Mental Health*, 13(1), 30–42, http://dx.doi.org/10.1080/18374905.2015.1023417

Cortis, C., MacDonald, F., Davidson, B. and Bentham, E. (2017). *Reasonable, Necessary and Valued: Pricing Disability Services for Quality Support and Decent Jobs*, Prepared for the Health Services Union, Australian Services Union and United Voice. SPRC Report (10/17). Sydney: Social Policy Research Centre, UNSW Sydney.

Glasby, J., LeGrand, J. and Duffy, S. (2009). A healthy choice? Direct payments and healthcare in the English NHS. *Policy & Politics*, 37(4), 481–97, https://doi.org/10.1332/030557309X434322

Green, J. and Mears, J. (2014). The implementation of the NDIS: Who wins, who loses?. *Cosmopolitan Civil Societies Journal*, 6(2), 25–39.

Hancock, A.M. (2016). *Intersectionality: An Intellectual History*. Oxford: Oxford University Press.

Howard, A., Agllias, K.B., Gray, M. and Schubert, L. (2016) Hovering above the stream: Perception, experience and identity at the frontline of work with unemployed clients. *International Social Work*. https://doi.org/10.1177/0020872815618767

Hutchison, P., Lord, J. and Salisbury, B. (2006). North American approaches to individualised planning and direct funding. In J. Leece and J. Bornat (Eds.), *Developments in Direct Payments* (pp. 49–62). Bristol: Policy Press.

Ireland, J. (2014). Teething problems do not justify cutbacks to NDIS says peak body, *Sydney Morning Herald*, 7 April.

Laragy, C., Fisher, K.R., Purcal, C. and Jenkinson, S. (2015). Australia's individualised disability funding packages: When do they provide greater choice and opportunity?. *Asian Social Work and Policy Review*, 9, 282–292.

McGrath, D. (2017). *The Implementation and Operation of Psychiatric Disability Elements of the Nation Disability Insurance Scheme: A Recommended Set of Approaches*. Deakin, ACT: Mental Health Australia.

NDIS (National Disability Insurance Scheme) IAC (Independent Advisory Council) (2013). *Choice and Control: Reflections on the Implementation of the Principle of Choice and Control under the NDIS*. NDIS IAC.

United Nations (2006). *Convention on the Rights of Persons with Disabilities*. http://www.un.org/disabilities/documents/convention/convoptprot-e.pdf

Warr, D., Dickinson, H., Olney, S., Hargrave, J., Karanikolas, A., Kasidis, V., Katsikis, G., Ozge, J., Peters, D., Wheeler, J. and Wilcox., M. (2017). *Choice, Control and the NDIS: Service Users Perspectives on Having Choice and Control in the NDIS*, Community Report. Melbourne: University of Melbourne.

15

Collisions Between the State and the Evil Spirit: Home Care in Indigenous Communities

Frank T.Y. Wang and Sheng-Pei Tsai

In the spirit of respect, the authors acknowledge the Traditional Owners of the land of the Tao people of Lanyu in Taiwan, who continue their ongoing custodianship of the land and waters. We acknowledge that we are on this land as beneficiaries of an uncompensated and unreconciled dispossession, which continues until today. We pay respect to Elders past, present and emerging, who have created many of the paths we now travel. Through acknowledgement, we remind ourselves to act in solidarity with the Tao people, along with other Indigenous peoples around Taiwan and the world to resist racism, oppression and colonisation, especially the nuclear waste that has been stored in Lanyu without informed consent of the Tao people for the past three decades.

This study started with Frank Wang's long-term friendship with the Tao nurse Si Yabosokanen, who devotes her life to elder care for Tao people. Based on the trust between Wang and Yabosokanen, Wang's student, Sheng-Pei Tsai, was able to conduct her fieldwork and finish her master's thesis. This chapter is written by Wang based on data collected by Tsai. Wang, a Han Chinese gay man, holds a position as a critical activist scholar and a social work educator, honouring the person's experience, perspective and strengths, and developing critical reflection for collective actions. Tsai, a Taiwanese woman and Social Work master's student, developed her passion for Indigenous people during her college years. Being aware of our privileged position as academics and Han Chinese, the authors continue to learn to listen to the unspoken and unheard voices of the Tao people with openness and modesty. As non-Indigenous activist researchers, we position ourselves as partners with the Tao communities to honour their perspectives and strengths in order to produce alternative discourses that challenge the colonial relations. Our study is an invitation to you as practitioners, researchers and students to enter the world of the Tao people, whose culture and perspective are systematically ignored and stigmatised by the state, and daily practices of front-line workers are excluded as illegal acts. Reframing these acts as creative and important resistance to the colonial relations among the Tao workers is the key to future transformation, a gift that we as academics can and should contribute in the process of future change.

Background

Indigenous people have different world views, which are often excluded in welfare policies. Social welfare that fails to confirm Indigenous world views tends to serve as a means of assimilating Indigenous people into mainstream society. Many Indigenous scholars have called such practices 'cultural genocide' (Kieken, 1999). Per Article 10 of Taiwan's Constitutional Provisions, social welfare, health care and long-term care (LTC) for Indigenous peoples are required to respect the will of Indigenous peoples. In other words, cultural safety in LTC policy for Indigenous peoples is required by the Constitution. In practice, there is no participatory mechanism for Indigenous peoples in the process of policy making. The promise of cultural safety for Indigenous peoples exists only on paper. The pattern of excluding the Indigenous perspective has produced an unequal relationship between Indigenous people and non-Indigenous Taiwanese over the past 400 years of colonial history. Making this mechanism of social exclusion visible is the first step towards change.

As home care is the backbone of long-term care, this study examines how the gap between LTC policy and Indigenous cultures shapes the practices of home care in Indigenous communities. The research question is how Indigenous ways of care are excluded in everyday home care practices and how this has produced inequality between the Taiwanese and Indigenous peoples.

Literature review

Institutional exclusion of Indigenous perspective

When asking how Indigenous communities can involve and decide the future of LTC for them, it is equally important to answer how Indigenous communities are excluded from the provision of LTC. Although public home care programs started in 1983, coverage is limited to urban areas. The Ministry of Health and Welfare (MOHW) provides a major proportion of funding and has set up service standards and regulations. The service standards, regulations and reimbursement scheme tend to reflect the lifeworld of urban experiences, in which Indigenous experiences are excluded. For example, the reimbursement scheme for home care is based on a fee-for-service model. Service hours do not cover travel time. In urban areas, travel time from site to site is about 10–20 minutes due to the availability of public transportation and the density of case location. However, travel time to and from Indigenous communities is high because of the scarcity of cases and the vast scale of the coverage area. Discounting travel time from the reimbursement scheme has significantly reduced the monthly income of home care workers in Indigenous communities (Wang, 2013).

Another barrier to Indigenous peoples' access to LTC is the implementation of co-payments in 2009. In order to satisfy demand, the public LTC program moved from means-tested/residual to universal, so that elderly people with functional disability could also have access. However, a co-payment of 40% was introduced in an attempt to prevent service abuse. The co-payment has become a financial barrier for Indigenous people as they have lower incomes. Tsai and Shih (2009) reported that two-thirds of case closures in the Indigenous communities in Pingtung County were due to the co-payment.

Contracting-out as a mechanism of social exclusion

The provision of LTC in Taiwan adopts the neoliberal contracting-out model, in which non-governmental organisations (NGOs) compete for public grants to provide services. The contracting-out system also serves as a mechanism to exclude Indigenous people. First of all, local governments tend to divide all the townships into several proposals, in which a coverage area includes several townships. This is often beyond the capacity of local Indigenous organisations; only external large-scale NGOs are capable of meeting the coverage requirement. Second, bidding requires proposal writing and personnel with professional qualifications. Local Indigenous community organisations often fail to meet these requirements, so the provision of LTC in Indigenous communities tends to depend on external non-Indigenous NGOs. It is in this context that the case of Lanyu is important because the provision of home care is provided by a local Tao organisation.

Research design

This study starts with the long-term friendship between the first author and Ms Si Yabosokanen, a Tao nurse, who has been committed to elder care in Lanyu since 1997. The Lanyu Public Health Center is the only medical service provider, providing emergency care and outpatient care. Individuals with cases that require intensive care, such as specialist and hospital care, will have to go to the main island. Si Yabosokanen had been working as a home health nurse in the Center. She had provided end-of-life care to about 40 elderly persons and then found herself alone, unable to meet the needs of these elderly people. She began to recruit a group of volunteers, mostly women, to provide home care to Tao elderly, leading to the establishment of the Orchid Association in 1999, the first local Indigenous organisation to provide LTC. The first author met Si Yabosokanen in the broadcasting of her first documentary film *And Deliver Us From Evil* in 2001 and supported her work by assisting the newly established organisation to get the government contract to provide home care in 2004.

Yet when the local government expanded the coverage area to cover more than Lanyu in 2008, the Orchid Association lost its qualifications for the bid. The NGO, St Mary's Hospital, which got the contract, decided to work with the Orchid Association to continue providing home care. The cooperation between St. Mary's and the Orchid Association continues to the present.

Based on the long-term trust between the first author and Si Yabosokanen, the authors were granted approval and support to conduct this research. The field study was conducted from March to June 2014 by the second author, and included a supervisor, three full-time and four part-time home care workers, with 35 cases.

The methodological approach used in the study is based on Dorothy Smith's institutional ethnography (Smith, 2005), which is aimed at people who are socially excluded. Her approach is an effort to expand on people's knowledge about the social organisation of their experiences, which in turn helps make the broader social relations based on class, gender and ethnicity that seek to rule our everyday lives become visible.

The Tao people and their Anito belief

The Tao people are one of 16 Indigenous tribes in Taiwan, comprising 4,408 Tao people living on Lanyu, a small island, which lies 90 km southeast of Taiwan, in the Pacific Ocean. Lanyu was preserved for anthropologist study in the Japanese colonial period (1895–1945), so the Tao people encountered modern civilisation only after World War II. Therefore, Tao is the latest Indigenous tribe to encounter Han Chinese/ Taiwanese culture and Taiwan's market economy. Since the 1950s, the Tao people have thus experienced cultural conflict and shock in the past 70 years (Tsai, 2009).

The Tao people have a different understanding of illness, death and ageing, through the traditional belief of Anito. 'Anito' is a Tao term for 'evil spirits', and carries different meanings, such as 'ghost', 'spirit', 'the dead', 'demon'. Furthermore, things that cannot be explained or things that are unfamiliar, such as twin babies or exotic insects, can be seen as Anito. Even the nuclear waste stored on Lanyu by the government since 1984 is now seen as a form of Anito. Anito does not designate certain types of things or persons, but rather a way of explaining how misfortune or disaster happens. It provides the basic framework for the Tao people to interpret things that are unpredictable and shape how they make sense of their everyday lives (Tsai, 2009).

The most typical case of Anito reflects on the Tao's understanding of illness, ageing and death. Before the introduction of modern medicine to Lanyu, illness and death were the most unpredictable and difficult things that the Tao people encountered in daily life. Wei and Liu (1962) state that the Tao people considered being sick to mean that the spirit of the sick person is struggling with Anito. If the spirit of the afflicted successfully escapes the capture of Anito, the sick person will recover. Otherwise, the sick person will die and his or her spirit will be taken away by Anito. The Tao people's fear of Anito comes from believing it not only to cause misery but also that it is contagious. Any person or thing close to the sick or dying is considered to be infected by Anito. The fear of Anito is fully expressed in the Tao funeral. The newly deceased is considered the most vicious Anito as a deceased person going to an unfamiliar domain will feel lonely and be eager to find companionship (Yu, 2004, p. 88). Therefore, only close family members will attend the funeral; others will avoid it.

In a time of scarce resources, the Tao people could feed themselves only through the hard work of fishing, farming and collecting. As a frail elderly person was unable to work, his existence became a liability to the family. The elderly person would ask his or her children to build a temporary house near the family or at the border of the community (see Figure 15.1). While the Tao people usually eat only twice a day, the adult children are responsible for providing one meal each day to the live-alone elderly person. Although the economic situation in Lanyu has improved so that food is sufficient for all, the practice of living alone continues among many Tao elderly.

Figure 15.1 Temporary house for a Tao elderly person

(Courtesy of Si Yabosokanen)

Findings

The 'living-alone' tradition as 'unfilial' behaviour

To access the need for home care is to determine what family responsibility is. The home care program in Taiwan is governed by what Wang (1998) called a 'three-generational-family' ideology in which family members should take care of their frail elderly parents. To apply for public home care is to put oneself under the scrutiny of family ideology. To be eligible for LTC, the elderly person needs to be assessed by a care manager, who tends to be Taiwanese. During home visits, care managers see an elderly person living alone in a very poor housing condition, with only one meal per day provided by the adult child, and tend to be surprised, condemning the Tao people as 'unfilial'. This misunderstanding of 'unfilial Tao children' is socially organised by the differences in cultural definitions of family care and the history of the housing policies in Lanyu, which are often unknown to Taiwanese.

The tradition of sick elderly Tao living alone is reflected in the traditional Tao housing arrangements. The traditional Tao house is composed of a main house and working room, the latter of which can be lived in by the elderly member. However, the government introduced a housing reconstruction project from 1966 to 1980. In 1974, Madame Kai-Shek Chiang, former first lady, visited Lanyu and viewed the traditional Tao house as barbarous and uncivilised. A large-scale public housing project was initiated afterwards, with a total of 566 units being built to replace traditional Tao houses in four of all six communities.

The housing reconstruction has had disastrous impacts on the Tao tradition as the living space was altered. The new public housing offers a modern home in which all the living space is under one roof. The extra room, that is, a working room, for the frail elderly to reside alone disappeared. This reconstruction has left no appropriate, safe space for the Tao elderly to practise their tradition of living alone.

The needs assessment regarding home care by non-Indigenous care managers tends to be biased by their racialised image of the unfilial Tao children, leading to a limited and unfair service plan in order to force the Tao family to take their responsibility. Without an awareness of the violent housing reconstruction, non-Indigenous care managers reinforce the stigma experienced by Indigenous people by denying the needs of elderly persons.

Not to be cared for is to be Indigenous

During needs assessments, if an elderly person refuses the service, such wishes will be respected. However, there is a category of clientele in the Orchid Association called 'cases rejecting services', so the volunteer continues to visit these elderly people without providing care. A supervisor who was in charge of managing the home care program told us: 'These elderly people reject our services not because they have no needs but because they insist on living their lives in the Tao way.' The tradition of living alone, based on the belief of Anito, in fact is an act of love and mercy in that the elderly Tao person leaves precious resources for future generations within the community. In addition, accepting care at such an old age, in Tao culture, is considered being selfish, taking food that belongs to the young. Tao elderly persons are encouraged to self-sacrifice for the continuation of their ethnic lifeline. In a culture where elderly people are encouraged to reject care, providing home care itself is an act that challenges their traditional beliefs, and redefines what 'elder care' means for the Tao people. This challenge and redefinition of Anito belief permeate the everyday practices of home care services.

Who are the home care workers?

Providing home care requires having home care workers who, according to MOHW regulations, must receive 90 hours of training and 100 hours of practicum in certified institutions. However, in a culture where caring for the elderly means also being in touch with Anito, being a home care worker also means that one's work will bring misfortune to the care worker and his or her family. Government-mandated training and personal willingness to do the work aside, the biggest challenge is that assuming a home care role requires approval and support from the whole family. Therefore, it is extremely difficult to find someone willing to be a home care worker. The supervisor described this as 'people saying that only those who are mad or crazy will be home care workers'.

If that is the case, who are the three full-time home care workers? How is it possible for them to work in this role? And how do they deal with the communities' belief in Anito and successfully complete their daily work? The supervisor described the home care workers as 'senior members of our church' and said that 'they are all elders in the church', eluding to their devotion to Christianity. They start work with a prayer every morning: 'May the Holy Spirit protect us from Anito.' Doing so collectively, they believe the Holy Spirit will protect both them and the elderly from Anito. From the perspective of a Christian, providing home care in this context is a testimony to their faith.

The government began allowing Christianity into Indigenous communities since its retreat from China in 1949. Indigenous people converted to Christianity on a large scale during 1945–1956. In 2013, about 70% of Indigenous people were Christian, compared with 6.53% of the total Taiwanese population (Chu, 2014). The introduction of Christianity provides a counter discourse to the traditional Anito, in that the Holy Spirit is capable of contending Anito.

Fraud or forgery, or act of resistance?

The Anito belief has created a caregiver hierarchy for the frail elderly person. Believing all bad things in life to be caused by an evil spirit, frail elderly people live separately from their family, and only close family members can provide care. The first priority is the elderly person's spouse, with same-sex adult children being second – that is, a mother is cared for by her daughter and a father by his son. If the spouse or adult children are not available, relatives are also allowed. However, the preference of care by close family members is in contradiction with government regulations on home care, in which the home care worker cannot be related to the client, as family members are legally obliged to care for their elderly parents, according to Article 1114 of the civil code. As Tao communities are composed of related family members, it becomes very difficult to find home care workers who meet both the government's requirements of non-relative carers and the elderly person's preference of close family members. The negotiation for a home care worker then becomes a task for the care supervisor.

Occasionally, there are cases that require home care workers to care for their elderly relatives. In order not to violate government regulations, the supervisor will ask another home care worker to sign the home care attendance sheet in the other's place. This exchange of signatures creates a textual reality that meets the government's ideology of family and allows the practice of traditional Anito for the elderly person at the same time.

The textual practice of swapping signatures can be recognised as the 'work knowledge' (Smith, 2005, p. 151) of Indigenous front-line workers. Work knowledge has two aspects: one is a person's experience of and in their work, and the other is the coordination of his or her work with the work of others. The supervisor coordinates the choice of an appropriate caregiver shaped by the Anito belief with the textual practices of the attendance sheet as required by MOHW regulations during an audit. Work knowledge such as this is essential to make the provision of home care possible. It may be seen as fraud or forgery, but instead it should be seen as an act of resistance by the front-line worker who is having to deal with the disjuncture between everyday life and the ruling ideology of family ethics.

As the Indigenous perspective of care is systematically excluded from government policy, the accumulation and diffusion of work knowledge like this is important for front-line workers in community-led organisations such as the Orchid Association. As the buffer between government policy and local Indigenous communities, front-line workers encounter situations such as needs of elderly persons that are not recognised by care managers, home care workers not being allowed to provide care, and textual practices deemed unacceptable to the local government. These practices tend to be kept secret by workers out of fear of being punished by the government. These practices, in fact, contain important work knowledge that should be shared within and between Indigenous communities and should be recognised as meaningful resistance to the ruling apparatus of home care.

How much time is allowed for taking a bath?

The function of 'number of service hours' in home care enables the development of the whole home care administrative regime, and thus renders the social lives of elderly persons and their families manageable by the state (Wang, 1998, p. 129). The elderly person is therefore objectified into an institutional term – the number of service hours. The number of service hours provides a unifying measurement to eliminate the variance that occurs and fluctuates from person to person.

Take 'assisting with bathing' as an example. An elderly person with 'physical dysfunction', in particular 'having difficulty moving about' is determined as 'in need of assistance with bathing'. The number of service hours allotted for assisting with bathing is 30 minutes to an hour, a standardised calculation between the type of care activity and the time needed. However, in our field study, we found that it takes three hours to finish the bathing for a Tao elderly person in Lanyu.

How does the gap between the knowledge regarding the time needed for taking a bath and the actual bathing in Lanyu occur? First of all, for the Tao elderly, bathing takes place outdoors as there is no bath tub in the temporary house. Taking a bath therefore requires fair weather.

Second, the home care worker has to find a flat spot for bathing and a path for the elderly person to walk outdoors safely. Once the bathing site is decided, the home care worker has to find neighbours who are willing to provide water and allow a hose to pass through their property so that water can be made available for the bath. This requires strong interpersonal skills on behalf of the home care worker because water for the sick elderly is seen as a carrier for Anito. To maintain good relationships with the neighbours, from time to time the home care worker has to bring gifts, such as yams he or she grows. During the bath, the home care worker also has to watch very carefully that the water does not go onto others' property as it may carry Anito.

Helping an elderly person in Lanyu with a bath is physically and emotionally taxing work and requires establishing and maintaining good interpersonal relationships. The whole process usually takes more than three hours, which also means overtime without pay for the worker. However, none of this 'work' can be recorded – simply a checkmark next to 'bath assistance' on the case record. Diamond (1995, p. 130) captured the rule of textual practice in modern social organisation of elderly care vividly in the phrase 'If it's not charted, it didn't happen'.

Discussion and conclusion

The Tao people have a unique interpretation of ageing, illness and death through the lens of the Anito belief, which in turn permeates the provision of home care. Without respect for their world view, disjuncture occurs in the process of home care provision, including the living-alone tradition being stigmatised as unfilial by Taiwanese care managers, as well as elderly people who need care refusing home care in order to maintain their Tao identity, textual practices of forging attendance sheets and the number of service hours allowed failing to cover care needs. Explication of these disjuncture experiences leads us to identify two institutional discourses that organise the everyday practices of home care. The first discourse is the Chinese family ideology, which sees 'unfilial' family members unworthy of help. The second discourse is the managerialism of care activities, leading to the devaluation of emotional work described by Hochschild (1983). The emphasis on measurability enables the standardised time allotted for care activities, which decontextualises care activities, makes care work in different contexts invisible and shifts costs of care to home care workers.

Work knowledge is produced by front-line workers, as they live with the contradictions between governmental policies and the Indigenous community on a daily basis. Practices based on this valuable work knowledge tend to be seen as unacceptable, illegal or unethical, and therefore can only be carried out without being recorded and must remain unknown to outsiders.

These practices should not be a sign of shame and guilt, but a sign of pride and triumph. They are possible because front-line workers have chosen the standpoint of Indigenous peoples instead of the government, and they are points of resistance and decolonisation for Indigenous peoples. This work knowledge should be shared among workers in Indigenous communities to raise the consciousness of those who are also struggling with similar problems. Armed with such awareness, other Indigenous communities can begin to engage in dialogue with the state and begin down the road towards self-determination.

The case of home care in Lanyu is unique because the Orchid Association is a community-led organisation, situated directly between government policy and the Indigenous community. Its practices of home care illustrate the fact that Indigenous culture is not fixed but fluid, and thus is subjected to a continuous process of defining and redefining. Although Anito still dominates how Tao people make sense of their everyday lives, especially the elderly, the Tao people's culture consists of more than the Anito belief. The introduction of Christianity in the 1950s has provided the Tao people with an alternative discourse, one in which the Holy Spirit can defeat Anito.

This leads to a series of thorny questions about the interpretation of Indigenous culture. Is the provision of home care in Lanyu destroying the traditional culture of the Tao Anito belief due to the introduction of Christianity? If the preservation of tradition is important, should the Tao elderly people, then, be left uncared for in order to live up to their Anito belief? These questions problematise how we understand what is Indigenous.

If being a Tao is to follow a way of living according to Anito belief, we fail to see culture as evolving and fluid in time and space. Regarding Anito as the essence of the Tao people is another form of cultural stereotyping. The function of culture is to provide a useful framework of meaning so that individuals of a group can be better adapted to the environment. The Anito belief has helped the Tao people survive in a time of scare resources, but its interpretation should not be locked into that period. Its revival needs interpretation by the people who identify as Tao. What is important is not the content of Anito being unchanged but that the power of interpretation is left in the hands of the Tao people, not outsiders.

If self-determination is the direction for LTC in Indigenous communities, what can we learn from Lanyu? The experiences of Lanyu offer a good example of how front-line workers can develop valuable work knowledge to bridge the gaps between government policy and local culture. Front-line workers are what Paulo Freire (1970) called 'culture worker' who develop critical consciousness for oppressed people. For the Tao people, the interpretation of Anito has the potential to develop into a decolonising discourse.

Home care workers have overcome their fear of Anito in their everyday practices of prayer. Anito is no longer as undefeatable as it used to be. What workers need is to further their resistance against not just Anito but also the government. Viewing the government as a form of Anito has been put forward by the nuclear waste movement.

The nuclear waste that the government has disposed of in Lanyu is considered by the Tao people to be Anito. The Tao people have fought for the removal of the nuclear waste for more than 30 years, rallying and protesting, and are determined to pass this fight on to the next generation. This social movement against the government making Lanyu a nuclear waste dump has become a catalyst for the Tao people seeing the government as another form of Anito, but not undefeatable if they unite in solidarity. By viewing the government as a form of Anito, the Anito discourse can serve as a discourse for decolonising the reproductive mechanism of racial inequality, that policies and regulations should be visible in order to be analysed, deconstructed and reconstructed for the Tao people. In this new discourse of the Anito, it is not the Holy Spirit that the Tao people need to defeat the Anito, but instead their solidarity.

Further readings

Allio, F. (1998). The Austronesian peoples of Taiwan: Building a political platform for themselves. *China Perspectives*, 18, 52–60.

Gao, I-An (2018). Indigenous peoples' self-determination and long-term care: Sápmi and Nunavut. *Social Work and Policy Studies: Social Justice, Practice and Theory*, 1(1) (online). https://openjournals.library.sydney.edu.au/index.php/SWPS/article/view/12415/1152

Simon, S. (2002). The underside of a miracle: Industrialization, land, and Taiwan's Indigenous peoples. *Cultural Survival Quarterly*, June. https://www.culturalsurvival.org/publications/cultural-survival-quarterly/underside-miracle-industrialization-land-and-taiwans

Taylor, K. and Guerin, P. (2010). *Health Care and Indigenous Australians: Cultural Safety in Practice*. Melbourne: Palgrave Macmillan.

References

Chu, J.S.T. (2014). *Taiwan Church Report 2013*. Taipei: Christian Resource Center. http://www.ccea.org.tw/cceaup/church/christianityreport/2013.pdf.

Diamond, T. (1995). *Making Grey Gold: Narratives of Nursing Home Care*. Chicago: Chicago University Press.

Freire, P. (1970). *Pedagogy of the Oppressed*. New York: Continuum.

Hochschild, A.R. (1983). *The Managed Heart: Commercialization of Human Feeling*. Berkeley: University of California Press.

Kieken, R.V. (1999). The stolen generations and cultural genocide: The forced removal of Australian Indigenous children from their families and its implications for the sociology of childhood. *Childhood*, 6(3), 297–311.

Kuan-Hong, Y. (2004). *Yamei Tribe*, Taipei: Sem Ming.

Smith, D.E. (2005). *Institutional Ethnography: A Sociology for People*. Toronto: University of Toronto Press.

Tsai, W.-F. and Shih, S.-J. (2009). Assessment of co-payment in home care in indigenous community: The case of Pingtung County. *Journal of Community Development*, 126, 226–239.

Tsai, Y.-Y. (2009). *Mental Disorder of the Tao Aboriginal Minority in Taiwan: Modernity, Social Change, and the Origin of Social Suffering*. Taipei: Lien-Chin Publishing.

Wang, F.T.Y. (1998). Disciplining Taiwanese families: A study of family ideology and home care practices, PhD Dissertation, University of Toronto.

Wang, F.T.Y. (2013). Exploring the possibility of self-determination in long term care by indigenous peoples. *Journal of Community Development*, 141, 284–295.

Wei, H. and Liu, B. (1962). *The Social Organization of Yami People in Lanyu*. Taipei: Institute of Ethnography, Acedimia Sinica.

PART SIX
RESISTANCES AND REFLECTIONS

16
Concepts, Theories and the Politics of Difference: A Discussion of Select Terms

Susan Goodwin

> *I acknowledge the Traditional Owners of the lands, skies and waterways where I have lived, learned and undertaken this work. I acknowledge that I am on this land as a beneficiary of an uncompensated and unreconciled dispossession, which continues today. I pay respect to Elders, past, present and emerging, and acknowledge the important role they play in caring for and forming my world.*

The critical interrogation of taken-for-granted terms, concepts and categories has been central to social justice politics: what people, things, places and institutions are labelled, and by whom, has been shown to matter. Indeed, the chapters in the book attest to the significance of knowledge and knowledge practices in shaping experiences of difference and inequity. This chapter provides an opportunity to interrogate and elaborate some of the key concepts that are used in the project of working across difference. In this chapter, I have assembled a selection of related concepts and ideas in use in the book to consider where they have come from and the work they do in establishing ways of thinking about difference and inequity. The idea is to explore 'how, when and why they emerged and became popular' (Talburt and Lesko, 2012, p. 11) and to discuss how they link to knowledge practices in social work and social policy more broadly.

Clearly, this interrogation of concepts and theories has involved making choices to include some concepts and approaches and exclude others. Given the approach taken to knowledge in this chapter, it is appropriate to also subject my choices to critical scrutiny. Two aspects of my 'own location within historically and culturally entrenched forms of knowledge' (Bacchi and Goodwin, 2016, p. 24) stand out as relevant: the first relates to my geographical positioning, and the second to my theoretical interest in social constructionist, poststructuralist and postcolonial perspectives on the world.

First, as an Australian researcher, I have been inculcated with Western ways of thinking and trained in social theory largely produced in Europe and North America, or what Connell refers to as 'the imperial centre' (Connell, 2015). Yet, in the context of the ongoing legacies of colonial violence towards Indigenous peoples and their knowledges, critiques of Western ways of knowing are politically potent for Australian researchers. Similarly, the prevalence of diaspora cultures, identities, religions and languages in Australia provides the impetus for considering the Anglo-Celtic mainstream as a dominant way of thinking rather than simply *the* way of thinking – in 2016, 49% of all Australians were either born overseas or had one parent born overseas (ABS, 2017). My geographic location, then, means I have highlighted terms from within a political and cultural framework that has generated particular critical preoccupations, particularly with cultural difference, settler colonialism, white privilege and decolonisation.

Second, my understanding of difference has been informed by social constructionist, poststructuralist and postcolonial theory that proposes that differences between people are central to processes of domination and subordination and are socially produced. From these perspectives, differences are not seen as neutral matters of fact that stem from biology or are embedded across societies in fixed ways. Instead, differences are produced in interaction with others and in the social context, through social processes. My theoretical perspective means that I have chosen to interrogate and elaborate terms that mesh with this perspective. The purpose of interrogating concepts-in-use such as, for example, 'binaries' and 'othering' is to demonstrate how they fit with particular theoretical traditions and also how they can be mobilised in social constructionist, poststructuralist and postcolonial politics of difference.

The key concepts and theories discussed in this chapter are:

➢ Binaries/binarism/binary thinking

➢ Decolonisation/decolonising theory

➢ Difference/the politics of difference

➢ Diversity

➢ Postcolonialism

➢ Poststructuralism

➢ Privilege/white privilege

➢ Other/Othering

➢ Settler Colonialism

Binaries/binarism/binary thinking

The concepts 'binary', 'binarism' and 'binary thinking' or 'binary logic' have come to be widely used in discussions of difference in social work and social policy. While the concept 'binary' simply means a pair or a combination of two things, it also has quite specific theoretical and conceptual roots. The concern with binarism can be traced to the French structural linguist Ferdinand de Saussure, who held that signs have meaning 'not by a simple reference to real objects, but by their opposition to other signs' (Ashcroft et al., p. 19). In Western cultural constructions of reality, binary oppositions are perceived as hierarchical, with one term valued (or privileged) and the other devalued (or marginalised).

A range of problems have been identified with binary systems or binary logics. First, they often entail the kind of hierarchy described above. Second, binaries suppress ambiguous spaces between the opposition, so that any overlap, say, between the categories man/woman, human/animal, child/adult, able-bodied/disabled, becomes impossible according to binary logic. One is either a man *or* a woman, a child *or* an adult, and so on. Third, binary oppositions repress additional and multiple categories, so that positions outside of the opposing categories are rendered invisible.

Feminists have drawn attention to the way binary logics entail a hierarchy in which one form of the male/female opposition is always dominant (man over woman) and that, in fact, the binary opposition itself exists to confirm that dominance. They have also drawn attention to the ways that binary logics fix behaviours and dispositions to the gender binary – male and female, men's work and women's work, masculinity and femininity, masculine things and feminine things, and so on – as a way of making gender orders appear 'natural' and logical (Connell and Messerschmidt, 2005; Huppatz and Goodwin, 2013; McPhail, 2004; Pease, 2011).

Postcolonial writers have demonstrated the tendency in Western thought to see and establish the world in terms of binary oppositions, and how this establishes relations of dominance and supports imperial ideology (Bhaba, 1992; Jack, 2015; Patel, 2006). Seeing the world in terms of coloniser/colonised, civilised/primitive, white/black has been crucial to the 'civilising missions' and exploitative practices of dominating and colonising cultures.

In social work and social policy, attention to binaries involves thinking about how language structures the world and the work that oppositions do, to both occlude variation and establish relations of dominance and subordination. For example, it has been argued that 'social workers must challenge the rigid gender binary, either by eliminating it or expanding it to include more gender possibilities' (Burdge, 2007, p. 247). Terms such as 'transgender', 'non-binary gender', meaning identifying as other than 'male' or 'female', and 'cisgender', to indicate a congruence between a person's gender identity and their socially recognised sex, disrupt binary thinking in important ways. The terms draw attention to the gender dualism *as a constructed dualism* and highlight the taken-for-granted hierarchy within it (Burdge, 2007; Connell, 2010). Similar challenges to dichotomous, binary thinking have been at the heart of critical race theory, critical disability studies and in anti-oppressive practice approaches to social work practice (Delgado and Stefancic, 2017; Meekosha and Shuttleworth, 2009; Morley, 2008; Razack, 2009; Walter et al., 2011).

Decolonisation/decolonising theory

In everyday discourse, the concept decolonisation is generally used to refer to the dismantling of colonial empires through changing the way that countries are formally ruled. In this sense, former colonies 'de-colonise' through struggles for independence or self-determination. However, decolonising theories also emphasise other dimensions of colonisation, demonstrating that colonisation involves the domination of populations through the imposition of ways of thinking. Decolonising theories push back against colonial assumptions about things like 'progress', what it is to be human (ontologies) and what knowledge is (epistemologies).

Decolonising social work involves *re-centring* Indigenous social thought or the long-standing traditions of ways of knowing such as knowledge about the Land, about people and about relationships and *de-centring* colonial ways of knowing. It also involves developing and supporting social work and social policy practices, such as research methodologies, that offer alternatives to Western paradigms and that eschew racism, ethnocentrism and exploitation (Bessarab and Ng'andu, 2010; Meekosha, 2011; Smith, 2013).

Difference/the politics of difference

In contemporary social work and social policy discussions, 'difference' operates as a keyword that does particular political work. Claims made on the basis of 'difference' are distinct to those made, for example, for 'equality' or 'diversity'. A 'politics of difference' also does more than make claims for recognition by identity groups; it brings into question the processes of differentiation, whereby differences are made meaningful. In a politics of difference, differences are not innocent but are actively deployed to both reflect and perpetuate or to resist or challenge the given social order.

Social constructionist approaches to difference can be contrasted to essentialist approaches, which see difference as related to the inner characteristics of individuals, which are relatively unified and consistent and often assumed to be 'natural' (Berger and Luckmann, 1991; Lewis, 2000). From an essentialist perspective, differences between individuals and social groups are held to pre-exist social life and are more or less predictive of behaviour and experience. In contrast, social constructionism holds that such differences are *made* and therefore focuses on 'how we come to be' as individuals and as members of social groups.

Feminist work has been important in outlining a social constructionist approach to difference through the establishment of the concept 'gender' which refers to socially formed traits that have come to be latched on to different types of bodies, so that inequalities between men and women are made to appear natural or related to real 'sex differences' based in biology. The concept gender proposes that gender inequality is not 'natural' and opens up possibilities for change in the social ordering of society (Connell, 2014).

Theorists of cultural difference have interrogated the concept 'race' as a social construct that emerged historically and involved reducing complex physical and cultural characteristics and a vast continuum of ethnic variation into narrow categories, and then sorting people into these categories. From the social constructionist perspective, the focus is not on race, ethnicity or religion, in and of themselves, but on the social consequences of the attribution of significance, exclusion and privilege by society to certain patterns of difference. Thus, the focus is racialisation – the ways in which racialised societies are sustained by racialised regimes that produce and reproduce boundaries based on biology, skin colour, language, links to real or presumed ancestors, religion and so on – and on racial inequality (Knowles, 2010).

Diversity

The concept 'diversity' is used in social work and social policy discourses, sometimes critically but often less so. Indeed, in organisational settings and organisational policies, 'diversity' is often used vaguely as a euphemism for 'race', and also for 'gender' or as a surrogate for equity and social justice (Dobusch, 2017). One of the key criticisms of the usage of 'diversity' rather than 'difference' is that it does not look at systems and is not designed to look at power, privilege and access to resources. As Sarah Ahmed (2012, p. 26) argues, the concept of 'diversity' is 'an empty container' into which all sorts of arbitrary and unrelated differences can be thrown in order to produce 'a happy image of diversity'. In social work and social policy, 'diversity' policies can result in a focus on *numbers* of people in the workforce or accessing a service, rather than deeper issues associated with exclusion. This can lead to strategies that focus on individuals (like diversity 'training') rather than addressing inequalities based on group membership. In addition, most groups that are 'marked as diversity-relevant' are treated as fixed, one-dimensional categories, often as 'target groups'.

Dobusch (2017, p. 1646) argues a feature of 'such homogenised and essentialist constructions of diversity target groups is that they mainly refer to 'those who "look different" such as women, people of colour or with "obvious" migration/ethnic background'. So, as well as homogenising those targeted, diversity discourses render the dominant group – that is, those *not* targeted – as unproblematic. White males do not have to be labelled. They are neither racialized nor gendered. White men are not represented as a group but as individuals (Nkomo and Stewart, 2006, p. 533). In addition, diversity discourses in organisations are often permeated by business rationales which argue that organisations *need* diversity, not for social justice reasons but for profitability. As Stuart Hall wrote about 'corporate multiculturalism': 'Corporate multiculturalism manages difference in the interests of the centre' (Hall, 2001, p. 3). It is in this sense that 'diversity-talk' can make social justice and equity discourses meaningless.

Other/Othering

In very basic terms, 'Other' is used to specify anyone who is separate from one's self and the term is crucial in locating oneself. The term 'Othering' was coined by Gayatri Spivak (1985, 1987) for the process by which imperial discourse creates its 'Others': Othering describes the various ways in which colonial discourse creates its subjects. In Spivak's explanation, Othering is a dialectical process because the colonising Other is established at the same time as its colonised Others are produced as subjects. The theory of identity formation inherent in the concept of Othering assumes that subordinate people are offered, and at the same time relegated to, subject positions as Others in discourse (Jensen, 2011). In these processes, it is the centre that has the power to describe, and the Other is constructed as inferior. The process of Othering does two things: it reduces groups who are 'Othered' to stereotypical characteristics and ultimately dehumanises them. At the same time, such discursive practices affirm the legitimacy and superiority of the powerful group: the dominant group thinks of itself as superior *because* it has constructed 'Others' as inferior.

Spivak's conceptualisation is in accordance with contemporary deployments of the concept, which is used across fields of social work to refer to differentiating discourses that lead to the defining of groups of people as problematic or 'inferior' by the group with the capacity to dominate. For instance, the concept has been applied to the way that people in poverty are thought about, talked about and treated as inferior to the rest of society. Ruth Lister (2005, p. 10) describes this process as 'Othering': 'A dividing line is drawn between "us" and "them" and the dividing line is imbued with negative judgements that construct "the poor" variously as a source of moral contamination, a threat, an undeserving economic burden, failures in the meritocratic race, an object of pity or even as an exotic species to be studied.'

Othering also has been an important concept in analyses of racism. Aileen Moreton-Robinson (2004) argues that white subjects have produced 'race' as belonging to the Other, in essence de-racialising whiteness. She argues (2004, p. 77) that systems of racial superiority hinge on white subjects producing the racialised Other 'in the liminal space between human/animal' as a way of universalising and normalising a very specific (white) representation of what 'humanity' is. Similar dehumanising processes have been identified in contemporary representations of other groups, for example 'the aged' and 'the disabled'. For example, Susan Wendell (1996, p. 60) has explained how non-disabled individuals who view themselves as the 'paradigm of humanity' produce the 'disabled-Other' through equating disability with sub-humanity. The concept 'Othering' is thus deployed to make visible how power operates in processes of discrimination or marginalisation. Writing about ableist Othering of disability, Reutlinger (2015, p. 26) explains:

> [T]he discourse of Othering becomes an exertion of heinous, subconscious, and invisible power over cultural groups considered different-from-the-norm. That is, the Othering of 'abnormal' groups occurs without anyone of-the-norm mindfully recognizing that the process is occurring because it has become commonplace to view someone 'different' in a negative way.

Postcolonialism

Postcolonial theorists focus on the ways that interactions between cultures in the context of colonialism produce cultural difference. As Kwok (2005, p. 43) explains, 'difference arises not because there are many pre-constituted cultures living side by side, but because it is manufactured in the interaction of cultures in the postcolonial world and, as such, is always imbued with relations of power and authority'. Postcolonial thinking has established the ways that issues of race, class, gender and sexuality are deeply tied in with the manufacture of cultural difference in colonialism (Baines, 2010; Mohanty, 1988). Postcolonial feminist social work perspectives, for example, have been developed and deployed in order to highlight the agency of women in third world and developing country contexts who have conventionally 'been characterized in discourses of colonialism and development as passive victims of timeless, oppressive religious and cultural traditions in need of being rescued' (Deepak, 2011, p. 2).

Poststructuralism

The poststructuralist concern with difference can be traced to borrowings from European social and political theory. Hegel, Lacan, Levinas and Derrida proposed that identities are grounded by their difference from that which they are not (often characterised as lack). Derrida, for example, emphasises difference as a negation between two items (Derrida, 1992). In this sense, difference is relational: 'For instance, being categorised as "female" or as having an "ethnic or migrant background" is inextricably linked to its assumed and simultaneously excluded opposite: the attribution as "male" or "white"/"non-ethnic"' (Dobusch, 2017, p. 1648) (see discussion of binaries earlier in the chapter). Foucault and Deleuze were also interested in how difference is produced. Rather than starting with the idea of fixed hierarchies of difference, no identity is seen as stable because boundaries between *what one is* and *what one is not* are asserted and erased through acts of power.

From the poststructuralist perspective, discourses shape the way that people are categorised (and categorise themselves) as different and/or similar. Following Foucault, discourses are understood as socially produced forms of knowledge rather than language. These knowledges set limits on what it is possible to think, write or speak about in terms of social objects and social practices and so it is through discourses that we are regulated and regulate ourselves. For example, discourses about what is 'normal' for an individual or group shape individuals, and in turn individuals perform and reiterate the social norms that regulate them. In social work and social policy, discourse analysis involves interrogating how knowledges, including our own, constitute normative realities and, in doing so, 'make' people (subjects) as well as social practices.

Queer theorists and gender theorists often draw on Judith Butler's theory of 'performativity' in discussions of how difference is established. The concept 'performativity' describes how sexed bodies create normative reality through repeated performance and the theory proposes that the expression of gender identity is 'a kind of persistent impersonation that passes as real' (Butler, 1990, p. viii). Thus, from this perspective people do not have *real* sexed identities but are 'interpellated' – they are signified or hailed into a subject position and then, through their own performances, come to occupy that position. In this sense, individuals and groups are positioned (by others and by themselves) as different.

This kind of thinking about *who we are* (identity) has had implications not just for gender theory but for theories of difference more generally. For example, Stuart Hall (1994) presents the idea of cultural identities as positionalities. The prevailing view of cultural identity has been that it is 'truly' rooted in a shared culture and it is often assumed that people with a shared ancestry share a true self in common. In contrast, Hall (1994, p. 225) argued that cultural identity consists of 'the names we give to the different ways we are positioned by, and position ourselves within, the narratives of the past'. As with sex and gender identity, cultural identity is not thought of as a fixed essence, but as a positioning. In this volume, authors refer to positioning using a range of terms, including referring to people and groups as 'marked' as different.

Privilege/white privilege

The concept 'privilege' focuses on the experience and effects of being privileged and has moved ways of thinking about difference beyond the predominant focus on the experiences of targets of prejudice and discrimination (Kennedy-Kish et al., 2017). As a concept, 'privilege' captures relationality in the politics of difference, whereby the disadvantaging of certain social groups is seen as always involving the advantaging of others. The concept captures the way that privilege is bestowed on groups of individuals categorised as male, white, heterosexual, middle class or able-bodied. It is also deployed to demonstrate the ways that 'the social norms of the privileged become the generalized normative expectations for marginalized groups, providing dominant group members the option of remaining ignorant and avoidant of awareness of both privilege and oppression' (Case et al., 2012, p. 3).

The concept privilege has enabled analyses of racialisation, racial difference and race inequality to focus on the dispositions and actions of white subjects in the making of white racial hegemony. One dimension of analyses of whiteness has been the notion of 'unearned privilege' (McIntosh, 1992). From this perspective, attention is drawn to the ways that white subjects accrue advantages simply by virtue of being constructed (or hailed, positioned or constituted) *as* white. This kind of everyday advantaging usually occurs through the valuation of white skin colour, but also through other characteristics that are read as 'white' such as hair texture, nose shape, religion, culture and language: in contexts where white racial hegemony saturates everyday life, just being recognised as 'white' multiplies privileges. The concept 'white privilege' draws attention to how privilege is granted to whites, but also to those who approximate them (Hunter, 2002). As with male privilege, white privilege is bestowed even without a subject's recognition that life is made easier for them and despite subjects' attempts to dis-identify with the white race.

The concepts 'privilege' and 'white privilege' centralise the role of dominant subjects in the process of domination (Bhopal, 2018; Bonds and Inwood, 2016; Leonardo, 2004). Attention is drawn to the direct processes that secure domination and the privileges associated with it, such as the acts, decisions and policies that white or masculine subjects perpetrate on 'Others'. Privilege studies in social work raise awareness of privilege as well as promote strategies for intervening in privileging processes (Bennett, 2015; Gair, 2016). The concept 'allyship', for example, has been developed as a way of thinking about how dominant group members can intervene in unjust social relations by challenging their own privilege at individual, community and institutional levels.

Settler colonialism

Settler colonialism is a distinctive way of thinking about the way nations have been formed. The concept provides a critical take on sovereign nations, making it impossible to think about countries that were established through colonisation without also acknowledging that this establishment involved an invasive settler society seeking to replace the Indigenous populations. Settler colonialism is the 'specific form of colonialism in which people come to a land inhabited by (Indigenous) people and declare that land to be their own' (Rowe and Tuck, 2017, p. 4). The concept makes visible what is involved in forming settler nations: the genocide of Indigenous peoples, the removal of people from their homelands and the reconfiguring of Indigenous land into settler property. Critical race theorist Patrick Wolfe (2006) argues that settler colonialism is a structure, not just a historical event in the past or the story of a nation state's origins. Instead, invasion persists. Indigenous social workers and social work scholars in Australia and elsewhere have made clear social work's complicity in colonialism and demonstrated – in depth – the settler knowledges and practices that continue to underpin contemporary mainstream social work and social policy.

Land is positioned at the crux of Indigenous–settler relationships in settler societies, as is the clash of understandings of what land means (Moreton-Robinson, 2015). For settlers, land is something to be occupied, to be possessed. In contrast, Indigenous understandings of Land (inclusive of water, skies, winds, the underground) are peoplehood – it is relational, and it is cosmological. Acknowledgements of Country and the traditional owners of Land pay respect and give recognition to Indigenous people, practices and knowledges. When the traditional owners of land welcome people to their Country, they provide visitors safe passage and spiritual protection while passing through that land. Thus, acknowledgements and welcomes disrupt dominant, repeated Western assumptions about lands, peoples and knowledges. In social work and social policy, explicitly stating relationship to Land also calls into question the notion that social workers represent a view from nowhere (Bell, 2017).

Conclusion

The purpose of this chapter was to clarify specific concepts-in-use in social work and social policy discussions of difference. Considering the theoretical genesis of commonly used concepts and theories helps clarify their use – and potential – in contemporary social work and social policy politics because *ways of thinking* impact on *ways of doing*. So, in addition to providing definitions and leads for further reading, this chapter was also intended to whet readers' interest in developing, extending and challenging *ways of thinking* about difference and inequity.

References

ABS (Australian Bureau of Statistics) (2017). *Census Reveals a Fast Changing, Culturally Diverse Nation*, Media Release. http://www.abs.gov.au/ausstats/abs@.nsf/lookup/Media%20Release3.

Ahmed, S. (2012). *On Being Included: Racism and Diversity in Institutional Life*. Durham, NC: Duke University Press.

Bacchi, C. and Goodwin, S. (2016). *Poststructural Policy Analysis: A Guide to Practice*. New York: Palgrave.

Baines, D. (2010). Gender mainstreaming in a development project: Intersectionality in a post-colonial un-doing?. *Gender, Work & Organization*, 17(2), 119–149.

Bell, A. (2017). Working from where we are: A response from Aotearoa New Zealand. *Higher Education Research & Development*, 36(1), 16–20.

Bennett, B. (2015). 'Stop deploying your white privilege on me!' Aboriginal and Torres Strait Islander engagement with the Australian Association of Social Workers. *Australian Social Work*, 68(1), 19–31.

Berger, P.L. and Luckmann, T. (1991). *The Social Construction of Reality: A Treatise in the Sociology of Knowledge*. London: Penguin.

Bessarab, D. and Ng'andu, B. (2010). Yarning about yarning as a legitimate method in Indigenous research. *International Journal of Critical Indigenous Studies*, 3(1), 37–50.

Bhabha, H.K. (1992). Freedom's Basis in the Indeterminate. *October*, 61, 46–57.

Bhopal, K. (2018). *White Privilege: The Myth of a Post-Racial Society*. London: Policy Press.

Bonds, A. and Inwood, J. (2016). Beyond white privilege: Geographies of white supremacy and settler colonialism. *Progress in Human Geography*, 40(6), 715–733.

Burdge, B.J. (2007). Bending gender, ending gender: Theoretical foundations for social work practice with the transgender community. *Social Work*, 52(3), 243–250.

Butler, J. (1990). *Gender Trouble: Feminism and the Subversion of Gender*. New York and Abingdon: Routledge.

Case, K.A., Iuzzini, J. and Hopkins, M. (2012). Systems of privilege: Intersections, awareness, and applications. *Journal of Social Issues*, 68(1), 1–10.

Connell, C. (2010). Doing, undoing, or redoing gender? Learning from the workplace experiences of transpeople. *Gender & Society*, 24(1), 31–55.

Connell, R. (2014). Margin becoming centre: For a world-centred rethinking of masculinities. *NORMA: International Journal for Masculinity Studies*, 9(4), 217–231.

Connell, R. (2015). Social science on a world scale: Connecting the pages. *Sociologies in Dialogue*, 1, 1.

Connell, R.W. and Messerschmidt, J.W. (2005). Hegemonic masculinity: Rethinking the concept. *Gender & Society*, 19(6), 829–859.

Deepak, A.C. (2011). Sustainability and population growth in the context of globalization: A postcolonial feminist social work perspective. *Journal of Research on Women and Gender*, 2, 2.

Delgado, R. and Stefancic, J. (2017). *Critical Race Theory: An Introduction*. New York: New York University Press.

Derrida, J. (1992). Force of law: The 'mystical foundation of authority'. In D. Cornell, M. Rosenfeld and D.G. Carlson (Eds.), *Deconstruction and the Possibility of Justice* (pp. 3–67). New York: Routledge.

Dobusch, J. (2017). Diversity discourses and the articulation of discrimination: The case of public organisations. *Journal of Ethnic and Migration Studies*, 43(10), 1644–1661.

Gair, S. (2016). Critical reflections on teaching challenging content: Do some students shoot the (white) messenger?. *Reflective Practice*, 17(5), 592–604.

Hall, S. (1994). Cultural identity and diaspora. In P. Williams and L. Chrisman (Eds.), *Colonial Discourse and Post-Colonial Theory: A Reader* (pp. 227–237). London: Harvester Wheatsheaf.

Hall, S. (2001). *The Multicultural Question*. London: Pavis Centre for Social and Cultural Research, The Open University.

Hunter, M.L. (2002). If you're light you're alright: Light skin color as social capital for women of color. *Gender & Society*, 16(2), 175–193.

Huppatz, K. and Goodwin, S. (2013). Masculinised jobs, feminised jobs and men's 'gender capital' experiences: Understanding occupational segregation in Australia. *Journal of Sociology*, 49(2–3), 291–308.

Jack, G. (2015). Postcolonial theory. In R. Mir, H. Willmott and M. Greenwood (Eds.), *The Routledge Companion to Philosophy in Organization Studies* (pp. 151–170). London: Routledge.

Jensen, S.Q. (2011). Othering, identity formation and agency. *Qualitative Studies*, 2(2), 63–78.

Kennedy-Kish, B., Sinclair, R., Carniol, B. and Baines, D. (2017). *Case Critical: Social Services and Social Justice in Canada*. Toronto: Between the Lines.

Knowles, C., J. Solomon and P.H. Collins (2010). Theorising race and ethnicity: Contemporary paradigms and perspectives. In *The SAGE Handbook of Race and Ethnic Studies* (pp. 23–42). London: Sage Publishing.

Kwok, P.L. (2005). *Postcolonial Imagination and Feminist Theology*. Westminster: John Knox Press.

Leonardo, Z. (2004). The color of supremacy: Beyond the discourse of 'white privilege'. *Educational Philosophy and Theory*, 36(2), 137–152.

Lesko, N. and Talburt, S. (Eds.) (2012). *Keywords in Youth Studies: Tracing Affects, Movements, Knowledges*. New York: Routledge.

Lewis, G. (2000). *'Race', Gender, Social Welfare: Encounters in a Postcolonial Society*. London: Polity Press.

Lister, R. (2005). *Poverty and Social Justice: Recognition and Respect*. Wales: Bevan Foundation.

McIntosh, P. (1992). White privilege and male privilege: A personal account of coming to see correspondences through work in women's studies. In M. Andersen and P.H. Collins (Eds.), *Race, Class, and Gender: An Anthology* (pp. 377–385). Belmont: Wadsworth.

McPhail, B.A. (2004). Questioning gender and sexuality binaries: What queer theorists, transgendered individuals, and sex researchers can teach social work. *Journal of Gay & Lesbian Social Services*, 17(1), 3–21.

Meekosha, H. (2011). Decolonising disability: Thinking and acting globally. *Disability & Society*, 26(6), 667–682.

Meekosha, H. and Shuttleworth, R. (2009). What's so 'critical' about critical disability studies?. *Australian Journal of Human Rights*, 15(1), 47–75.

Mohanty, C.T. (1988). Under Western eyes: Feminist scholarship and colonial discourses. *Feminist Review*, 30, 61–88.

Moreton-Robinson, A. (2004). Whiteness, epistemology and Indigenous representation. *Whitening Race: Essays in Social and Cultural Criticism*, 1, 75–88.

Moreton-Robinson, A. (2015). *The White Possessive: Property, Power, and Indigenous Sovereignty*. Minneapolis: University of Minnesota Press.

Morley, C. (2008). Teaching critical practice: Resisting structural domination through critical reflection. *Social Work Education*, 27(4), 407–421.

Nkomo, S. and Stewart, M. (2006). Diverse identities in organizations In S. Clegg, C. Hardy, T. Lawrence and W. Nord (Eds.), *The SAGE Handbook of Organization Studies*, 2nd Edition (pp. 520–540). London: Sage Publishing.

Patel, S. (2006). Beyond binaries: A case for self-reflexive sociologies. *Current Sociology*, 54(3), 381–395.

Pease, B. (2011). Men in social work: Challenging or reproducing an unequal gender regime?. *Affilia*, 26(4), 406–418.

Razack, N. (2009). Decolonizing the pedagogy and practice of international social work. *International Social Work*, 52(1), 9–21.

Reutlinger, C.J. (2015). The ableist Othering of disability in the classroom: An experiential investigation of academic adjustments in higher education. Doctoral dissertation, Kansas State University.

Rowe, A.C. and Tuck, E. (2017). Settler colonialism and cultural studies: Ongoing settlement, cultural production, and resistance. *Cultural Studies ↔ Critical Methodologies*, 17(1), 3–13.

Smith, L.T. (2012). *Decolonizing Methodologies: Research and Indigenous Peoples*. London: Zed Books.

Spivak, G. (1987). *In Other Worlds: Essays in Cultural Politics*. London: Methuen.

Spivak, G.C. (1985). Can the subaltern speak?. *Wedge*, 7(8), 120–130.

Walter, M., Taylor, S. and Habibis, D. (2011). How white is social work in Australia?. *Australian Social Work*, 64(1), 6–19.

Wendell, S. (1996). *The Rejected Body: Feminist Philosophical Reflections on Disability*. New York: Routledge.

Wolfe, P. (2006). Settler colonialism and the elimination of the native. *Journal of Genocide Research*, 8, 387–409.

17
Afterword: Resistance, White Fragility and Late Neoliberalism

Donna Baines and Fran Waugh

As part of the many waves of settlers, and as white women, the authors acknowledge and pay respect to the Traditional Owners and Custodians of the land now known as Australia, as well as their knowledge and care, and the unearned privilege of all those living in and benefiting from the un-ceded lands, winds and waters which we share.

Introduction

Xenophobia, anti-immigrant backlash and racism are an increasingly present aspect of our society and growing more acute in the context of more than 30 years of neoliberalism, rising disparity between rich and poor countries, and growing polarisation between the rich and poor within most nations. Some have termed this era 'late neoliberalism' and associated it with permanent austerity and the inter-group tensions that are exacerbated by inadequate resources for social programs and supports, a weak economy, growing unemployment and social explanations that blame the victims of policies that vilify those who cannot compete successfully in the unregulated private market (Evans and Albo, 2010; Peck, 2010; Pierson, 2002).

Within the wealthy nations, moves such as Brexit in the United Kingdom and the election of Donald Trump in the United States have been seen to unleash and legitimise fascist and ultra-right forces that openly call for an end to diversity, inclusion and equity – in other words, an end to social justice policies and practices that social work has avidly pursued as part of its moral and ethical code. Similarly, though the need for safe havens for those fleeing wars and natural disasters has never been higher, anti-immigrant and anti-refugee sentiments are reflected in calls to limit and expel non-citizens (Briskman et al., 2009; Peck, 2010).

One of many sources underlying this deeply disturbing backlash is a set of social relations and discourses that are coming to be known as white fragility (DiAngelo, 2011; Keger, 2016; Waters, 2016). White fragility involves the inability of those from dominant groups, principally people with white privilege, to accept critique from subordinated groups, to ally themselves with social justice, and to embrace the leadership of those who are marginalised. White fragility shuts down conversations, blames the victims and protects existing relations of dominance, violence and inequality (DiAngelo, 2011; Waters, 2016).

White fragility is like racism in that it functions to deny the experience of those who are impacted by racialised practices of power and to perpetuate that inequity (Dominelli, 2017). It is also related to white dominance and white privilege in that it maintains existing inequitable power relations, policies and practices (Jeffery, 2005). It is very much a part of colonial debates that deny the genocide perpetuated on Indigenous peoples and their continued oppression and exclusion (Bennett et al., 2011; Sinclair et al., 2009). White fragility has been analysed as part of communication patterns in situations where racism is raised as a problem by non-white groups and then turned back on those groups, without resolving issues and often blaming inequity on those targeted by oppression (DiAngelo, 2011; Keger, 2016).

Male fragility is a linked term that is often heard in recent years in relation to male-identified persons' responses to much needed discussions of gender inequity and power, particularly in relation to unwanted sexual attentions and assault. It operates in a similar manner to white fragility and frequently intersects with it, shutting down debate and making it appear that those seeking solutions to social injustice are perpetrating harm by simply raising the subject. Consistent with the other chapters in this book, this chapter adopts an intersectional lens. White fragility is undergirded, strengthened and protected by colonial fragility, heteronormative fragility, male fragility and so forth. However, for purposes of analytic clarity and given the tidal wave of white fragility released and legitimised by events such as those discussed above (Brexit, Trump, refugee crises), this chapter will contribute to theory on white fragility by exploring its operation within the apparently neutral policies and practices that are part of social services organisations in the context of neoliberalism.

Social work agencies and organisations often encounter the cutting edge of emerging social issues and tensions, such as the refugee crises noted above. In order to be responsive and ethical, this means that they need to take leadership in changing their approaches to the difficult questions facing humankind in the current context. However, more than 30 years of neoliberalism has meant that many social service agencies have been restructured to reflect private market ideology, meaning that there are few spaces left in which to debate issues openly within the workplace and to collectively develop strategies to address emerging needs and rising social tensions (Briskman et al., 2009; Fook, 2016; Kennedy-Kish et al., 2017).

This also means that social workers have to use other strategies and other spaces to foster critical reflection on how white fragility, xenophobia, ongoing colonialism, sexism, ableism and homophobia may have been, quietly and possibly unintentionally, woven into practice and policies and have become the accepted norm (see Morley, 2011). These practices and policies need to be examined, critiqued and replaced by positive visions of equity and social participation. However, what tools can social workers use, and are using, in the context of late neoliberalism to find these spaces for critical reflection and to legitimise and generate alternative, social justice-engaged, diversity-embracing practices and policies?

This chapter argues that, though often flawed in its application, the Social Work Code of Ethics remains a significant tool in the struggle for a more equitable world and resistance within the social services workplace. The chapter also explores strategies that social workers are using to disrupt and challenge discourses and practices that legitimise white fragility, racism, xenophobia and other oppressive relations, and to find spaces in which to build more socially just approaches.

Code of Ethics and the neoliberal context of practice

Social work is a rare profession in that it recognises the pursuit of human rights and social justice as central ethical practices (International Federation of Social Work, 2018). However, as Mullaly (2010) notes, there is little consensus around what constitutes socially just or human rights-based social work practice. Similarly, Ife (2012) warns of the danger that human rights and equity become optional aspects of practice. Moreover, though not presented as optional or relativist, the social justice and human rights sections of Codes of Ethics are never used to sanction the behaviour of those promoting the status quo, though many agree that the status quo is fundamentally unjust. Similarly, these sections of the Code are not invoked against those failing to promote social justice and equity.

Codes of professional ethics, the various United Nations Declarations of Human Rights and government-level human rights codes are intended as absolute, decisive resolutions rather than optional suggestions open to a wide swath of interpretations (Ife, 2012). Indeed, other aspects of professional Codes of Ethics such as conflict of interest or professional comportment can and are invoked as unbendable laws under which professionals receive discipline, including excluding them from professional practice, temporarily or permanently (Carey, 2011; Mullaly, 2010).

Despite this, the social justice and human rights aspects of social work codes of ethics have always been practised as if they are discretionary, interpretive and aspirational. This happens at three levels: (1) the level of the social service agency or organisation; (2) the level of theory; and (3) the level of social work practice. At the level of the organisation or agency, though almost all social service organisations would claim a strong commitment to social justice and human rights, most agencies adopt a bureaucratic, corporate model, with workplace power and control centred in management (Baines, 2017; Kennedy-Kish et al., 2017; Webb and Gray, 2013). This necessarily excludes communities, service users and employees from participation in policy, planning and operational decisions (Ferguson, 2007; Ife, 2012). These structures do not come out of nowhere; they are generally required by government legislation (regarding corporations, including non-profit organisations), and they are also re-enforced through the details of funding contracts from government and other funders (Baines, 2017; Gray and Webb, 2013).

In additional, government funding has rarely kept up with the need for service, resulting in social service agencies that are stretched and inadequate in comparison to need. Based, as they are, in the priorities of government and far-off experts rather than in the local knowledge of service users and communities, social services agencies are frequently funded to provide the wrong kinds of services and/or services that reproduce or attenuate many of the problems they purport to address (Carey, 2014; Pease et al., 2016).

Neoliberalism has accentuated these problems. Neoliberalism is a set of overlapping and mutually reinforcing policies, practices and ideologies that valorises market solutions and places continuous emphasis on cost-saving and efficiencies (Peck, 2010). New Public Management and managerialism are workplace-level organisational models that government funding contracts have required of social service agencies (Davies, 2008). Though these models claim to promote best practices and reduce waste, in reality they standardise practice through the required use of outcome measures and targets. The adoption of these seemingly neutral measurement practices has meant that most social service agencies have reduced or removed social work practices that are hard to quantify and measure, such as the many open-ended practices associated with building social justice and sustaining community participation (Baines, 2017; Briskman et al., 2009; Ferguson, 2007). What cannot be measured soon ceases to exist. One of the main victims of this rationalisation of practice has been the hallmark trust-based, dignity-enhancing, time-intensive relationships generally thought to form the impetus and means for change within the social work endeavour (Carey, 2014; Fook, 2016). Rather than building the social justice, human rights orientation encoded in social work codes of ethics (Ife, 2010), the reduction or absence of these open-ended relationships with service users and communities pushes practice towards the pro-market individualising and victim blaming ethos of neoliberalism.

Rationalisation and standardisation of practice also result in work speed-up, increased caseloads and an emphasis on compliance that delegitimises alternative, more social justice-engaged ways of working and resisting unjust policies and practices (Carey, 2014). Standardisation also 'dumbs down' social work practice to replicable, bite-sized, technical activities that can be accomplished by less skilled, less credentialed and lower paid workers, or even unpaid family members and volunteers (Kennedy-Kish et al., 2017; Mullaly, 2010). This further erodes the already low wages and challenging working conditions in social service agencies and makes it more difficult for workers to feel sufficiently secure to challenge inequities and injustices in practice and in policy (Pease et al., 2016; Webb and Gray, 2013). However, as will be discussed in the balance of the chapter, these spaces for resistance can still be found and activities undertaken.

Not surprisingly, the dominance of privileged groups is preserved within standardised practices that appear neutral on the surface but reflect the interests of those intent on reducing social spending and maintaining the existing distribution of power and prestige in society. In their putative neutrality, these practices depoliticise social work practice, remaking it as a technical profession rather than a social justice-engaged vocation (Baines, 2017). This makes it difficult to speak about, critically reflect or act on social work practices in ways that address structural differences such as race, white fragility, class, gender, sexual orientation, (dis)ability, and the social practices and discourses accompanying them (Fook, 2016; Ife, 2012; Morley, 2011).

Equity requires non-standardised practices and policies that recognise that different groups and individuals have different needs based on historical and contemporary contexts (Kennedy-Kish et al., 2017; Webb and Gray, 2013). Failing to recognise or redress inequities perpetuates them (Thompson, 2016) and, simultaneously, perpetuates the white fragility and other oppressive relations that benefit from the ongoing inequity of larger society. Thus, by ignoring difference, standardised practice silently weaves white fragility, racism, classism, sexism and other axes of injustice into everyday social work practice.

The balance of this chapter draws on case study vignettes and the voices of service users and community members to address how to engage with these tensions and contractions in everyday social work practice. Case studies are analysed to address (1) the tools that can and are used by social workers in the context of late neoliberalism to find spaces for critical reflection and to legitimise and generate alternative, social justice-engaged, diversity-embracing practices aimed at working across difference, and (2) strategies that social workers are using to disrupt and challenge discourses and practices that legitimise white fragility, racism, xenophobia and other oppressive relations.

Vignettes from practice

Vignette 1

Simone works in a small shelter for women escaping domestic violence. The shelter has small, individual flats for the women and their children. The program is part of a larger multi-service agency that is funded by a constantly changing set of government contracts. These contracts require frequent reporting of outcome measures in order to maintain funding. Simone's supervisor feels under strong pressure to meet these measures and passes this stress on to Simone and the other workers she supervises. The funding contract states that the women should be ready to move out of the shelter after one month's stay. This is impossible for most of the service users, as housing is rarely available and they feel unsettled in many aspects of their rapidly changing lives. The lack of housing options is particularly acute for the families who are not white. Though many of the women and children, particularly those who are not white, require three or more bedrooms, the housing authority has few units with more than two bedrooms and will not 'under-house' applicants. This means that the white families are rehoused quickly relative to the Indigenous and non-white families, who often have to wait a very long time to get their lives restarted after violence. Though her supervisor wants her to meet outcome targets, Simone will not evict women who lack housing and finds ways to 'massage' her statistics and outcome measures to evade detection for as long as possible.

Many of the families, but particularly the families who are not part of the dominant culture, sleep in one room as they did at home or to provide comfort to traumatised children in their new living situation. The only way to do this is to move mattresses to the living room and sleep on the floor. Simone's supervisor instructs her that this is not acceptable and to tell the women to put children in individual rooms in their individual beds. Simone explains that it is important to recognise the diversity of experience around sleeping arrangements in different families, particularly among other cultural and language groups, and that it is more helpful to let the families use the living space in the ways that best meet their needs. Her supervisor tells Simone that her views are too radical and directs Simone to move the mattresses if the women will not. Simone spends some time thinking this over and decides to explain the situation to the women and asks them what they want to do. They agree that Simone will tell them when the supervisor is coming for an inspection and Simone will help them move their mattresses to the accepted white, middle-class practice of individual beds and bedrooms.

This example highlights the way that standardised metrics and practices in the first part of the narrative, and common sense and practice expectations in the second part of the narrative, act to enforce white, straight, middle-class norms. The standardisation and the norms serve to marginalise and devalue the experiences of excluded groups. In the first part of the vignette, standardised practices and outcome measures amplify the racism contained in the housing authority's policies. Though the policy's aim is good, that is, that people should not be under-housed, its effect is that small families (more often white families) are more quickly rehoused than families with more children (mostly Indigenous and immigrant families). This neutral-appearing policy has racist impacts. Though the pressure that Simone and her supervisor are under to meet funding metrics and move service users quickly through the program are real, they, too, reinforce subordination of groups that do not meet the white, middle-class norm. So, it is both the housing authority policy and the metrics of the funding contracts that erase and devalue differences and reinforce white, classed, gendered privilege (gendered in that it impacts on women more frequently and more intensely than men).

In the second part of the narrative, Simone's advocacy on the part of the women and children advances a case for equity and a respectful way to work across differences. However, her supervisor's response that her views are too radical is a response typical of white fragility where challenges to the systems that support white hegemony are silenced, debate is shut down and white norms and hegemonic practices (white dominance) are reasserted. Taking this dilemma to the women to discuss and seek solutions is a way of sharing power with service users and supporting their capacity to act for themselves in close alliance with social justice-oriented social workers. It is also a form of resistance that shares power, defends service users and legitimises, rather than attempts to erase, difference.

Arguably, these resistance practices will not change policies or agency-level practices, as they are covert (Smith, 2007). However, as Baines (2017) notes, though we may be committed activists for social justice, our tactics will vary through the course of our lives, depending on what other responsibilities and demands we are juggling in our busy lives. In a situation where service users have escaped violence and face the overwhelming task of rebuilding their lives, most will not have the energy for formal, systemic resistance. Undertaking covert resistance is still beneficial. It protects the practices and dignity of a group of marginalised service users, while simultaneously building a shared analysis of problems in the social services system and how service users and social workers working in alliance can make things slightly better, challenge white fragility and resist inequity at the level of everyday life.

In both parts of the narrative, inequities that reinforce white privilege and other oppressive relations are perpetuated by the operation of seemingly neutral, bureaucratic processes, such as standardised reporting and outcome measures, and policies, such as the housing authority's under-housing policy. They serve to systemically distance people from much needed resources, dignity and fairness. They also put Simone in the position of needing to find the space to critically reflect on practice and decide where she stands in terms of ethics, social justice and herself as a moral actor in an unequal, xenophobic and oppressive set of relations.

Simone collectivises this critical reflection when she takes the question of allegedly atypical and pathological sleeping arrangements back to the service users and asks them what they want to do. Though the space for critical action and resistance is not extensive in this scenario, Simone gently pushes back at the boundaries placed on her, covertly 'massages' her documentation to protect service users who are being marginalised by housing authority policy and shares power with service users in ways that build fairer, respect-based, anti-oppressive practices.

Vignette 2

Eileen has recently been appointed the chief executive officer of a large non-government child welfare agency whose staff provide a range of family integrated services in diverse, disadvantaged multi-cultural communities, in both metropolitan and regional areas. There are multiple and diverse social problems and opportunities facing children, young people, parents, workers and the agency as a consequence of changes in government policies, growing inequities, shrinking resources and innovative technologies.

There are approximately 300 staff working in the agency of whom 60% are from Anglo Australian backgrounds, 30% from other cultural backgrounds and 10% identify as Aboriginal. The agency is primarily funded by the state government and supplemented with monies from private donors and corporate sponsors. Each of these carries its own set of expectations in terms of accountabilities in the form of compliance requirements, outcome measures and upholding the excellent reputation of the agency in order to continue to attract private donations.

Eileen holds a Master's in both Social Work and Business and places importance on having research and mentorship inform her leadership. She provided strong evidence to the board of directors, during her hiring interview, of her experiences, abilities, expertise, networking, understandings of complexities facing children and families, and the need for welfare agencies to balance their legislative responsibilities with the development of innovative programs that are responsive to the changing needs of children and families. According to Eileen, her strong commitment to social justice and human rights was key to her successful leadership in her previous position, where she led cultural change and the enhancement of a respectful, inclusive, collaborative and participatory workplace where service users were welcomed and the staff were celebrated for their commitment to providing high-quality services.

Listening to workers and service users and valuing their contributions to the agency were the principal means through which Eileen achieved this. In her new role, Eileen set about doing the same things. First, she met with the senior leadership team to understand the current organisational structures, resources and systems. Concurrently, Eileen commenced a series of town hall meetings with all the staff across the metropolitan and regional centres, to consult about what they perceived to be the strengths, limitations, gaps in the services they offered, and how informed and involved they were in influencing the agency's practices and future directions. In addition, Eileen was interested in mechanisms the agency had to keep track of changing issues for the diverse groups of children and their families and if there are groups who were missing out. In particular, she was interested to know how the agency included and responded to issues raised by vulnerable services users who often are 'voiceless'.

While the board of directors considered organisational cultural change to be an important area of Eileen's work, at the first board meeting they informed her that their major priority for her was to review and develop strategies to reduce risks in all facets of the agency's operations with service users but, in particular, financial risks because of the threat of reduced government funding, increased services costs, complaints from service users and increasing insurance premiums following payments to staff experiencing excessive stress. While Eileen appreciates the need to ensure systems are in place to reduce potential risks, it is evident to her that the views of several of the board directors are dominated by a risk-averse discourse and they have limited knowledge and understanding of the complexities, uncertainties and emerging problems facing the diverse communities that the agency serves. Though the board words all their concerns in a neutral way, it is clear that the priorities they set have little to do with equity and, hence, their priorities leave inequity unaddressed and invisible. This invisibility of equity concerns protects white fragility and other contemporary practices of dominance, and instead prioritises the neoliberal discourse of risk avoidance.

Following the board meeting, Eileen finds space in her busy schedule to spend some time critically reflecting on the risk-avoidance strategy. She then discusses her concerns with the senior leadership team who share her sense that the board does not fully understand the need for cultural change or the way that social justice-linked, cultural/organisational changes will help ensure that the agency avoids reproducing oppression. Making a narrow understanding of risk management Eileen's priority 'risks' unintentionally harming the diverse group of service users involved with the agency, and centring white, middle-class practice. It does this in part by continuing to operate as if risk has nothing to do with structural and social inequity, that all service users are the same and that their needs are met well enough under the current set of practices. In reality, many contemporary services operate on a white, middle-class norm that erases the experience of those outside the norm and delegitimises their concerns and experience.

To better inform the board and in hopes of having them recognise that organisational cultural change is a form of reducing risk through improved, diversity-embracing practice, Eileen consults with the chair of the board of directors. A decision is made to include a brief report from each of the services for board members at all meetings. In addition, each board meeting will commence with a short presentation by senior leaders outlining the strengths, limitations and need for change in the services for which they are responsible. The reports will also identify the emerging needs of children and their families in the communities the agency serves. The reports will introduce the board members, many of whom are from dominant groups, to the lives and challenges of the diverse, under-served and systemically marginalised communities the agency serves. The reports are also aimed at helping the board members develop a critical social analysis around anti-oppressive social practice and service delivery.

This vignette highlights the competing tensions leaders face as they strive to enact socially just practices across all aspects of the agency's operations. It also shows the challenges they face in trying to be responsive to the multiple needs of diverse service users and to introduce changes that shift practices and policies to more inclusive, anti-oppressive approaches rather than the ostensibly neutral, funding-driven, bureaucratic practices that dominate most agencies. Importantly, leaders must constantly grapple with questions around who has the power to set the agenda and priorities in any organisation, and how leaders meaningfully involve service users and front-line workers, and how to privilege the input of marginalised voices in the development of future practices. In other words, leaders must engage closely and explicitly in working across differences.

Eileen has made it clear this is a priority in her work with the agency and her driving passion. However, rather than being able to dive into this work, instead, the board directs her to prioritise the review of systems and strategies in terms of narrowly defined 'risks'. Risk is narrowly understood by the board, and though it may be necessary for the ongoing viability and sustainability of the agency, it needs to be understood in the fullest possible way, so that strategies can be developed to lower the risk of marginalising and silencing diverse service users, reinstating white dominance and other practices of inequity and failing to meet emerging and existing community needs. These concerns need to be seen to be just as important as avoiding losing funding contracts and documenting outcome metrics.

Eileen is not downplaying the need for sound risk assessment. However, she is aware of the research that critiques risk assessment tools as, often, culturally biased processes that erase the larger context and silence the voices of those with diverse needs. Developing an organisational culture which is open, flexible and responsive to the multiple stakeholders, in particular the service users, is core to how Eileen addresses these competing tensions. While white fragility is not overtly evident in the current policies and procedures in the agency, white privilege quietly saturates most Western societies. As such, it underlies the outwardly neutral emphasis on risk avoidance rather than on anti-oppressive organisational change.

Recent research undertaken by the agency has identified unmet needs of young people from African and Middle Eastern countries. If the agency fails to take action to address these emerging needs, it will reflect a white fragility in terms of erasing and delegitimising the priorities and concerns of those outside the white, middle-class norm.

Eileen is keen for the board directors to be educated on the complexities and uncertainties facing services users and the need for workers to be responsive to the changing situations of service users. Adopting her critically reflexive, collaborative, participatory leadership style, Eileen consults with the board members, the senior leadership team, pertinent staff and relevant networks engaged in offering services to this diverse group of young people. She draws on her critical social analysis to challenge people to think beyond the bureaucratic requirements of the funding contracts and board directives to reflect on what socially just practices and policies would look like at every level of the agency. Eileen is also keen to provide staff with professional development opportunities that enhance culturally sensitive, anti-oppressive practice with diverse groups. In order to do this workers require a keen social analysis; time and encouragement to undertake critical reflexive practice; organisational support, in the form of regular supervision and sufficient resources to undertake their work; regular communication about professional development opportunities and agency changes and plans; meaningful participation in agency planning; the support of co-workers and supervisors in strong teams where contributions and achievements are valued and celebrated; and fair remuneration and industrial conditions to help the staff feel valued by the agency.

Conclusion

The discussion above confirms that seemingly neutral, standardised practices and policies are often saturated with inequities and, in their operation, reproduce and quietly legitimise white privilege and other overlapping forms of oppression. Challenges to the dominance of these practices and policies are often met with responses that reflect white fragility and an inability to critically reflect on how dominance, exclusion and marginalisation are maintained in our society, even when people of goodwill would prefer to operate in more constructive and liberatory ways. Our vignettes underscore the importance of a social analysis, individual and collective critical reflection, and a willingness to 'massage' practices that reproduce inequities and exclusion (Fook, 2016; Pease et al., 2016). Though spaces for critical reflection and resistance are difficult to find in neoliberal, managerialised workplaces (Baines, 2017; Carey, 2014; Morley, 2011), our vignettes show that this is still possible, and that strong leaders can help enlarge and legitimise this space. The workers and managers in these vignettes found creative ways to covertly or overtly shift power and agency to staff and service users, and to live in tandem with the values that drew them to the field in the first place. The Social Work Code of Ethics plays an important symbolic role in social justice efforts, as it provides a bulwark against xenophobia, growing racism and inequity; a way to explain why one is taking and encouraging others to undertake resistance to oppressive policies and practices; and a ratification for those seeking to build a more socially just world.

Further readings

Baines, D. (Ed.) (2017). *Doing Anti-Oppressive Practice: Social Justice Social Work*, 3rd Edition. Halifax: Fernwood.

DiAngelo, R. (2011). White fragility. *The International Journal of Critical Pedagogy*, 3(3), 54–70.

Dominelli, L. (2017). *Anti-Racist Social Work*. London: Palgrave.

References

Baines, D. (2017). Is progressive, critical, anti-oppressive social work possible in today's context? Exhausting ethical action + revitalizing resistance. In E. Spencer, J. Gough and D. Massing (Eds.), *Progressive, Critical, Anti-Oppressive Social Work: Ethical Action* (pp. 56–68). Toronto: Oxford University Press.

Bennett, B., Zubrzcki, J. and Bacon, V. (2011). What do we know? The experiences of social workers working alongside aboriginal people. *Australian Social Work*, 64(1), 20–37.

Briskman, L., Pease, B. and Allan, J. (2009). Introducing critical theories for social work in a neo-liberal context. In J. Allan, L. Briskman and B. Pease (Eds.), *Critical Social Work: Theories and Practices for a Socially Just World*, 2nd Edition (pp. 3–14). St. Leonards, NSW: Allen & Unwin.

Carey, M. (2011). Here today, gone tomorrow? The ambivalent ethics of contingency social work. *Critical Social Policy*, 31(4), 540–561.

Carey, M. (2014). The fragmentation of social work and social care: Some ramifications and a critique. *British Journal of Social Work*, 45(8), 2406–2422.

Davies, S. (2008). Contracting out employment services to the third and private sectors: A critique. *Critical Social Policy*, 28(2), 136–164.

Evans, B. and Albo, G. (2010). Permanent austerity: The politics of the Canadian exit strategy from fiscal stimulus. *Alternate Routes: A Journal of Critical Social Research*, 22. http://www.alternateroutes.ca/index.php/ar/article/view/14414/12899.

Ferguson, I. (2007). *Reclaiming Social Work: Challenging Neo-Liberalism and Promoting Social Justice*. London: Sage Publishing.

Fook, J. (2016). *Social Work: A Critical Approach to Practice*. London: Sage Publishing.

Gray, M. and Webb, S.A. (2013). *The New Politics of Social Work*. London: Macmillan International Higher Education.

Ife, J. (2012). *Human Rights and Social Work: Towards Rights-Based Practice*. Cambridge: Cambridge University Press.

International Federation of Social Work (2018). *Global Social Work Statement of Ethical Principles*. https://www.ifsw.org/global-social-work-statement-of-ethical-principles/.

Jeffery, D. (2005). 'What good is anti-racist social work if you can't master it'?: Exploring a paradox in anti-racist social work education. *Race Ethnicity and Education*, 8(4), 409–425.

Keger, A. (2016) The Sugarcoated Language of White Fragility, *The Huffington Post*. 22 July. http://www.huffingtonpost.com/anna-kegler/the-sugarcoated-language-of-white-fragility_b_10909350.html.

Kennedy-Kish, B., Sinclair, R., Carniol, B. and Baines, D. (2017). *Case Critical: Social Services and Social Justice in Canada*. Toronto: Between the Lines.

Morley, C. (2011). How does critical reflection develop possibilities for emancipatory change? An example from an empirical research project. *British Journal of Social Work*, 42(8), 1513–1532.

Mullaly, B. (2010). *Challenging Oppression and Confronting Privilege*. Toronto: Oxford University Press.

Pease, B., Goldinjay, S., Hosken, N. and Nipperess, S. (2016). *Doing critical social work. Transformative practices for social justice*. Melbourne: Allen & Unwin.

Peck, J. (2010). Zombie neoliberalism and the ambidextrous state. *Theoretical Criminology*, 14(1), 104–110.

Pierson, P. (2002). Coping with permanent austerity: Welfare state restructuring in affluent democracies. *Revue française de sociologie*, 369–406.

Sinclair, R., Hart, M.A. and Bruyere, G. (2009). *Wicihitowin: Aboriginal Social Work in Canada*. Halifax, NS: Fernwood Publishing.

Smith, K. (2007). Social work, restructuring and resistance: 'Best practices' gone underground. In D. Baines (Ed.), *Doing Anti-Oppressive Practice: Building Transformative, Politicized Social Work* (pp. 145–149). Halifax, NS: Fernwood Books.

Thompson, N. (2016). *Anti-Discriminatory Practice: Equality, Diversity and Social Justice*. London: Palgrave Macmillan.

Waters, M. (2016) White fragility, white fear: the crisis of racial identity in Australia, and beyond. *The Guardian*, 23 November. https://www.theguardian.com/commentisfree/2016/nov/23/white-fragility-white-fear-the-crisis-of-racial-identity-in-australia-and-beyond.

Webb, S.A. and Gray, M. (Eds.) (2013). *The New Politics of Social Work*. London: Palgrave Macmillan.

Index

Aboriginal and Torres Strait Islanders
  Aboriginal perspectives, 11–48
  anti-oppressive practice and, 21–3
  education and, 26–37
  historical treatment, 13–16, 18, 27, 29–31
  housing and, 253
Aboriginal and Torres Strait Islander women
  in domestic violence refuges, 196–7
  in old age, 127–8
  use of ACCHSs, 18–23
Aboriginal community-controlled health services, 13–23
Aboriginal culture, 15–16, 18, 20, 22, 30, 127
Aboriginal kinship system, 15, 30–1
Aboriginal knowledge, 1, 13, 15–16, 30, 39–48
aging
  elder care in the Tao community, 218–29
  privilege and oppression of older women, 120–33
allyship
  liberation and, 88
  men as allies to women, 103–15
  working across difference and, 6
Anito belief, 218–29
anti-immigrant backlash, 71–3, 77, 81–2, 247; *see also* xenophobia
anti-Muslim sentiment *see* Islamophobia
anti-oppressive practice
  binaries and, 236
  distractions from, 257
  Aboriginal people and, 14–15, 21–3
  culture and, 254
  women and, 114–15
  tenets of, 1–6

anti-racism
  allyship, 105
  in practice, 22–3, 252–4, 258
anti-refugee backlash, 247; *see also* anti-immigrant backlash
anti-stigma education
  disability and, 180–1
  mental health and, 155–67
  women's refuges and, 198
anti-terrorism laws *see* Countering Violent Extremism Policy
austerity, 4, 247
Australian Association of Social Workers (AASW), 41, 55–6, 60, 63–7

Bennett, Bindi on Aboriginal knowledge, 39–49
Binaries/binarism
  border identities, 105
  construction of, 87, 235–6, 240
  LGBTQI+ people and, 141–2
  in mental health, 160; *see also* non-binary people

capacity-building, 88–9
care, 35, 123, 126–7
  carers, 65, 178; *see also* health care; home care; social work profession
chicken and egg analogy, 39–41
choice and control in the NDIS, 204–16
cis-gender
  feminism and, 104, 108
  gender diverse people and, 137–8, 147, 236
classism, 73, 158, 252–3, 256–7; *see also* socioeconomic marginalisation

Code of Ethics in social work, 66–7, 249–58
collaboration
  with Aboriginal people, 40–3, 46–8
  in feminism, 198–9
  with gender diverse people, 139
  in social work, 255, 257
collective action
  attacks on, 4, 249
  collective accountability, 139, 148–9
  harnessing, 66–7, 258
collective learning, 34, 91, 93
colonialism
  Aboriginal people and, 13–14, 16, 27–32, 39–42, 197
  Muslims and, 58
  Tao people and, 218–19, 222
  othering and, 238
  in social work, 249
  white fragility and, 248; *see also* decolonisation; postcolonialism; settler colonialism
colour-blind approach, 64–5
community, 78, 128, 141
  development, 48, 86; *see also* Aboriginal community-controlled health services
community engagement
  in CVE, 60–1
  for people with disabilities, 170–81; *see also* anti-stigma education
conflict, 37, 66, 222; *see also* violence
Countering Violent Extremism Policy, 55–65
critical mental health theory, 156–8, 163, 167
critical pedagogy, 6, 28
critical social work, 65–7, 85–6, 132–3, 167
critical thinking
  about gender, 112, 138–40, 146
  about mental health, 156, 158, 163–4, 167
  about older women, 121–2
  about terms, 233
  in allyship, 104
  critical perspectives on cultural difference, 53–100
  critical perspectives on gender difference, 101–49

critical perspectives on normality and difference, 153–81
  in education, 93, 97
  importance of, 2–5
  knowledge and, 87
  in practice, 255–7; *see also* reflection and reflexivity
cultural appropriation, 42–4
cultural humility, 1, 35
cultural knowledge *see* Aboriginal knowledge
culturally and linguistically diverse people, 72; *see also* immigrants; Indigenous people; religion
cultural safety
  in classrooms, 26–37, 95
  in providing care, 21–3, 219
culture
  Aboriginal, 15–16, 18, 20, 22, 30, 127
  critical perspectives on cultural difference, 53–100
  cultural humility, 1
  cultural identity, 241
  cultural solutions, 5
  cultural vitality, 36–7
  domestic violence and, 73, 78, 80–2
  othering of, 239–40
  in practice, 252–7
  race and, 237
  Tao, 219, 223–4
  Western, 158, 235
  working with cultural differences, 85–98; *see also* immigrants; Indigenous people; monoculture; religion; Western ways of knowing and thinking; whiteness
curricula, 30, 34, 46, 90

decolonisation, 228–9, 236; *see also* colonialism
Derrida, Jacques, 86–7, 240
difference
  critical perspectives on cultural difference, 53–100
  critical perspectives on gender difference, 101–49
  critical perspectives on normality and difference, 153–81
  cultural, 88, 240
  disability and, 176–80

domestic violence and, 185–6, 199
in epistemologies of ignorance, 89
extremism as, 62
focus on, 56
formation of, 1–3
mental health and, 167
policy work across difference, 183–229
politics of, 1, 233–43
in practice, 251–3, 256
supporting, 3–6, 85–6
tolerance for, 159; *see also* diversity; intersectionality
disabilities, people with
dehumanisation of, 239
supported employment and social inclusion for, 170–81; *see also* National Disability Insurance Scheme
disciplinary power, 62–3
discrimination
in education, 90
othering and, 239
quotas to reduce, 181
theories of, 241
against trans people, 143, 145; *see also* anti-immigrant backlash; Islamophobia; racism; sexism
disempowerment, 14, 35, 121, 126, 199; *see also* power
diversity
in education, 26, 35, 37, 91
of experiences, 189
in practice, 251–2, 254–7
sampling for, 130
supporting, 85–6, 249
use of term, 236–8
of women, 121–2, 127, 130–3; *see also* difference
domestic violence
Muslim immigrants' experiences of domestic violence, 71–82
shelters, 185–200, 252–4
dominant discourse, 15, 85, 89, 123, 126, 165

education
Aboriginal, 14, 46
culturally safe, 26–37
CVE in, 62–4, 68
on domestic violence, 81
gender and, 110, 127
ideal, 87
of social workers, 85–98, 257; *see also* anti-stigma education; critical pedagogy; knowledge; learning
egg and chicken analogy, 39–41
employment
competition for, 247
for people with disabilities, 170–81
for survivors of domestic violence, 188
empowerment *see* power
epistemology of ignorance, 89–90
equity
for Aboriginal people, 27, 46
backlash against, 247
intersectionality and, 126
for people with disabilities, 171, 203, 207
in practice, 249, 251, 253, 255; *see also* inequality
ethics *see* Code of Ethics in social work; values
evil spirit (Anito) belief, 218–29
exclusion
of Aboriginal people, 14, 16, 30
cultural, 237–8, 247–8
gendered, 107, 109, 121, 123
of immigrants, 88
of mentally ill people, 158
of Muslims, 64, 66
of people with disabilities, 170–81, 204, 209
social work and, 5, 253, 258
of Tao people, 219–20, 226; *see also* marginalisation

family ideology, 223, 228
feminism
allyship and, 103–4, 106–15
feminist gains lost in domestic violence refuges, 185–200
feminist theory, 73, 121–3, 235, 237
older women and, 121–3, 126, 129, 131
women in developing countries and, 240
First Peoples *see* Indigenous people

Foucault, Michel, 62–3, 87, 240; *see also* Games of Truth
front-line workers, 86, 229

Games of Truth, 137–46, 148–9
gender
   binaries and, 235–6
   critical perspectives on gender difference, 101–49
   identity, 112–13, 140, 142, 146, 240
   male fragility, 248
   social construction of, 237; *see also* non-binary people; sexism; trans people; women
gendered violence
   challenging, 103–15
   pervasiveness of, 124; *see also* domestic violence
government
   housing for survivors of domestic violence, 185–200
   impact on social work, 4, 250, 252, 254–5
   response to ACCHSs, 16
   response to immigration, 71
   of the Tao people, 225–6, 228–9; *see also* colonialism; Countering Violent Extremism Policy; National Disability Insurance Scheme

Hall, Stuart, 88, 238
health, 123–4, 127, 194; *see also* mental illness
health care
   for gender diverse people, 137–49; *see also* Aboriginal community-controlled health services; National Disability Insurance Scheme
home care
   for Tao people, 218–29
   workers, 224–5
housing
   domestic violence shelters, 185–200, 252–4
   for gender diverse people, 148
   for older women, 120, 124
   for Tao people, 222–4
human rights
   Aboriginal people and, 27–8, 31–2, 34, 36–7
   allyship and, 104
   disability and, 171, 205, 207–9, 215–16
   domestic violence and, 188
   to knowledge, 43–6
   mental health and, 161
   in social work, 4, 249–50, 255
humility, cultural, 1, 35

identity
   cultural, 35–6, 41, 61
   fluid, 127
   gender, 112–13, 140, 142, 146
   mental health and, 160, 164
   neoliberalism and, 4–5
   of older women, 122–3
   poststructuralism and, 240
   professional, 86, 89, 126
immigrants
   domestic violence towards immigrant women, 71–82, 196–7, 253
   immigration policy, 71, 77, 81–2, 196–7; *see also* anti-immigrant backlash
inclusion *see* exclusion
Indigenous people *see* Aboriginal...; colonialism; Tao people
individualisation
   of aging, 128
   of disability policy, 203–4, 207–9, 213, 215–16
   gender and, 146, 186
   of mental health, 122, 156, 161, 163
   reasons for, 251
   work and, 171
inequality
   of Aboriginal people, 16, 21
   difference and, 1–6
   in education, 85–6, 88–9
   gender, 72, 80–1, 105–7, 115, 124, 127, 133, 167, 186, 237, 248
   intersectional, 120–3
   of mentally ill people, 160
   of Muslims, 56, 68
   of people with disabilities, 179–80
   in practice, 253–5, 258

racial, 229, 237–8, 248, 253–4
of survivors of domestic violence, 80–1
of the Tao people, 219
terminology of, 233–43; *see also* equity
intellectual disabilities, people with
NDIS and, 214
supported employment and social inclusion for, 170–81
intellectual property, 43–6
intersectionality
culture and, 14, 65–6, 73–4, 76, 80, 82
disability and, 171, 186, 214
gender and, 120–33, 139, 145
importance of, 3, 5, 161
privilege and, 104–5
teaching and, 94
interventions
Aboriginal people and, 1, 17, 22, 30
CVE, 60
mental health and, 159, 164, 167
for people with disabilities, 210
privilege and, 242
violence and, 111, 113, 115, 188–9, 200
invisibility
of Aboriginal people, 13–23, 42
binarism and, 235
of colonialism, 197
of difference, 123
of equity, 255
of gender diversity, 144
mental health and, 158, 162–3
NDIS and, 204
of neoliberalism, 4
of older women, 132
of privilege, 3, 104
of whiteness, 66
of women's needs, 192; *see also* visibility
Islamophobia
Countering Violent Extremism Policy, 59–65
Islamophobia industry, 56, 65
Islamophobic incidents, 56, 72

learning, 22, 115, 176–7; *see also* education; knowledge

LGBTQI+, 73, 146, 148, 240; *see also* non-binary people; trans people
liberation
allyship in, 88, 109, 113
disability and, 208
in education, 28–9, 33
Mad activism, 159
listening, 68, 139, 146–9
lived experience, 125, 140, 156, 163–4
long-term care *see* home care
Lorde, Audre, 2, 5, 107–8

Mad studies, 156, 158–9
male fragility, 248
male violence *see* gendered violence
managerialism, 228, 250, 258; *see also* private market
marginalisation
of CALD people, 21, 71, 81–2, 253–4
of disability, 172, 180
discourses of, 87–9
educating about, 93
mental health and, 155, 159
of non-hegemonic masculinity, 108
of older women, 120, 132
othering and, 88, 239
social work and, 67–8, 253–4, 257–8; *see also* exclusion; othering; segregation; socioeconomic marginalisation
marketisation
feminism and, 186, 198
NDIS and, 205, 207–16; *see also* managerialism; private market
men's violence *see* gendered violence
mental distress, 156, 158, 163, 167
mental illness
anti-stigma education, 155–67
cultural safety and, 35
gender and, 139–43, 145
NDIS and, 211–12
in refuges, 197
monoculture, 4
Mullaly, Bob, 4–5, 249, 251
Muslim people
women's experiences of domestic violence, 71–82; *see also* Islamophobia

National Disability Insurance Scheme
 (NDIS), issues with, 203–16
neoliberalism
 social work and, 4–6, 66, 247–58
 disability and, 171–2, 205, 207–8
 domestic violence and, 186
 effect on health care, 138–9, 146, 148
 effect on older women, 120–1, 123,
  125–6, 128, 132
 effect on Tao people, 220
 mental health and, 159–60, 162, 167
neurodiversity, 156; *see also* mental
 illness
non-binary people
 disrupting binarism, 236
 health care for, 137–49
 violence against, 104

othering
 in education, 93
 marginalisation and, 88, 239
 racial, 13–14, 17–18, 65, 238–9
 social work's response to, 3, 5
 theory behind, 238–9

participation
 in education, 91
 of people with disabilities, 172–4,
  177–9, 206
 sexism and, 105
 social work and, 60–1, 68, 249–50,
  255, 257
Pease, Bob, 137–8
people with disabilities *see* disabilities
 challenging inequality, 2–6, 247,
  250–1, 256
 disability in, 203–16
 discourse analysis in, 240
 in education, 27, 96
 health, 127
 Indigenous people in, 13, 16–18, 30,
  228, 236, 243
 inequitable, 248–9, 256–8
 mental health, 156
 neoliberal, 120, 123, 126
 older women in, 130, 132
 policy work across difference,
  183–229

regarding domestic violence, 81,
 185–200
regarding employment, 181; *see
 also* colour-blind approach;
 Countering Violent Extremism
 Policy
politics
 of difference, 1, 233–43
 gender diverse people and, 146–7
 of mental health, 158–60, 163
 of social work, 5, 66, 251
 women and, 103, 105–6, 114–15,
  121–3, 125–7, 185; *see also*
  government; neoliberalism; ultra-
  right
postcolonialism, 233–5, 239–40
postmodernism, 5, 121–2, 139
poststructuralism, 5, 86, 129, 233–4,
 240
poverty
 of older women, 120, 123–4, 126,
  131
 view of, 4, 239, 247; *see also*
  classism; socioeconomic
  marginalisation
power
 of Aboriginal people, 14, 16, 20, 22
 in allyship, 104
 cultural, 35
 domestic violence and, 186, 191,
  199
 in education, 86–90, 93, 97–8
 fragility and, 248
 of gender diverse people, 140–3,
  145–9
 in intersectionality, 65
 of mentally ill people, 160–3, 166–7
 of older women, 121–3, 125–7,
  132–3
 of people with disabilities, 172, 174,
  181, 204–8
 in social work, 3–4, 6, 240, 250–1,
  253–4, 256
 of Tao people, 229
 theories of, 2–4, 87, 238–40; *see
 also* disempowerment; dominant
 discourse; privilege; *see also* anti-
 oppressive practice; Countering

Violent Extremism Policy; standardisation
private market, 159, 247–8, 250–1; *see also* employment; marketisation
privilege
  in education, 89–90
  gender and, 138–9, 142–4, 146
  male, 73, 107–8, 110–14
  mental health and, 160
  Muslims and, 62, 65
  of older women, 120–33
  in social work, 3–6, 58, 67, 103–4, 251
  theories of, 87, 235, 237–8, 241–2
  throughout time, 120–33
  white, 16, 42, 58, 65, 241–2, 248, 254, 257–8; *see also* power
professionalisation, 66, 162
professionalism, 90
professions *see* employment; social work profession
psychiatry *see* mental illness

Racial Discrimination Act 1975 (Cth), 16
racism
  othering and, 239
  psychology and, 158
  rise of, 247
  social construction of, 237
  towards Aboriginal people, 13–14, 17–23, 27–9, 30–1
  towards immigrants, 88
  towards Muslims, 56, 58, 64, 72–3
  towards Tao people, 223–4; *see also* anti-immigrant backlash; anti-racism; Islamophobia; white fragility
recovery, 156–7, 161–2
reflection and reflexivity
  about gender, 107, 110–11, 149
  about mental health, 163–4
  about older women, 129, 132–3
  critical, 67, 90–1, 104, 110–11, 129, 133, 149, 249, 251, 254–5, 257
  in education, 35–6, 96
  resistance and, 231–58
  towards oneself, 91, 104, 149

refugees, 247; *see also* immigrants
religion, 78–9, 81, 197; *see also* Muslim people; spirituality
resilience, 60, 75
resistance
  of Aboriginal people, 21, 42
  to depoliticisation, 114–15
  to domestic violence, 75, 79
  marginalisation and, 88
  of mentally ill people, 140, 167
  of Muslims, 62
  to neoliberalism, 125
  of older women, 125
  reflection and, 231–58
  of social work, 3–5, 66, 237, 247–58
  of Tao people, 219, 225–6, 228–9
resources
  for Aboriginal people, 22
  diversity and, 238
  for gender diverse people, 147–8
  for learning, 32–3
  for mentally ill people, 160–2
  for older women, 123, 127
  for people with disabilities *see* National Disability Insurance Scheme
  redistributing, 2, 5
  for survivors of domestic violence, 81, 185, 190
  for Tao people, 224, 229
risk
  disability and, 204, 211–12
  domestic violence and, 189, 193, 195–6, 199
  LGBTQI+ people and, 141, 147
  mental health and, 161
  older women and, 126
  in practice, 255–7

safety
  in ACCHSs, 20
  of domestic violence refuges, 187–9, 192, 196–7, 200
  of gender diverse people, 147
  of people with disabilities, 210
  of the Tao elderly, 224; *see also* cultural safety

segregation, 13, 171, 176, 179–80; *see also* exclusion
service users
   LGBTQI+, 141–3, 146–8
   mentally ill, 158, 160–2
   in social work, 250–8
settler colonialism, 3, 140–1, 242–3; *see also* colonialism
sexism
   male allyship challenging, 103–15; *see also* gender
silencing of voices, 59, 75, 162, 186, 253, 257
social cohesion, 55, 60, 98, 181
social construction, 1, 3, 65, 87, 234, 237
social disadvantage, 189; *see also* inequality; socioeconomic marginalisation
social exclusion *see* exclusion
social justice
   allyship challenging sexism, 103–15
   backlash against, 247–9
   disability and, 173, 181
   education, 28, 34, 86, 89–92
   feminist, 125–6, 132
   mental health and, 158
   in social work, 1–6, 66–8, 98, 120–1, 247–51, 253–5, 258
   terminology of, 233
social model of disability, 172, 180
social work collusion
   with Islamophobia, 55–68
   neoliberalism and, 126
   privilege and, 3
social work profession
   Aboriginal people and, 21–2
   aim of, 103
   Code of Ethics, 249–58
   developing a professional identity, 86
   domestic violence and, 81–2, 111, 115, 197–8
   education for, 36–7, 85–98
   gender and, 148
   older women and, 121
   tenets of, 2–6, 247–9
   terminology of, 233–43; *see also* Australian Association of Social Workers (AASW); care; critical social work; policies of social work; practice of social work
socioeconomic marginalisation, 63, 77, 93, 247, 252–3; *see also* marginalisation; poverty
solidarity, 37, 149
spirituality, 15, 35, 78–9, 81; *see also* Anito belief; religion
standardisation, 4–5, 17, 251, 253–4, 258
stolen generation, 5, 18
structural inequalities, 3, 5–6, 21–2, 80–1, 103, 105, 113, 115, 132, 215
supported employment, issues with, 170–81
systems
   affecting Aboriginal people, 13–14, 17–18, 21, 30, 32, 65
   affecting disability, 203, 207, 211, 213
   affecting older women, 121
   affecting social work, 254–5
   affecting Tao people, 226
   gender-based, 105, 112, 140
   neoliberal, 149
   quotas, 181
   racial, 127, 253
   representational, 88
   response to inequality, 2, 4, 89

Tao people, elder care for, 218–29
terrorism, CVE policy regarding, 55–65
Torres Strait Islanders *see* Aboriginal...
trans people
   binarism and, 236
   health care for, 137–49
trauma-informed perspectives, 14, 192
trust, 18–19, 35, 218, 250

ultra-right, 247
'unfilial', view of Tao people as, 223–4

values
   cultural, 15, 35, 78–80
   in education, 90
   patriarchal, 105
   of social work, 21
   societal structure and, 85, 87–8; *see also* ethics

violence, 15, 145, 160, 165, 167, 248; *see also* gendered violence
visibility, 82, 104, 127, 139, 146; *see also* invisibility

wellbeing
  of Aboriginal people, 15, 29
  in education, 35
  of gender diverse people, 147
  of mentally ill people, 161, 167
  of older women, 132
  of survivors of domestic violence, 194; *see also* health
Western ways of knowing and thinking
  Aboriginality and, 15, 30, 32, 41, 45–6
  about gender, 140
  about Islam, 58, 68
  binaries and, 235
  dominance of, 234
  regarding knowledge and learning, 32, 45–6, 236
white fragility
  regarding ACCHSs, 17
  social work's response to, 56, 249, 251–8
  workings of, 247–8
whiteness
  CVE and, 64–7
  diversity and, 238
  dominance of, 31
  in education, 26
  of health care, 16–22
  intersectionality and, 66, 73
  othering, 239
  of social work, 58, 66–7, 252–4, 256–8
  white privilege, 16, 42, 58, 65, 241–2, 248, 254, 257–8
women
  male allyship with, 103–15
  mental health of, 164–7
  Muslim, 56–9, 66
  in old age, 120–33; *see also* Aboriginal and Torres Strait Islander women; feminism; gendered violence; sexism
work knowledge, 66, 226, 228–9, 233

xenophobia
  disrupting, 249, 252–8
  rise of, 247; *see also* anti-immigrant backlash; Islamophobia; racism

young people
  domestic violence and, 194–5
  health care and support for, 137–49
  policing of, 57, 60–4

CPSIA information can be obtained
at www.ICGtesting.com
Printed in the USA
LVHW021136110523
746711LV00004B/159